The Picaresque Saint

By R. W. B. Lewis

❧

THE PICARESQUE SAINT

THE AMERICAN ADAM

THE
PICARESQUE
SAINT

Representative Figures
in Contemporary Fiction

R. W. B. LEWIS

1959
J. B. LIPPINCOTT COMPANY
Philadelphia & New York

For Nancy
especially remembering Florence
October, 1954, and September, 1957

Contents

7

PREFATORY NOTE

THE AIM of this book is to identify and to describe a particular generation of novelists in Europe and America. The writers I have selected seem to me the most significant members of that generation; and because of the important differences between them of theme and style, they suggest the variety and indeed the contradictions that the generation expresses. I have tried to do justice to the unique qualities of each writer and each work. At the same time, these writers tend to communicate—across four countries and two hemispheres—within the same world of literary discourse. And my larger purpose has been to identify the generation by exploring the nature of the imaginative world it has succeeded in creating.

In doing so, I have had to explore a world fundamentally different from the world created by the novels of the previous generation—the generation of Joyce and Proust and Mann. For the latter, perhaps the simplest adjective would be "artistic." It was a world in which the aesthetic experience was supreme, and one which criticism dealt with properly enough by means of close technical analysis, by delicate discriminations of texture and design. But for the world of Silone and Camus, of Faulkner and Moravia and Greene and Malraux, perhaps the best single word is "human." It is a world in which the chief experience has been the discovery of what it means to be a human being and to be alive. Criticism, examining this world, is drawn to the more radically human considerations of life and death, and of the aspiring, sinful nature of man. The two generations overlap, to be sure, both chronologically and thematically; nevertheless the basic distinction should be emphasized.

These remarks indicate, I hope, that I am not offering in this

9

book a collection of random essays on assorted literary topics. Nor, at the other extreme, am I offering a thoroughgoing survey of all the novels and novelists of recent decades. The book was conceived as a single continuing discussion of several intimately related themes. What I take to be the most fertile of these several themes is named in the book's title. That phrase refers to a number of things: to the paradoxical hero I see emerging from the works selected, implicit in some of them and explicit in others—a person who is something of a saint, in the contemporary manner of sainthood, but who is also something of a rogue; it refers also, by implication, to the human image that this generation has honored in its literature; and it refers to the kind or the genre of fiction—the old-fashioned picaresque novel, the episodic account of the rogue on his journeys—which has been revived and greatly modified for contemporary narrative purposes.

I should add, perhaps, that the word "figures" in the subtitle refers to figures of speech, to the characteristic metaphors of the generation; as well as to the human figures within the novels and to the figures of the writers themselves. To detect those figures and to describe the world they serve to compose is, as I understand it, a major function of criticism in the present time.

ACKNOWLEDGMENTS

Portions of this book have appeared in *Kenyon Review*, *Modern Writing* and *Modern Fiction Studies*; in most cases they have been considerably revised. I am especially grateful to *Kenyon Review* for its award to me, in 1954, of a Fellowship in Criticism, under which I was able to begin work on the book.

Quotations from *The Power and the Glory*, by Graham Greene, are made with the permission of The Viking Press; and those from *Bread and Wine*, by Ignazio Silone, with the permission of Harper & Brothers. Though my analysis of all texts is based upon a reading of the originals, I have gratefully made use of the following translations for the purpose of quotation: Moravia's *The Time of Indifference* and *The Woman of Rome*, by Angus Davidson; Camus's *The Fall*, by Justin O'Brien; Silone's *Fontamara*, by Michael Wharf,

Bread and Wine by Gwenda David and Eric Mosbacher and *A Handful of Blackberries,* by Darina Silone; and Malraux's *The Royal Way,* by Stuart Gilbert. Other translations are by the present writer.

Personal indebtedness is equally pleasant to record. I am grateful to Albert Camus and Alberto Moravia, who have talked and written generously about their literary concerns. I am profoundly indebted to Ignazio Silone for help and friendship over a number of years. Much of the book would have been impossible without that help, which was invariably offered both swiftly and patiently; and one of the rewards of writing about Silone has been the opportunity of knowing him. To Charles J. Rolo, I am obliged for two key suggestions, as well as for encouragement. Other contributions of critics and scholars have, I trust, been carefully noted in the text; they are numerous and invaluable. My students at Newark College in Rutgers University and at the School of Letters in the University of Indiana have been of the greatest assistance by their friendly comments on and their stimulating resistance to my ideas about fiction.

My most important acknowledgment is named in the dedication. More than critical studies usually are, this one is a work of collaboration.

The poet essentially *can't* be concerned with dying. Let him deal with the sickest of the sick, it is still by the act of living that they appeal to him, and appeal the more as the conditions plot against them and prescribe the battle. The process of life gives way fighting, and often may so shine out on the lost ground as in no other connexion.

HENRY JAMES, Preface to *The Wings of the Dove*

I hate self-satisfied virtue. I hate the despicable morality of the world, and I hate it because, just like cynicism, it ends by depriving man of hope and preventing him from assuming responsibility for his own life with all its terrible burden of crimes and grandeur.

ALBERT CAMUS

The Picaresque Saint

CHAPTER 1

The Sense of Life

> To lose one's life is a little thing. . . . But to see
> the sense of this life dissipated, to see our reason
> for existence disappear: that is what is insup-
> portable.
>
> CAMUS, *Caligula*

TWENTIETH CENTURY literature began on the note of death. The
first page of the first book by James Joyce established the subject
and tone for an entire generation, at least for an entire European
generation—the opening lines of *Dubliners* (written in 1904), in
which a young boy describes his feelings about a dying priest:

> There was no hope for him this time: it was the third stroke.
> Night after night I had passed the house (it was vacation time) and
> studied the lighted square of window: and night after night I had
> found it lighted in the same way, faintly and evenly. . . . Every
> night as I gazed up at the window I said softly to myself the word
> paralysis. It had always sounded strangely in my ears, like the word
> gnomon in the Euclid and the word simony in the Catechism. But
> now it sounded to me like the name of some maleficent and sinful
> being. It filled me with fear, and yet I longed to be nearer to it and
> to look upon its deadly work.

The name of the paralyzed priest is Father Flynn; but he is also,
as we know, an image of darkening Ireland, culturally withered and

17

priest-ridden, in Joyce's view of it.[1] And in the larger perspective
of the twentieth century novel, the priest is not only modern Ireland,
he is modern Europe—the modern world. "There was no hope for
him this time: it was the third stroke." However they happen to
count their strokes—whether by wars or revolutions or by striking
symptoms of spiritual decay—that is the impression of things with
which most of the century's talents have begun. And the world or
Europe or some fragment of Europe or America is depicted thereafter as maleficent and sinful, paralyzed and dying.

Yet there is an endless fascination in the effort so to depict it.
The boy's reaction is that of the modern artist as he is drawn
helplessly to portraying the death-world he looks out upon: "It
filled me with fear, and yet I longed to be nearer to it and to look
upon its deadly work." The same longing is reflected in the substance and even the titles of a whole range of writing by the generation to which Joyce belonged. Titles like *Death in Venice* or *The
Wasteland* or "The Dead" are suggestive enough; and the content
we discover almost everywhere confirms what they hint at. The
decaying atmosphere of Proust's Paris and Combray, his characters
with the sign of death upon them—doomed more obviously than
ourselves, as E. M. Forster once remarked, to decay, and with no
new life flowering amidst the corrosive mortality of the aging;[2]
the sickness unto death of persons and of places as well, the disease
that commonly afflicts Hans Castorp and Gustav van Aschenbach
and Adrian Leverkühn in the fiction of Thomas Mann; the fading
fragilities, the sigh that extends into a delicate death rattle in the
novels of Virginia Woolf: over them all, and over the slighter
worlds and lesser creations of the generation's minor talents, we
seem to see snow falling steadily. It is the snow that comes down
like a final curtain to conclude Joyce's *Dubliners*, the last lines of
that book fulfilling and universalizing the image projected in its first
lines: "the snow falling faintly through the universe and faintly
falling, like the descent of their last end, upon all the living and the
dead."

Death is the beginning, often it is the middle, and sometimes, as in
"The Dead," it seems to be the end of the century's most splendid
works of the literary art. We hardly need to ask why this should be
so. It is still the business of the artist (in the words of Hamlet's

advice to the players) to show the age and body of his time its form
and pressure; and the first fact of modern historic life is the death
that presses in on it from all sides: death in battle, death in prison,
death in the pit of the soul and the very heart of the culture. Death
is the word we use for all those tendencies and events that led so
vibrant a spirit as Antoine de St-Exupéry to exclaim, "I hate my
epoch!" And on the basis of death Albert Camus can write, with
cold accuracy, that the secret of modern Europe is that it no longer
loves life. America no longer loves it either, though only its harried
artists dare to say so. There is little wonder that death is the beginning of art in this century. And yet, after all, death is *not* the end,
in the masterpieces of our time, when we look at the matter more
closely. The true artist is constantly seeking ways to confound
death. Indeed, the best way to distinguish the two or three literary
generations of our century is in their manner of responding to the
fact of death—that is, in their manner of somehow getting beyond it.

That there have been several distinct literary generations in this
century is itself something increasingly noted of late. The first
generation, that of Joyce and Proust and Mann, has in fact been
more and more isolated for inspection in recent years, and, as usually happens with an individual writer recently deceased, isolated
rather for disapproval than for praise.[3] The ground of disapproval is
customarily this: that the generation failed to attend to the visible
life of men, to the shape of their actions, the motives of their hope.
From the work of Joyce and his colleagues—according to one com-
mentator—we receive "an impression of hopelessness."

> There is often something confusing, something hazy about them,
> something hostile to the reality which they represent. We not in-
> frequently find a turning away from the practical will to live, or
> delight in portraying it under its most brutal forms. There is a
> hatred of culture and civilization, brought out by means of the
> subtlest stylistic devices which culture and civilization have de-
> veloped, and often a radical and fanatical urge to destroy.[4]

This is the judgment of Erich Auerbach, the disheartening conclusion of his survey of literary masterpieces from Homer and the
authors of the Old Testament to Joyce and Proust and Virginia
Woolf. The reality represented by twentieth century fiction, says
Professor Auerbach, differs from that of any earlier period in its

coloration by the disdain and the revulsion of its observers.

The critic Yvor Winters offers another reason for what he takes to be the failures of Joyce and the others. All of them have done a serious disservice to the narrative art, Winters argues, not so much through their obsession with death as through their obsession with the sheer mechanics of fiction and with visual detail.[5] Plot and character have largely departed from the novel, he believes, and the glory of fiction is departed with them; a proliferating verbal fussiness has become the prime characteristic of all that we read. Henry James was chiefly responsible, according to Winters; but James's successors completed the job (Winters is among those who think the novel is dying; and on the whole, he implies, a good thing too):

> Of James I think we may safely say this: that he is the greatest master in our literature of the most limited kind of narrative matter combined with the most unsound narrative technique antedating Joyce, Miss Richardson, and Mrs. Woolf; and in our time this is no small achievement, but I would hope for better.

Amid all that angry syntax, the reference intended by "this" in the penultimate clause is perhaps unclear. But the general point is clear enough, and Winters goes on to reinforce it: "In the later Joyce, in Miss Richardson and in Mrs. Woolf, plot, in various ways and degrees, has become less important; the particular detail and the progression from detail to detail have largely taken charge of the novel"—a sorry confusion, he concludes, of means and of ends.

These men are distinguished and valuable witnesses, and I believe we can mainly assent to their findings—without, however, giving up our regard for the novelists in question. If, as Auerbach rightly says, Joyce and his contemporaries did turn away from the practical will to live, it was because they turned toward the practical will to create—toward a vital concern with those elements Winters disapproves of. And if, as Winters rightly says, they busied themselves with the techniques of language and construction, it was because plot and character had already departed from the life they could observe; and in the paltry time they were honest enough to mirror, art appeared as the supreme consolation—with technique as the creative force that made it effective. Art was even more than that. Art was the answer given back by the first generation to the universal

pressure of death. There was at work something deeper than the
ancient formula that Art is long and Life is fleeting. Life was ugly
as well; life was not even lively, not even real. And art was not
merely long and not merely shapely: it was the one remaining
channel into a living reality.[6] Turning away, therefore, from the
City of Man, which was dying, the writer of that time entered
alone into the deathless City of Art. The poet, as Henry James
asserted in a noble passage, essentially *can't* be concerned with dying.[7] And for all the paralysis and the deadly work looked upon
with fear and longing by Joyce, by Proust, by Virginia Woolf,
by Thomas Mann, death was not at all their true or final subject
matter. Their final subject was art itself. "Poetry," as Wallace
Stevens was once candid enough to say, "is the subject of the poem,"
and the force which rescues man's dying dream from the mud.[8]
In Proust, it is the art of fiction, operating on memory, that is the
very absolute, the fixity amid flux, that memory has all the time
been seeking; and beyond the shambles of soul and body into which
The Magic Mountain seems finally to disintegrate, there is the art of
Thomas Mann, holding the fragments in their place in an inviolable
order, an order of wisdom and purity beyond the possibility of
change.

This movement away from actual life as fatally infected by death
and toward an imaginative life made whole and luminous by art—
this *is* the plot, and a very exciting plot it is, of Joyce's novel *A
Portrait of the Artist as a Young Man*. It is developed less in the
traditional manner of narrative than in those same exquisitely careful verbal techniques Yvor Winters has criticized. Here are two
passages, almost identical in formal structure, that occur only a
couple of pages apart during the grand "epiphany" of the fourth
chapter and which contain the novel's entire plot in essence. The
first describes boys swimming in the river, representing the deathy
life Stephen Dedalus must escape from; the second describes a girl
wading in the river, representing the redemption of the actual by
the poetic.

The mere sight of that medley of nakedness chilled him to the
bone. Their bodies, corpsewhite or suffused with a pallid golden
light or rawly tanned by the suns, gleamed with the wet of the sea.
Their divingstone poised on its rude supports and rocking under

their plunges, and the rough-hewn stones of the sloping break-water over which they scrambled in their horseplay, gleamed with cold wet lustre. The towels with which they smacked their bodies were heavy with cold seawater; and drenched with cold brine was their matted hair.

These are Stephen's schoolmates, his permanent companions if he stays in Ireland—repulsive little boys, all snakes and snails and puppy-dogs' tails: life as a mode of death. Here is the vision he comes upon a few moments later, a young girl seen in solitude as everything nice: an emblem of art.

A girl stood before him in midstream: alone and still, gazing out to sea. She seemed like one whom magic had changed into the like-ness of a strange and beautiful sea-bird. Her long slender bare legs were delicate as a crane's and pure save where an emerald trail of seaweed had fashioned itself as a sign upon the flesh. Her thighs, fuller and softhued as ivory, were bared almost to the hips where the white fringes of her drawers were like feathering of soft white down. Her slate-blue skirts were kilted boldly about her waist and dovetailed behind her. Her bosom was a bird's, soft and slight, slight and soft as the breast of some dark-plumaged dove. But her long fair hair was girlish; and girlish, and touched with the wonder of mortal beauty, her face.

The progression is achieved by the language of visual detail, rather than by the language of statement; but the progression itself is emphatic. On the one hand, the imagery of cold and of corpses, of rough-hewn stones and of *plunging*, of heavy wet towels, matted hair, and cold sea brine. On the other, the imagery of magical change, of precious stones and of *soaring*, of cranes and doves, of long fair hair and the wonder of mortal beauty. One passage sinks, and actual life with it; the other passage rises, on the wings of art. And the rising *is* the real subject and figuratively the final word: in this sense, at least, as affirmative as the seven words that conclude Joyce's *Ulysses* and which celebrate not only Molly Bloom's sexual surrender but Joyce's novelistic art that has transfigured it: "Yes I said yes I will yes."

The generation of writers that followed that of Joyce began no less urgently with the sensibility of death; but the answer that it has given is radically different. I take as representative of the second generation the following (and in an order the book will eventually justify): Alberto Moravia, Albert Camus, Ignazio Silone, William Faulkner, and Graham Greene. These are (for me) representative men in the meaning Emerson intended when he titled his book *Representative Men* (1850)—not typical or average writers, but precisely writers who give final expression to tendencies and motifs that are elsewhere in their time only latent or partial. What each of them does in fact represent will be the subject of the following chapters; I have tried to offer hints in their titles. What is to be remarked upon here is the initial awareness they shared in common, and the common solution—if that is not too strong a term—they independently have moved toward.

"Today my mother died. Or perhaps yesterday. I don't know. I received a telegram from the Home: 'Mother deceased. Burial tomorrow. Sincere condolences.'" These are the opening spasms of Camus's short novel, his first work of fiction, *The Stranger*. The frenzied action of the play *Caligula*, by the same writer, emerges from the atmosphere of darkness, absence and death (the death of the Emperor's sister) that disturbs the senses in the opening scene; and *The Plague* unfolds from the first symptoms of the epidemic, the rats in Oran tumbling out into the streets to die. The entire career of the hero of Moravia's *The Conformist* is the consequence of the murder he has committed (or rather, believes he has committed) in the book's prologue; though it is more characteristic of Moravia to begin with the heavy aroma of death—as in *The Time of Indifference*—rather than with actual instances of it. Much of Faulkner's fiction, too, takes its start in atmospheric rather than physical death; but Greene and Silone, like Camus, are more literal. "Hale knew, before he had been in Brighton three hours, that they meant to murder him." That is the introductory sentence of Greene's *Brighton Rock;* and his next novel, *The Power and the Glory* is bestirred in its first paragraph by a vulture flapping across the town under the blazing Mexican sun in search of carrion. Greene's ironically titled play *The Living Room* discloses at the outset an image of life almost totally invaded by a series of deaths; and the outer plot of *The Potting Shed* begins with the imminent death of an elderly intellectual, while its interior action departs from the suicide of his son. The death not of one or two individuals but of an entire village is the abrupt overture to *Fontamara* by Ignazio Silone; and that amateurish yet moving little novel progresses through an explanation of that death to the question it insistently raises—the question death raises in all the representative fiction of the first and second generation: "What can we do?"

For a variety of reasons, the question has cut deeper than ever into the consciousness of Camus and his contemporaries: a matter of degree, perhaps, but of a degree that has evolved into a difference. One reason is suggested by the tormented words of the tribune, Cherea, in *Caligula:* "To lose one's life is a little thing. . . . But to see the sense of this life dissipated, to see our reason for existence disappear: that is what is insupportable." The doubts and fears of the first generation, the wavering premonitions of some deep disaster,[9] have expanded over years of war, of public and private treachery, of the fatal shaking of all cultural and spiritual foundations into an abyss of nihilism that the ideal of art can no longer serve to span. Legal murder, Camus has stated flatly, is the prime characteristic of the time. But it is not murder but the nihilism that makes murder legal—the dissipation of the very sense or reason of life—which the second generation has had to confront as its supreme challenge. Art may provide a haven among ruins, but it cannot supply a basis for sheer existence. And indeed one of the significant symptoms of recent years has been exactly the harrowing succession of suicides among our most gifted and sensitive writers and artists—as well as in the pages of their books. There has been nothing comparable in modern culture since the wave of real and fictional suicides in late nineteenth century Russia. But to find a more accurate parallel, one must go back to the sixteenth and early seventeenth centuries, to Reformation Germany and Elizabethan England. A representative document of that age was John Donne's meditation on suicide, a little treatise called *Biathanatos,* written about 1610 but not published until 1644. Possibly the representative work of the contemporary epoch is an essay called *The Myth of Sisyphus* (1943), in which Albert Camus with a sort of passionate logic examines the case for and against the taking of one's own life— in a universe from which not only plot and character but reason itself has departed.

I think the analogy between the two periods and the crisis each

had to meet should be stressed, for it indicates something of the
scope and depth of the present cultural revolution and helps us, however grimly, to see where we are. In both periods we can see a
shattering not only of belief and custom, but—and in a manner happily unknown for long periods before—of the very structure of the
human psyche and the shape of its relation to the universe. Not
since the Renaissance, for instance, has the word "nothing" been
so often employed or carried so much dreadful weight. The freezing epitaph of Shakespeare's Timon of Athens:

> My long sickness
> Of health and living now begins to mend,
> And nothing brings me all things

finds its echo in the perverse celebration of "nothing" throughout
the play *Caligula*, and its analogy in the closing lines of Camus's
play *Cross-Purposes*. The lines are spoken by Maria, a woman half
crazed by horror, and a deaf old servant who seems to represent
God in the singular theology of Albert Camus:

Maria: . . . Help me, I need someone to help me. Have pity on me,
  help me!
Servant (in a dry firm voice): No!

There is perhaps an implication, which here I only mention, to be
drawn from the historic comparison at this point. Several competent
historians have related the suicides of the sixteenth century to the
Protestant Reformation—to the truncated doctrine of grace that it
promulgated, and to the overpowering anxiety that new doctrine
inevitably begot among the faithful, lest they be cut off from the
traditional sources of absolution and salvation. Whether the anxiety
was justified and whether the doctrine was valid or no are questions
we need not now inquire into—it is the psychology of the thing that
counted. And if persons in the sixteenth century felt that God had
been somehow withdrawn and the sense of life along with Him,
certain persons at least in the twentieth century have felt correspondingly that—in Nietzsche's phrase—God is dead, and that with
Him there died the perceptible reason for living.

An abysmal sense of loss, anyhow, is what permeates the atmosphere of the day and what is uttered and dramatized so often in
the opening pages of our second generation fiction. The form it

takes varies impressively, though in most instances the form is human; and I reveal only a personal opinion when I suggest that behind all forms of the sense of loss is the felt loss of the presence or even the life of God. But fiction deals in human affairs; and perhaps the most suitable metaphor to condense the varying metaphors that our novelists employ to convey the sense of loss is that of a lost paradise—"a paradise of reality and truth," as Michele tells himself in Moravia's first novel, *The Time of Indifference;* "a paradise where everything —gestures, words, feelings—would have a direct connection with the reality in which they originated." That is everywhere the point: the relation, or rather the severance of the relation between man and whatever reality he is willing to acknowledge. The condition in which the relation holds firm is a kind of paradise—"Wasn't that Eden, *cher monsieur?*" Clamence ironically asks his ghostly interlocutor in Camus's *The Fall;* "Wasn't that Eden . . . no intermediary between life and me?"

Camus, of course, bespeaks the largest philosophical, even metaphysical version of the loss: in the tortured progression from his early book of essays, *Noces (Nuptials),* the very title of which affirms the marriage between man and his environment, to the bleak period of divorce represented by *The Stranger, The Myth of Sisyphus,* and *Caligula.* The relation described by Camus in these works is nothing less than that between the voice of human reason and the universe that remains deaf to it; it is Camus who has best and most famously described what is known as "cosmic homelessness." Silone's view is simpler, more human, and in a delicate sense more persuasive: what has been lost, as Silone sees it, is the intimate relation between man and man, a relation recoverable only amidst primitive simplicities, in a hut on the mountainside, during long walks across the valley. Faulkner's account—especially in "The Bear" —is traditional, American, and biblical. He looks back with intensity and the sense of outrage to a period of innocence and honor, humility and pride—a highly moral Eden that might have been re-established in the New World but, irrevocably, was not; and for that loss, his characters are driven as though by a dream to atone. In Graham Greene what is felt most passionately is the loss of a world, of a condition, wherein—as he says in his Liberian travel book—the sense of pleasure was keener, the sense of terror deeper and purer;

a place, in short, where supernatural good and supernatural evil
made their direct and energizing impact upon the living individual;
a place now altogether buried (except for a few primitive portions
of the earth) beneath "the sinless empty graceless chromium world"
of modern civilized society.

What has been the response of the second generation to these
varieties of loss—loss felt so sharply in the imagination and spirit
that some mode of death has appeared as the natural starting point
of the contemporary novel? With an unconsciously common impulse, the writers of this generation have resorted to a rather desperate strategy. They have been forced to find, or try to find,
certain grounds for living *in life itself.* In order to write at all, they
must continue to live; the grave's a fine and quiet place (as we
might, without undue frivolity, paraphrase Marvell), but none I
think do there compose. They have, not unnaturally, taken as the
main subject of their work not the citadel of art but the demon-
strable reason, the accessible sources of human existence. Because
they have mirrored in their novels, the nihilism, the murders, and
the self-annihilations they see in the world about them, they have
been accused of morbidity. They should have been honored for
gallantry. For proceeding as they do, Camus and Greene, Faulkner
and Silone and Moravia have been faithful not only to the principle
of the thesis laid down by Henry James and mentioned above, but
to the whole text: "The poet essentially *can't* be concerned with
dying. Let him deal with the sickest of the sick, it is still by the act
of living that they appeal to him, and appeal the more as the conditions plot against them and prescribe the battle. The process of life
gives way fighting, and often may so shine out on the lost ground
as in no other connexion." Whether they have known it or not, the
representative novelists of the second generation have accepted that
passage as vital dogma; and they have centered not upon the ubiquity
of sickness and of death but on the act of living. Where, in the first
generation, the image of disintegration was redeemed by the absolute value of art, the sense of nothingness has been transcended, in
the second generation, by an agonizing dedication to life. What the
poet Alexander Blok said in 1918 about the Russian masters of a
century ago may be applied to our contemporaries: "They were
submerged in darkness, but it was never their will to stay hidden in

it, for they believed in the light. . . . Each one of them . . . ground his teeth in the darkness, seized by despair and fury. Yet they knew that sooner or later life will be renewed because life is beautiful." [10] This is the precise emotion expressed through Quentin Compson by William Faulkner in the final lines of *Absalom, Absalom:* " 'I dont hate it,' Quentin said, quickly, at once, immediately; 'I dont hate it,' he said. *I dont hate it* he thought, panting in the cold air, the iron New England dark; *I dont. I dont! I dont hate it! I dont hate it!*"

A belief in the act of living is not, then, something given to the contemporary novelist as his natural legacy, as it has been in less disturbed generations. It is something achieved by a desperate struggle; and the successive phases of the struggle provide the representative plot of the contemporary novel. The plot varies widely from writer to writer; but in all the novelists I have chosen we eventually come upon an experience at least analogous to the personal experience recorded by Graham Greene in his book about Liberia, *Journey Without Maps*. Toward the end of that journey, Greene had a severe bout of malaria, a miserable and even frightening business that led, however, to an astonishing discovery when the fever was sweated out of him. It was the wholly unexpected discovery of "a passionate interest in living."

It was, Greene adds significantly, "like a conversion." For the other writers, too, the revelation of the value, indeed the very possibility, of living—as against the initial absorption with death—came with the shock of conversion, and always at the moment each novelist had hit upon terms for repairing the tragic loss. Conversion is one of the great representative events enacted in the contemporary novel: if, by conversion, we mean not merely religious conversion, but any kind of radical, wholehearted shift of allegiance and belief. (Another and related species of conversion, to be examined later, is equally relevant to our discussion—artistic conversion, or the writer's *technique for portraying* the shift of allegiance, and, more generally, for artistically substituting one set of values and metaphors for another.) Here again, we observe and must stress important differences; but in all cases, the conversion that occurs is from something like death to the outlines of something like life—from a felt loss to a potential gain. "It is not a matter of putting new

formulas, new gestures, or shirts of a different color into circulation"
—so Silone's Pietro Spina addresses his young disciple Murica in
Bread and Wine—"but rather a matter of a new way of living. To
use an old expression, it is a matter of conversion. It is a matter of
becoming a new man."

For Silone, becoming a new man has meant primarily entering
into a new and authentic human friendship. And indeed, if we
reach for a single phrase to explain the basis for the renewed sense
of life, discovered in most, if not all of these instances, the one that
comes to mind is the seemingly tame one: human companionship.
Mild as it sounds, and dangerously close as it comes to fashionable
piety, the phrase is perhaps more accurate than that ambiguous
vocable "love." And it should be sharply distinguished at once
from those caricatures of itself that every forceful and moving idea
instantly begets: in this case, current concepts like togetherness,
which has dripped offensively into the fiber of popular culture; or
belongingness, which belies in the guttural croak of its sound the
notion it seeks to name; or the dehumanization implied in the word
"teamwork." Companionship, as dramatized in the contemporary
novel, should suggest in its prefix the idea of sharing; but it echoes
in its syllables the matter whose sharing it requires—by echoing the
note of compassion (that is, literally and etymologically, of *suffering with*). The key impulse I am describing requires the sharing of
pain; but the word itself also retains its own root meaning of the
sharing of bread—of *panis* broken in common. A companion
is a person who shares with you all that is nourishing to
body and soul, whose sharing may even be that nourishment. There
is, so to speak, a companion word to companionship, which one
wishes might still be used in its splendid original meaning: symposium, or a drinking together. The most effective celebration of
companionship in recent decades is also, as its title indicates, a celebration of symposium: Ignazio Silone's *Bread and Wine*, a novel
that finds in the human relation the seeds of a truly sacramental
sensibility.

The idea of companionship appears a trifle more obsessive among
the Continental writers than it does with the Englishman, Greene,
or the American, Faulkner, though there is evidence enough, espe-

cially with the latter, that the same concern is not far from the center of their view of things. Faulkner, indeed—in *As I Lay Dying* and elsewhere—carries forward, under hectic new pressures, the classic American theme of the solitary individual striving at all costs and often to his own calamity to open an intercourse with the human world: the theme that, in the major writings of the nineteenth century, helped determine the character of an American literature.[11] And we remark, for later consideration, that the contemporary European novel has arrived, out of its own awareness of dislocation and collapse, at a note curiously similar to the note struck again and again in America a century ago. It was characteristic of André Gide, in the first generation, to reprimand Henry James because his characters "never seem to exist except in relation to each other"; just as it was characteristic of James, working in the American tradition, to have aimed precisely at that image of genuine existence. Gide represented the longing of his time to escape into solitude from the suffocating weight, the corrupted and corrupting power of an age-old social and family fabric—to search for the sense of life in privacy or in the desert. But for Gide's Continental successors, for men like Moravia and Camus and Silone, that fabric appears to be all in shreds; and they have allied themselves, as it were accidentally, with the compelling need for relation expressed in nineteenth century America, and even with the sorry dream of a lost Eden that underlay the need.

In the three chapters following, I try to show the development and to some limited extent the fulfillment of that need by tracing a thematic (*not* a chronological) progression from Moravia to Camus and then to Silone: that is, from the sexual effort to the intellectual effort to the effort that, in Silone, begins with politics and is transformed into charity. Dramatically, the effort to achieve relationship is projected as a representative and recurring encounter —a sexual encounter, an intellectual encounter, and so on. But when, in chapters five and six, we examine Faulkner and Greene, we shall see that the encounters in their novels have tended to be increasingly religious in nature—quite literally involving priests and the doctrines of Catholic Christianity in Greene; and, in Faulkner, involving persons bent on shaping their lives in a conscious imitation of Christ. Yet the religious motif does not really separate the English language novelists from the others—it simply extends and makes explicit something shared by all of them. This something is not so much a theme as a personality—a representative human figure that seems to me *the* representative figure of the contemporary novel.

It is the figure of a saint: a very peculiar kind of saint, embodying a peculiar sanctity that has provided the title of this book. More, perhaps, than by anything else, it is by means of this figure—this strange, recurring, half-hidden or wholly realized, sometimes antic, and in at least one instance godless figure of sainthood—that the sense of life in second generation fiction has been ultimately conveyed. In fiction, traditionally, the sense of life is communicated not so much by statement as by character and by action. The figure I am calling the picaresque saint tries to hold in balance (as we shall see), by the very contradictions of his character, both the observed truths of contemporary experience and the vital aspiration to transcend them.

Paradoxical as he is, the picaresque saint is the logical hero of our paradoxical age. Every age of fiction develops its own representative hero: its own human image of the values it acknowledges and the force or power it respects and responds to. The heroes of Sir Walter Scott, for example, embody the power of a ceremonial religion and the ethics of chivalry, the virtues of honor and courage and fidelity and reverence. Those of Charles Dickens, on the other hand, represent the newer, urban forces of law and commerce; the powerful figures in Dickens are skilled in legal maneuvering and the handling of money.[12] The best of twentieth century fiction, turning away from more obvious symbols of force in the modern world, has contrived two versions of what we might call "trans-economic man." In the first generation, the hero was usually an artist, or a man of artistic sensibility: Joyce's Stephen Dedalus or Proust's Charles Swann; men who bespoke their authors' conviction that art was the one genuinely redemptive power of the day. In the second generation, no less revealingly, the hero has tended to be an apprentice saint or a saint *manqué*.

The figure turns up almost everywhere. Here is a man called Tarrou, talking to his friend Dr. Rieux in Camus's *The Plague:* "In short, what interests me is to know how to become a saint." Here is Pietro Spina, announcing his personal ambition in a high-school essay in Silone's *Bread and Wine:* "If the prospect of being displayed on altars after one's death, and being prayed to and worshipped by a lot of unknown people, mostly ugly old ladies, were not very unpleasant, I should like to be a saint." Here is the nameless priest, on the eve of his execution, in Greene's *The Power and the Glory:* "It seemed to him, at that moment, that it would have been quite easy to have been a saint." Where the intention is not plainly to be some kind of saint, it is frequently to be some kind of Christ. Here is Isaac McCaslin in Faulkner's "The Bear," who took up the trade of carpentering "not in mere static and hopeful emulation of the Nazarene . . . [but] because if the Nazarene had found carpentering good for the life and ends He had assumed and elected to serve, it would be all right too for Isaac McCaslin." And we recall the French corporal in Faulkner's *A Fable,* who—prodded by a still more strained and redundant prose—seems to be almost literally Christ in a second coming.

That summary is too brief to indicate the wide divergence between the notions of sainthood at work in these novels; and perhaps no single formula can truthfully embrace them all. But this may be suggested in advance, and prior to illustration: that the fictional saints of second generation fiction are men dedicated not so much, or not immediately, to a supernatural god as to what yet remains of the sacred in the ravaged human community. Pietro Spina argues that "the ideal of social justice that animates the masses" may itself be the current disguised visage of God; so that the form sainthood might currently take would be a whole-souled devotion to just that ideal. Nowhere else is the case put in such nakedly political and social terms; but in most other instances, too, the image of the saintly is the image of participation in the sufferings of mankind— as a way of touching and of submitting to what is most *real* in the world today. At the same time, in what seem to me the most fully developed portraits of the contemporary hero, he is apt to share not only in the miseries of humanity, but in its gravest weaknesses, too, and even in its sins. He is not only a saint, as the novelists have been describing him. He is a picaresque saint.

"Picaresque" is an adjective deriving from the word *picaro,* meaning "rogue." Most of these men have a touch of roguery about them, sometimes a touch of criminality; the more roguery, I dare say, the more representative. Joe Christmas, the bootlegger and murderer in *Light in August*, is more representative and more compelling a fictional creation than the excessively pure corporal in *A Fable*. Pietro Spina is a criminal subversive, according to the statutes of Italian fascism, and his influence is often disastrous to those who would follow him: in a manner reminiscent, for American readers, of Tom Joad, the outlaw redeemer in John Steinbeck's *The Grapes of Wrath*. Greene's priest is not only a criminal to be hunted and shot down by the totalitarian government of Tabasco, he is also a sinner against the ecclesiastical laws of his Church. It is in the nature of things that men like these should be outsiders—criminals to be pursued, escapees on the run, strangers in an alien world.

It is exactly in their impurity—whether it is reckoned by official morality or by any other kind—that the saintly characters achieve, and in fact incarnate, that trust in life and that companionship that the contemporary novel so emphasizes. They are outsiders who share; they are outcasts who enter in. It is just by taking on some of the wretchedness of the sinful, the persecuted and the dispossessed that they can experience what Henry James once called a "tragic fellowship" with suffering humanity. It is also through their roguishness that these figures become not only recognizable human beings but persuasive and impressive fictional creations. Part of the intensity of the contemporary novel is drawn at once from the artist's effort to depict and the created character's effort to become (as we may put it) both a saint and a sinner, both transcendent and companionable, to embody both the observed truth and the hidden aspiration. The effort is by no means always successful, and where successful by no means equally so. It is so easy to "fall" in the direction of the all too human or the all too saintly: Ike McCaslin no doubt suffers artistically from the latter mistake, and Adriana, Moravia's Roman prostitute, from the former—though Adriana, with her dedication to *living* in a world characterized by death, and with her compassionate effort to reach a relation with others, is probably Moravia's closest approximation to date of the representative heroic image. But through all these novels, the struggle to hold the elements in dramatic balance is one of the great and most meaningful creative struggles of our time.

The tragic fellowship I speak of is accomplished, in narrative terms, by a series of encounters—encounters between the hero and the beings and customs it is his purpose to outwit; and between the hero and those rare beings with whom communion may be fleetingly possible. The representative story of the second generation is thus the story of a journey, or more often of a chase: the story of the saintly rogue on his hurried and perilous travels. The genre of fiction which has re-emerged to carry the adventures of the picaresque saint is the old and sometimes disreputable genre of the picaresque novel—the traditional account of the journeying rogue.

To reach a fairer perspective, it should be noted that one writer of the first generation and at least one writer of what in context should perhaps be called the third generation have also presented us in recent years with picaresque novels—and of an unmistakably traditional character. *The Confessions of Felix Krull* (1954), the last work to be published by Thomas Mann during his lifetime, is an exemplary version of the familiar tale, the story of a talented and high-spirited confidence-man traveling the world en route to great and stupendously comic achievements. It is one of Mann's masterpieces. Younger writers in both England and America are discovering fresh resources in this ancient vein. One thinks especially of Saul Bellow and *The Adventures of Augie March* (1953), a novel which—even more than *Henderson The Rain King*, which follows it—is a knowing extension on to the anarchic modern scene of the picaresque plot and character. Both *Felix Krull* and *Augie March* are purer instances of the traditional genre than any of the works we are examining: and just because the picaresque element remains unmixed in them. It remains boldly comic, undisturbed by any leaning toward the saintly—that is, in the modern paradox, by any leaning toward the passionate involvement with human misery. To say so is to pass no adverse judgment on *Felix Krull* and *Augie March*, which are, respectively, works of the highest and of very high distinction. It is only to distinguish them from novels like *Bread and Wine*, *The Power and the Glory* and *The Fall;* and hence to see more clearly into the nature of the latter and their artistic aim.

In the second generation, in any case, the formal perfections characteristic of its predecessor have given way to the bumpy

episodes of the picaresque. At the same time, second generation fiction engages perhaps a more recognizable chunk of humanity, and its jerky rhythms have after all (as I shall hope to show)
their own peculiar and achieved design. I do not venture to predict
how long these novels will endure, but they have helped make it
possible for fiction itself to endure. In their fidelity at once to our
common roguery and our instinct to transcend it and in their profound concern with the realities of the human condition—"with
its terrible burden of crimes and grandeur," as Camus has put it—
these novels have given us back a solid sense of this earthly life.
And without that sense, fiction would seem as moribund as the
world it refuses to abandon.

CHAPTER 2

Alberto Moravia: Eros and Existence

"So as to have a new life": was what she wanted
to answer; but she had not the courage. That remote reason of hers, now that she saw nothing
was changed except her surrendered body, appeared to her ridiculous and unworthy.

MORAVIA, *The Time of Indifference*

THE SEXUAL ASPECT

ALBERTO MORAVIA is the most precocious and among the most gifted
and prolific of the novelists now referred to by younger Italians as
the second generation. Italian intellectuals in their twenties have
taken to calling themselves the third generation (a periodical bearing that name was even founded to promote the notion [1]); and they
are now lumping together, as their elders if not betters, all those
novelists whose art was formed out of the experience of the Fascist
era: Silone, Moravia, Elio Vittorini, Cesare Pavese, Vitaliano Bran-
cati, Carlo Levi, Mario Soldati, and a number of others. Moravia
belongs properly with this group and is probably its leading prac-
titioner of the craft of fiction. But beyond that, he is perhaps the
most emphatic annalist anywhere of one widely featured explanation
of life.

The explanation seems to have come to him, all rounded and

complete, at the moment he first became aware of his own literary talent, and this was a very early moment indeed. He has complained with apparent seriousness that he was able to write nothing from his ninth to his seventeenth years; but his first and perhaps best novel, *The Time of Indifference*, was written before he was eighteen (though not published until 1928, when he reached his majority), and his first story—"Tired Courtesan"—came out in the Italian journal *Novecento* in 1927, when he was twenty years old. "Tired Courtesan" was published in French, in line with the magazine's policy of supporting a pan-European culture by offering its wares in any of the major languages. A good deal of Moravia was announced in the subject and tone of the title itself, and in the sophisticated trickery of the French translation. The substance of the tale—a murky assignation during an illicit affair that both parties, for diverse financial reasons, are anxious to terminate—introduced much of what has ever since been Moravia's controlling image of experience.

It is an image of the world in its sexual aspect: or at least of that part of the world that, according to Moravia, is touched and accounted for by the sexual aspect. To say merely that Moravia's fiction is erotic is a truism that can stifle rather than enlarge our sense of his achievement: like saying, with a final simplicity, that Dante's poetry is religious. For Moravia's fiction provides a major treatment of a minor but honorable and suggestive view of things: the sexual view, the view of human relations and of everything that arises in or impinges upon human relations as beginning and ending in the sexual encounter. Everything other than sex is, in the stories of Moravia, an extension of sex; or perhaps better, everything other than sex is sooner or later converted into it. Moravia, in fact, is a minor master of the strategy of conversion in literature: that is, of *artistic* conversion, of the transformation of one set of values into another. The typical Moravian narrative shows us, not the precise and detailed moment of the sexual encounter (in this respect, there is less "sex" in Moravia than in a good many other modern writers; much of the time the "sex" remains hidden, like the divinity in certain religious poems), but the full amount of life that culminates in the sexual encounter or is an observable deflection from it. And the purpose behind Moravia's strategy is strikingly similar to that of the other novelists we are considering. If Moravia's encounters are sexual rather than political, as in Silone, or religious, as in Greene, the aim is identical—to recover a more faithful image of man at a time when that image has been singularly deformed and betrayed. Measured against that purpose, Moravia's achievement is impressive but partial.

"The use of man as a means and not as an end," Moravia has insisted, "is the root of all evil." An ancient and recently urgent European tradition echoes in the remark; and in the case of Moravia, the urgency arose from the Fascist habit of reversing the formula. It was chiefly because fascism was the enemy of man that it was also the enemy of art. Moravia had to discover, as Silone rapidly discovered, that human reality in art was heresy in the Fascist view. *The Time of Indifference* was a notable public success, but its combination of clinical honesty and lyrical sadness went so against the official vulgar heartiness sponsored by the Italian government that an order was issued forbidding the mention of the author's name in any newspaper or magazine. His next novel, *Mistaken Ambitions* (1935), consequently went unreviewed, and Moravia was forced, like Silone, to adopt a pen name, "Pseudo," for articles, and the mild evasion of "Alberto Moravia" for stories (the author's real name is Alberto Pincherle-Moravia). Moravia traveled a good deal during the thirties—to Mexico, China and the United States.[2] In the same period he abandoned realism for more indirect and furtive pictures of the contemporary scene. Several of his literary colleagues were driven by the political climate of the day into the same area of the fantastic and the hermetic, and not always to their disadvantage;[3] but Moravia's surrealistic and satirical writings in the thirties (*L'Epidemia*, for example) do not, in my opinion, show him at his best.

Moravia's sufferings under Mussolini were not abnormal, nor was his early life unduly adventurous; what was abnormal was Moravia's creative sensitivity. He was born in Rome in 1907, and much of his childhood was colored by a painful bone disease that required a prolonged stay in a sanitarium and the use first of crutches and later of a cane. He still walks with discomfort; but his illness was to serve him by recompense, and in a manner not uncommon in the history of literature, both as stimulus and as sheer material for his fiction: *Sick Boy's Winter* (1930) was a brilliant early fruit of the days at the Istituto Codavilla in Cortina. His worst experience during the war came toward the end of it, when he tried to flee southward from Rome to Allied-occupied Naples, in 1943, and got stuck en route. He spent nine months of hideous boredom, hiding out with his wife and some shepherds in a kind of covered pigsty, silent, inactive, watching the endless rain descend (as he has said) "like a liquid wall and always the same." This episode, too, was to be fruitful. Out of the discomfort and the boredom, Moravia, fourteen years later, fashioned one of his solidest novels: *Two Women*, a meticulous account of the winter he still vividly remembered.

He had written *The Fancy Dress Party*, a curious short novel, in 1941, and the eloquent *Agostino* three years later; but his uninterruptedly fertile period began with the arrival of spring and the Allied armies in 1944. *The Woman of Rome* followed in 1947; *Luca* (another short novel, coupled with *Agostino* as *Two Adolescents* in English) in 1948; *Conjugal Love* in 1949, *The Conformist* in 1950, and *A Ghost at Noon* in 1954. It is in these works (along with *Two Women*) that Moravia's image of human nature and human experience—though present, as I have said, from the beginning—assumed its full and unmistakably Moravian shape.

The Strategy of Conversion

Perhaps the element most often vitalized by the sexual impulse, in Moravia's treatment of it, is money—the element closest indeed to sex in the center of Moravia's vision of human affairs. Moravia's characters are relentlessly grasping; but they or their observers intermittently realize that it is not the acquisitive but the sexual instinct that grasps after satisfaction. One of *Racconti Romani*,[4] for example, shows us a real-estate agent with designs upon a beautiful and aristocratic young widow, some of whose property he has been asked to sell. His hopes fade as he discovers that the woman derives her sexual gratification not from men but from money—from the very fantasy of making money, from demanding many times more money for the property than she can possibly expect to get. The lines cross skillfully: the widow's interviews with prospective buyers are forms of flirtation aimed at increasing the price in the pursuit of an essentially nonfinancial pleasure. The agent gives up. "I had been the agent in a business affair, but now she had made me become the agent in a sordid love affair. Before I knew what I was doing, I burst out, 'Princess, I am a broker, not a pimp'; and red in the face, I hurried away."

The child Agostino (in the novella bearing his name), reveals only his innocence when he wonders—gazing at a country villa turned into a brothel—"what the relation was between money, which usually served to acquire well-defined objects of measurable quantity, and caresses, nudity, female flesh." A connection is readily intuited by the initiated. Adriana, the woman of Rome, remembers her surprising willingness to accept money the first time it is offered her—and by a man she dislikes, at a moment she believes herself "engaged" (in the fine free Italian meaning of the word) to someone else:

> The feeling I experienced at the moment bewildered me . . . a feeling of complicity and sensual conspiracy such as none of his caresses in the restaurant bedroom had been able to arouse in me. It was a feeling of inevitable subjection. . . . I knew, of course, that I ought to refuse the money; but at the same time I wanted to accept it. And not so much from greed, as from the new kind of pleasure which his offering had afforded me.

The young woman who narrates "The English Officer" (1946) recalls, like Adriana, the "spontaneity" and "attitude of surrender" with which she took the first money offered her for going to bed with an Allied soldier.

Moravia's repertoire is not a large one; in fact, he has insisted that it must not be. "I never trust a writer who can say too many things," he has told a *New Yorker* interviewer. "By that I mean a writer who has too many tunes to play. One good tune is enough. Good writers are monotonous, like good composers. Their truth is self-repeating. They keep rewriting the same book. That is to say, they keep trying to perfect their expression of the one problem they were born to understand." [5]

The political dimension of life yields not much less easily than does the economic. Fascism and underground anti-Fascist activities enter *The Woman of Rome* as a shadowy other world; they are made to seem an unreal intrusion—via the insubstantial character of Mino—into the reality of the heroine's sexual history. In an essay on communism and the West (1954), Moravia alluded resentfully to the recent "politicization" (his word) of life; and he has attempted, in his own writings, to reverse that tendency. "Moravia distrusts politics," his friend and colleague Paolo Milano has said about him; "and he has a qualified indifference towards history—individual men interest him, not crowded events." [6] Moravia's distrust leads, in his fiction, to the conversion, or attempted conversion, of the political into the sexual: an effort which compares interestingly to that of Silone, who, as we shall see, has sought to transform the political into the charitable, out of an even more radical distrust of the former.

Moravia's attempt is projected with entertaining directness in "Bitter Honeymoon" (1951), in which a young couple, starting on their honeymoon, run into one of the bride's political colleagues, a fellow worker in "the Party." The husband, Giacomo, is (he says) not interested in politics, though he is vitally interested in consummating the marriage after a failure to do so the night before. The Communist intruder, Livio, argues that everything has its political implications: "How could it be otherwise? Politics is everything." Simona, the wife, wobbles between the two men in a state of uncertain potentiality; she had failed to report her marriage to the Party, but she had also resisted her husband's advances. Listening to the two comrades talking together, Giacomo suspects gloomily that "comrade" may represent a more intimate relation than "lover." But love conquers all, or nearly so; at least, the human element seems vindicated; and the story ends with the first instant of consummation. In *The Conformist*, an admirably ambitious but on the whole unsuccessful novel, Moravia attempts nothing less than a philosophical demonstration in narrative of the sexual origins of political commitment—the Fascist temperament as rooted in a youthful homosexual trauma. And in his *Portrait of Machiavelli* (1950), Moravia intimates that the peculiar quality of Machiavelli's political passion was the consequence of sexual frustration, or the consequence at least of an utter moral exhaustion that Moravia perceives in Machiavelli's cold comedy of seduction, *Man-*

dragola, and which he defines by means of a close comparison with the Marquis de Sade.

Friendship, to judge from Moravia's fiction, is determined and measured by a man's sexual conduct toward his friend's wife or mistress: several rather amiable items from the *Racconti Romani* underline this criterion. Family relations are shaped in the same manner. The theme of *Agostino* is examined in the context of the predominantly, almost overtly sexual relation between a young mother and her child. An awareness of that relation is the beginning of Agostino's transition to manhood, of the decline of his innocence and the toughening of his heart: when, secretly watching his mother undress, he says to himself—with an attitude that "seemed to him almost scientific but which in fact owed its false objectivity to the cruelty of sentiment which inspired it"—"She is a woman . . . nothing but a woman." In *The Time of Indifference,* the relations between mother and daughter, mother and son, and sister and brother are elaborately defined by the sexual aspect: as incarnate in the businessman, Leo, who moves in the novel from an affair with the mother to an affair with the daughter, while the brother looks on, alternating between a dreary effort to feel morally indignant over his family's behavior and the thought that he might turn his sister's quasi-incestuous degradation to his own account by borrowing money from her new lover. "*L'Architetto*" (1935) is a lighter and less contorted variation on this same singular design. And when Moravia wrote his first original play (he had already dramatized his short novel *The Fancy Dress Party*), he was drawn quite naturally to the tale of Beatrice Cenci and her repulsive father— "since," as he has remarked, "the relations between father and daughter . . . lend themselves to a psychological interpretation very close to the modern sensibility, and have indeed an almost existentialist flavor."

These illustrations are typical. These are the inhabitants and these the characteristic involvements in the somewhat lopsided Moravian universe. It is to be noted that there is no historical or religious or mythological dimension to this universe, either pure or converted; this is one of the many ways in which Moravia should be differentiated from D. H. Lawrence, who may also be said to have described the world in its sexual aspect, but with a sense of incipient force and with a rich and tender carelessness altogether distinct from the meticulously ordered proceedings of Alberto Moravia. Nothing, for example, could be more alien to Moravia than Lawrence's own achievement of deep-flowing artistic conversion in *The Man Who Died*, in which the crucified but not wholly dead Christ is restored to life by the sexual devotion of a priestess of Isis. The religious impulse is thus converted into the erotic impulse in a manner that converts near death into a *vita nuova*. Moravia's view of the mythic as well of life in general and of family relations was plainly indicated in the comment introducing his second novel, *Mistaken Ambitions*, in 1935. "In *The Time of Indifference*," he wrote, "the author tried to create tragedy based on traditional motives—those, so to say, which grow out of the tensions and disequilibria of a badly tangled family situation: those for example of Aeschylus in the *Oresteia*, or of Shakespeare in *Hamlet*." [7] It should be added, in fairness, that Moravia has recently satirized his earlier attitude by including, in *A Ghost at Noon*, a preposterous interpretation of the *Odyssey* as a bleak story of sexual incompatibility—a view of that spacious poem that Moravia's hero-narrator is permitted violently to reject.

But the literary allusions are none the less significant: for perhaps the major tactic within Moravia's broad strategy of conversion—of transforming a familiar moral note into an essentially sexual note—is to invoke the literary echo, in a partly joking and partly jaundiced manner. He is quoted as relating the scene in *The Time of Indifference* in which Leo and Carla embrace behind the curtains, their guilty pleasure heightened by peeking out at the betrayed but unsuspecting mother, to the famous "curtain scene" in *Hamlet;* and it may be, as Daniel Aaron has suggested,[8] that the seduction of Leda by the barber in *Conjugal Love* wryly re-enacts, and willfully debases, the more ancient seduction of Leda by the god as swan. In *The Time of Indifference* again, there is a manifest echo—within the context of an affair gone stale before it has started—of one of the best-known and most poignant soliloquies in Italian literature. It is the classic *addio monti* passage in chapter eight of Manzoni's *I Promessi Sposi*, the farewell of chaste Lucia to her homeland and her lover: "Farewell mountains springing from the waters and rising to the sky . . . farewell house that was still not hers. . . ." This turns up in *The Time of Indifference*, echoed by Carla's soliloquy as she hastens through the inevitable rain toward her mother's lover: "Farewell streets, farewell deserted quarters," and so on. The transformation implicit in the echo depends crucially upon the purity, the firm moral character of the original.

THE TRAGICOMEDY OF EXISTENCE

All of this brings us to a central quality, or combination of qualities, in Moravia's fiction, a recognition of which must modify our first impression of frankness and realism. I mean its literary and especially its theatrical quality, and its pervasive semicomic mood.

Moravia's work is to some extent impressively realistic, and it has an exceptional vividness of presentation. His words at their best provide instantaneous openings on to the actions they describe; persons and things are observed with a camera-eye exactness, tinged all the while with an elusive wistfulness; but the style rarely *rises*, for there seems to be nothing, as it were, for the style to rise to— the here-and-now, sharply delineated and sadly contemplated, is everything. But his scenes stay fixed in our minds, and our recollection is that we have seen them, not read them; we recall people and places, not words and pages. This is to say, precisely, that his writing is theatrical—and theatrical, it should be insisted, rather than dramatic. Italians for twenty years have been speaking of "the Rome of Moravia"—a crowded, hurried, modernized, and mechanized Rome, full of brief cases and cocktails and very different from the Rome of somewhat older Italian literature; for example, the poetic, heroic, archeological Rome of D'Annunzio.[9] It is true that Moravia has accomplished one of the great feats of the artist in narrative; he has created a world, and he calls it Rome. But Giuseppe Borgese was probably right when, reviewing *The Time of Indifference* in 1929, he contended against the claim for Moravia of sociological accuracy in his portrait of Rome: "There is not much Rome here . . . the scene is made up of lights and draperies, as in certain contemporary *mises en scénes*."

When Moravia won the Marzotto award for fiction in 1954, he was introduced, aptly enough, as "the last Goldonian in Italy." The reference was to the eighteenth century Venetian playwright, author of several scores of comedies of intrigue and manners. Moravia works assiduously in the whole tradition of Italian culture; Boccaccio, Machiavelli, Ariosto, Manzoni, and many others are very notably reflected in his writing, and he is, in fact, one of the most incorrigibly *literary* novelists of his generation; but he is perhaps closest to Goldoni, and reading Moravia's stories we come upon many signs of his affection. The rhythmic comings and goings, the startling confrontations, the heated dinner conversations, the mistaken identities, the cross-purposes, the deceits, the peepings, the gifts or billets-doux received and mislaid and inopportunely discovered: these are what move the plot in a narrative by Moravia, and they are the devices of conventional farce.

Above all, the device of the accidental witness to the intimate or even the shameful act. The use of it is endless: Agostino, lurking outside the window of a country brothel, peering in at a prostitute and her customer; Marcello, in *The Conformist*, returned unexpectedly to his Paris apartment, hiding in the dark to watch a Lesbian make overtures to his wife; the protagonist of *Conjugal Love* happening, during an evening stroll, upon an adulterous interchange between his wife and the local barber—and a host of other such occasions. One sign of the interesting development represented by Moravia's novel, *A Ghost at Noon*, is—along with the implicit satire it contains of Moravia's own earlier attitude to myth, as mentioned above —the way the hidden-witness motif is turned back on itself. The husband in *A Ghost at Noon* finds himself on one occasion seated next to his wife, badly rattled by her obdurate attitude toward him and furtively watching the fall of her *négligé*. "Suddenly . . . I told myself that this was what I had come to at last: to look at my wife's nakedness in hiding, with the pleasure of forbidden things, like a boy who peeps through a crack in the cabin of a beach resort." That reflection, typical of *A Ghost at Noon*, suggests a deepened moral estimate of the erotic theatricality with which Moravia has for long busied himself. But for much of his earlier work, the device of the secret observer was a valid necessity. It is, to be sure, a classic motif of pornographic literature as well as of farce; but in Moravia, it is primarily a piece of theatrical mechanics, not lingered over for its own sake (if there is a truly pornographic ele-

ment in any of our five novelists, it is within the paradoxes of
Graham Greene) but essential to the progress of the action. It
is the turning point or even the climax. For the very core of Moravia's fiction *is* theatrical. He begins not on a clearly felt literal
level, nor even on the so-called symbolic level; he begins on a
theatrical level, with the dramatis personae poised toward each other
in postures of skilled artifice; and the moral content follows from
there. His fiction, that is, moves under the compulsive effort of
both author and character to squeeze genuine sentiment out of
traditional stage business.

Now genuine sentiment, in these stories, is the first dependable
mark of being alive. In fact, given the human condition reflected
by Moravia, it is precisely a sentiment·*about* being alive; the Moravian character suffers from the need attributed by Moravia to
Machiavelli—the need "to feel himself alive." [10] What is gradually
revealed to us as Moravia's pervasive theme, a theme even more
pervasive than sex and in fact served by the erotic theme, is nothing
else than the sensation of existence. This is the end to which
Moravia's fiction may be seen to be pressing; and it is to this that the
sexual encounter regularly and treacherously seems to promise the
clue.[11] As a consequence of his theme, Moravia's stories are more
ridden by anxiety than the Goldonian comedies they draw upon;
the stake is so much more important. Goldoni's work, too, had its
measure of realism, along with a certain hardness of tone; Goldoni
lacked the warm romantic humor, say, of Goldsmith or the rational
gaiety of Beaumarchais. But his comedies were firm in outline and
unstrained in manner; they centered on the complicated steps of
the intrigue in question, and intrigue could provide Goldoni with a
set pattern of action in which he might take a detached, if sometimes uncharitable, delight. But despite the morbid amusement they
may contain, Moravia's tragicomedies of intrigue are (like *Man-
dragola*) darker and more desperate; for Moravia focuses not upon
the intrigue but—through the intrigue—upon the encounter the
intrigue was to bring about, and upon the reward the encounter
was to assure; and comedy dissipates in panic as the outcome of the
adventure seems ever more dubious.

Or perhaps we should say that only the laughter dissipates: the
comic mood, however discolored, remains. Traditional comedy,

from the Greek stage onward, has defined a particular rhythm of experience that concludes with the unmasking of impostors and the celebration of marriage. Impostors are for the most part unmasked in the fiction of Moravia, but anything like a marriage is just what dismally fails to take place. That is why his stories may more properly be called tragicomedies; and why, in this respect, they are like many of the narratives of Henry James (a writer with whom Moravia might not otherwise be easily associated)—in particular, like *The Ambassadors*, where the imposthume represented by the adultery of Chad Newsome and Mme. de Vionnet is exposed, but where the potential marriage between Strether and Miss Gostrey is fastidiously renounced. The tone of that novel is explicitly stated at the moment of renunciation: "She sighed it at last all tragically, all comically away." With a shift in pronoun, the sentence could conclude Moravia's *Conjugal Love*.

James was congenitally interested in the question of living. Moravia has been obsessed with a more radical mystery—the mystery of existence itself, the fundamental enigma that, I venture to say, has been the chief concern of Moravia's literary generation, both in Italy and elsewhere: as this book will, I trust, sufficiently testify. What the concern amounts to in Moravia's case may best be suggested by tracing through his stories the process by which he arrived at it; as the sexual intention gradually invades the whole of observable life only to pause before the threshold of the source of life itself. I have rehearsed the "sexualization" of money, politics, friendship, and family relations; to these may be added the moral virtues—courage, honor, good will, kindness, truthfulness, self-respect, all of them tested and given their meaning in sexual terms. And even beyond those, the trivial rituals of the daily round: dressing and undressing, shaving, bathing, eating and drinking, the trip to the seashore, the afternoon walk, the leisurely times in the neighborhood cafe. The same inclination energizes them all, the same atmosphere surrounds them. But here and there we detect a deepening of penetration to the more elementary conditions of human survival. Health and sickness, for example: we can cite the rapidly sketched "*Infermiera*" (*Racconti Romani*), in which the gardener of a Roman villa fails in the courtship of his patron's nurse because the latter was more attracted by sickness than by health. Her taste was "to make love with sick people; but I, un-happily, was healthy, and so there was absolutely no hope for me." Better than that, and one of Moravia's finest novellas, is *Sick Boy's Winter*, the whole of which takes place in a sanitarium, with the narrative prose fairly breathing the sterilized air of its corridors. Here, the progress of the young hero's convalescence is entirely implicated in the development and expression of his sexual pride; he seduces a wan little English girl, a fellow patient, and both he and his mute pitiful victim suffer nearly fatal relapses. In *Luca*, adolescent sexuality leads through a grave illness to the longing for death, and then onward to partial recovery and the meager promise of a new life.

Dealing as he does so persistently with the sexual element, Moravia could scarcely help sounding the note already familiar in modern literature: the ambiguous relation between sex and death; and he has not failed to offer his own erotic variation on the grand pattern of death and rebirth—for instance, the combination of murder, suicide, and impending childbirth that turgidly concludes *The Woman of Rome*. But life and death are stripped by Moravia to their innermost essence. They are very simply existence and non-existence. They are the plus and minus of radical vitality, as affected by sexual action. In the fiction of Moravia, we have a recurring picture of Eros moving between being and nonbeing. It is this that distinguishes the fiction once and for all from pornography; for the incessant peepings and pryings in Moravia's stories are, beyond pornography and even beyond farce, symptoms of an insatiable desire to catch a glimpse of the secret reality of human beings—their primary existence, what is hidden or misrepresented by public morality, conventions and clothing. They are symptoms, in short, of a hectic and self-conscious and yet ambiguous romanticism; they are symptomatic, too, of an author whose characters, as inveterate spies, are surrogates for their creator, whose work may be called the most thoroughgoing job of private espionage in modern fiction. But again, a distinction must be pressed; for as to Moravia's ana-tomical concern, his repeated and detailed descriptions of the naked body, what this suggests, as more than one critic has asserted, is not a salacious interest in nudity but an aptitude for still-life paint-ing. The Italian phrase for still-life, more telling than ours, is *natura morta;* and it is exactly Moravia's ambition and that of his principal characters to transform *natura morta* into *natura viva.*

The ambition offers a peculiar challenge to Moravia's artistic talent, for existence, as it seems to be conceived in the Moravian ethic, is anything but a dramatic subject. The ethic itself contains few seeds of the dramatic; it is personal and nonphilosophical in its nature; it is a feeling, rather than a theory; a mood and a tone, rather than a discourse. We could perhaps say that it is a fragment of existentialism that evaporates at the critical moments; for while Moravia's characters, like those in certain of the writings of Sartre and Camus, reach for wholeness and identity *through* action (through cautiously staged sexual action, in the case of Moravia), they almost always fail.[12] Carla, the heroine of *The Time of Indifference,* enters the affair with Leo out of muddled desire for a "new life": a phrase that, in typical Moravian fashion, sings ironically in Italian with its flattened reminder of Dante's *Vita Nuova,* an account of spiritual rebirth through ennobling love. And Carla fails so abysmally that she cannot answer her brother Michele when he asks her why she had behaved so. Life, as she had anticipated it, was too scanty a thing to have striven for. " 'So as to have a new life': was what she wanted to answer; but she had not the courage. That remote reason of hers, now that she saw nothing was changed except her surrendered body, appeared to her ridiculous and unworthy." Michele and his sister are the first in Moravia's long catalogue of failures: mostly masculine failures, be it noted in passing, for Moravia's women are occasionally endowed with a sort of hulking secret, just as they are given personal names (Leda, Adriana, etc.) more consistently than are the men. Moravia's heroes are apt to be small, indistinct, ill-favored, and hesitant; and there is a portion of verisimilitude here that I will not labor, both in the portrayal of Italian women and men and in the exposure everywhere on the chosen scene of the sexual preoccupation. But what the men do acquire is the consolation of a rueful humor, a still faintly comic reflection of *This is the way things are;* how foolish, ultimately, is the human posture and the human destiny. For the price of failure is to be condemned to a second-class existence, a form of nonexistence, something that is to be suffered rather than enacted. Moravia's stories are therefore, and by design, pathetic rather than dramatic;

pathos is the middle and the end of his characteristic narrative.

In *Luca*, a little sum of existence is actually retrieved: enough to give this excellent short novel a rarely positive and almost (but not quite) a hopeful quality. Luca, an adolescent of good family, undergoes a nervous breakdown and is brought back from the edge of nonexistence by a robust woman who nurses him, bathes him, and finally makes love to him; but his recovery is isolated and private, almost metaphysical; it relates him to existing things qua existing, but in no sense does it relate him to humanity. The suggestion of a Camus or a Silone, that the answer to the sense of non-existence is companionship and compassion, has yet to appear in the pages of Moravia. Hence the dispirited, prematurely exhausted quality that so often pervades these pages: the absence, that is, of creative tension. Such tension as his fiction does manage to generate is elaborately exemplified in *The Woman of Rome*, in the contrast between the natural, inframoral bias toward life of Adriana, the Roman prostitute, and the bias toward death of her succession of lovers.

Adriana has a simple capacity for existence; and it is that capacity —rather than any rage to live—that is challenged, bruised, and seduced, but never destroyed in the course of her recorded experiences. For along with a talent for existence, Adriana has a distinct taste for the deathly. Her lovers are death symbols, symbols of anti-existence, recognizable variations on deadliness: and the drama they engage her in is an antic, sensual, and highly traditional *danse macabre*. The men in her life cavort ominously before her, beckoning and grinning: Astarita, the police administrator, who looks like a death's-head and who speaks of himself as a "garbage-can for rubbish" and curses the day he was born; Sonzogno, the murderer, in whose embrace Adriana "felt a pleasure made sinister and atrocious by fear [so that] I could not restrain a long wailing cry in the dark, as if the final clasp had been the clasp of death, not of love, and my cry was life departing from me"; Mino, the hapless revolutionist, who is faithless to his calling and who tells Adriana in bed that he has "died—just died. Died forever." For her part, on her side of the bed, Adriana acknowledges the deeply seductive appeal of nothingness in a meditation of singularly erotic detail:

I began to think about the sea again and was overcome by the longing to drown myself. I imagined it would only be a moment's suffering, and then my lifeless body would float from wave to wave beneath the sun for ages. The gulls would peck my eyes, the sun would burn my breast and belly, the fish would gnaw my back. At last I would sink to the bottom, would be dragged head downwards towards some icy blue current that would carry me along the seabed for months and years among submarine rocks, fish and seaweed, and floods of limpid salt water would wash my forehead, my breast and my belly, my legs, slowly wearing away my flesh, smoothing and refining me continually. And at last some wave would cast me up on some shore, nothing but a handful of fragile, white bones . . . and perhaps someone without noticing it would walk on my bones and crush them to white powder. With these sad, voluptuous thoughts, I fell asleep.

But Adriana survives the self-annihilating impulse of her lovers; and while Mino commits suicide and Astarita and Sonzogno deliberately get themselves killed, Adriana's tribute is the only pregnancy I can recall in Moravia's fiction.

THE SUPREMACY OF SADNESS

The Woman of Rome is, on balance, a distinguished piece of fiction; but it is distinguished, I suggest, in the terms proposed above, as an image of Eros moving between being and nonbeing. To speak of its affinities with French realism, as some readers have done, or to identify it as an Italian *Moll Flanders*, is to miss its real quality by extracting the subject matter from the texture. The tone of Daniel Defoe and the world it informs (hard, dry, virile, and epiphenomenal) have almost nothing in common with the lyrical reflectiveness, the muffled nostalgia, that modify the happenings in *The Woman of Rome*, or any other work by Alberto Moravia. That tone is most effectively rendered, perhaps, in *Conjugal Love;* over which we may briefly linger, by way of conclusion, since it seems to me his most elegantly wrought romance of existence.

Conjugal Love has a kind of subdued perfection; and it illustrates memorably Moravia's personal sense of the poignant foolishness of human aspiration and illusion. It tends, too, to confirm the suspicion aroused by *Agostino* and *Luca* that Moravia is usually happier with the short novel (and the short story) than with the novel proper;

his resources and his themes appear to lack the variety and the inward momentum that novels require. *Conjugal Love* seems aware of these limitations, and never seeks to extend itself. The husband's narration gives the impression of some tidy person leafing through his private scrapbook. For what happens in the book—more important than its plot, which is a reshuffle of Moravia's theatrical stock in trade—is the creation through the arts of narrative of a feeling or a mood: the sense of existence as suffering.

The story introduces us to a married couple of independent means, enjoying the graceful leisure of a Tuscan villa. The wife, Leda, is a fastidious and affectionate person, marked however by an observably ambivalent attitude—a combination of attraction and disgust—toward the sordid and ugly in human experience. The husband is marked by the sort of taste, intelligence, and fussy kindness —all genuine, but when taken together, pathetically inadequate— that characterized Lambert Strether, whose unlucky fate it was also, in James's *The Ambassadors*, to stumble upon an adultery that his very kindness and taste had prevented him from guessing at. Like Strether, the husband is a man of mild literary pretensions; and when we meet him, he is settling down to the composition of a story—a small work of art that will be called, of course, *Conjugal Love*. Creative power and sexual power are established in the familiar but always fertile tension of similarity and hostility: the husband's brief fit of artistic energy demands from him a marital abstinence, as his entire fund of potency is given over to his writing. We are not left in doubt over the outcome, for the tone from the beginning has reduced drama to pathos; and we foresee, without the need for bracing, the evening when the husband will discover at once his wife's infidelity and his own irrevocable failure as a novelist. But the moral of the book—and perhaps it is the moral of Moravia's fiction in general—has been reached several chapters earlier.

The husband has been puzzled by some elusive quality in Antonio, the barber who comes to shave him daily and who will eventually cuckold him—dragging from his wife the full physical expression of her fascinated revulsion. The barber's secret, the husband learns, is simply that his demure and courteous exterior masks an indefatigable Don Juan, an erotomaniac. But the husband goes on to realize that the discovery answers nothing; and his meditation at this point is almost a personal apologia of the author.

> The mystery I had noticed when I knew nothing about him survived even now when I thought I knew everything. That mystery had been pushed backwards into a less accessible zone, that was all. It was a little, I began to think, like the mystery of all things, the big and the small: you can explain everything except their existence.

The perception of the enigma of existence beneath the puzzle of devouring sexuality shapes the husband's final attitude and hence the feeling diffused through the book. The disasters, such as they are, do not spring from vicious or chronically self-willed deceitfulness. They are due to an impersonal fraudulence in the nature of things, the way things ineluctably are; and so the book closes on a note of simple acceptance—not with anger or bitterness, but with rue for remembrance and sadness for all the imaginable future. The husband confides at the end his acceptance of a second class existence, a shrunken assignment to perpetual mediocrity; he will become "a much more modest man."

Sadness is thus the supreme emotion in the Moravian universe. It is the one emotion that transcends indifference—as indifference itself is an achieved condition that transcends the vulgar credulity, the unexamined faith in human debasement, of the Antonios and the Leos. Indifference is the final response to the world in its sexual aspect; but sadness is what a man feels when he has "pushed [the mystery] backwards into a less accessible zone"; it is the only sentiment remaining to those who have arrived at the condition realized at a stroke by Moravia in the first of his novels, *The Time of Indifference*. This is why, as some Italian critics have complained, there is not much "story" to Moravia's career: his themes, his characters, his devices, his moral range were all exemplified by the time he was twenty. His story is the story of an endeavor to move beyond indifference, and for reasons of art as well as morality. Sadness is as far as he has been able to get. For what Moravia is unable to portray—because in all honesty he is unable to detect it—is a moral world more real and resilient than the condensed and decaying world in which his characters glumly move: a more remote machinery, even if it turns out to be infernal machinery, at work behind the stage machinery so prominent in the middle distance.

The absence of such a counterworld means the absence, too, of any sharply defined vision of evil; for the betrayals Moravia describes are not flanked by the persuasive imagery of innocence and conscience. There is consequently only a slight and shadowy moral tension, little actual resistance and no tragedy. At most, the minds of his characters are fleetingly troubled, not by a sense of sin, but by a sense of having forgotten something that might once have been a sense of sin. "The fault was Carla's as well," muses Michele, ". . . and his mother's too. The fault was everyone's; impossible to discover its source, the original cause of it." And behind that, a sense, fainter than perfume in an empty room, of a lost paradise: "a paradise of reality and truth," as Michele vaguely tells himself; "a paradise where everything—gestures, words, feelings—would have a direct connection with the reality in which they had originated."

The memory of this paradise appears as an occasional mirage in the stories of Moravia, something to serve as the basis for resentment but not strong enough to promote rebellion. The representative hero of Moravia, like modern man himself in Camus's definition, feels himself a stranger "in a universe suddenly emptied of illusion and light," an exile fatally deprived "of the memories of a lost home country or the hope of a promised land." In the world of Albert Camus, revolt has gradually emerged as man's only dignifying act; but Moravia's is a world in which revolt is improbable. It lies dormant, a painless hell, undisturbed by the expectancy of a fresh revelation, a larger conversion: the conversion, perhaps, of existence into life. The contents of that world are fairly indicated in the very language of Moravia's titles (especially in the original), with their invariable allusion to indifference, contempt, sickness, weariness, poor judgment, equivocation, deceit, crime, smallness, ugliness, conformity, bitterness, unhappiness, or solitude. The word "hope" or anything like it has never appeared except once, and then in the title of an essay rather than a narrative: "La Speranza." But La Speranza is not an affirmation of hope, it is a skeptical analysis of its phenomenon, and an analysis that—by defining hope as the illusory impulse that spurs men on in the endless pursuit of the impossible—permits Moravia to identify *The Castle* of Franz Kafka as the very type of hope-filled book.

The aspects of Moravia stressed in this chapter are the ones which ought to be stressed at this reckoning of him; they have been the defining aspects of his work over nearly three decades. But his estimate of the world has grown increasingly complex. In his most recent novel, *Two Women*, Moravia concludes by a clear sounding of the themes that mark him unmistakably as a central participant in the novelistic "world of discourse" of the second generation. They are the themes which will especially concern us during the rest of our discussion—the radically simple interlocking themes of human compassion and of the motion from death to life which compassion may stimulate. *Two Women* is the detailed account of life in a refugee hideout in the mountains during the long months between the Allied invasion of Italy and the liberation of Rome. The experience of Cesira (the lower-class woman who tells the story) and her daughter Rosetta—the confusion and danger and discomfort, the singularly brutal violation of the daughter and her subsequent moral collapse, the shocks and betrayals: all this seems to the mother in retrospect to have been an experience of death itself. But returning to Rome at last, she remembers the reading by a heroic young neighbor-in-hiding of the Bible story of Lazarus, the man raised from the dead by Jesus. In the book's final words, Cesira seems to find in Lazarus a symbol for herself and her daughter.

> Now I understood that Michele was right; and that for some time we had been dead, Rosetta and I, dead to the compassion we owe to others and to ourselves. But grief had saved us at the last moment; and so, in a certain sense, what had happened to Lazarus was true for us also; since, thanks to grief, we had come out of the war which had shut us up in its tomb of indifference and cruelty. We had begun once again to go forward in our own life, a poor life full of uncertainty and error, but the only life we had to live. . . .

It was not by accident that Ignazio Silone, as we shall see, chose the name of Lazarus for the Italian peasant-farmer who, in *A Handful of Blackberries*, would represent the possibility of rebirth through the force of compassion. Both Silone and Moravia were drawing on one of the greatest recorded symbols of human resurrection; and both are associating the event symbolized with the sharing of pain. Nor is it, as I shall suggest, a mere coincidence that Graham Greene's most recent work, *The Potting Shed*, should turn on another instance, not less miraculous than that of Lazarus, of a man actually and physically restored to life. An involvement with that extraordinary event, whether it be seen as literal or metaphorical, is a determining feature of second generation writing.

But Moravia's last sentence should not be overlooked, either: "a poor life, full of uncertainty and error. . . ." No gay and splendid triumph has been envisaged or described. The human reality Moravia looks upon and delineates for us remains soiled and it remains stunted; for that is the way it does look to a writer of courage, tenacity, intelligence and very considerable talent. There is a measure of gallantry in Moravia's picture of things, and in his resolute refusal to make his picture any handsomer, or to draw on sustenance from afar. We find in his work little evidence of that larger human heroism, the sacrificial devotion to the miseries of mankind that characterizes betimes the fiction of Camus and Silone, of Faulkner and Greene and to which the word "saintly" so ambiguously applies. In this respect, too, we acknowledge Moravia's stubborn gallantry. Not everyone who says to him, "Lord, Lord," will persuade Moravia that the awaiting reality is, or in any manner resembles, the kingdom of heaven.

CHAPTER 3

Albert Camus:
The Compassionate Mind

Descender plus bas pour monter plus hautement.
MARGUERITE DE NAVARRE, *Chanson Spirituelle*

THE FORCE OF INDIFFERENCE

THE INDIFFERENCE that for Moravia of Italy led usually to sadness of heart and a final retreat from ambition becomes instead, for Albert Camus of France, a hard clarity of mind that makes advance once again possible and even imperative. "Everything starts from clear-sighted indifference," Camus wrote in *The Myth of Sisyphus* (1942 —French edition); for he has found in indifference a point of departure, a sort of creative sterility out of which a limited portion of understanding, the objects of a faith, and the sources of a guarded contentment may be drawn. In his view, also, indifference is something one laboriously arrives at, by the scrupulous shedding of inborn illusions. But now it is no longer an end, it is a prerequisite to wisdom. The indifference bespoken by Camus not only relates him momentarily to Moravia. As Camus has elaborated and examined that condition, it places him at the close of the more than century-long European tradition of *malaise*, that deep and growing uneasiness of spirit, with its spasmodic expression of the sense of *le néant* (nothingness) and its disempowering doubt of the validity of all moral distinctions. But Camus's dramatic and philosophical inquiries mark an impressive turn in the career of recent Western culture. By possessing himself of that career and by going far behind it in his own ever-enlarging—and, as I shall suggest, highly idiosyncratic—view of it, Camus has found some of the terms for going at least a small distance beyond it.

Camus has carried his inquiry into the human condition to a depth of nihilism far below the sad frustration described by Moravia. But the aim is always in some sense positive: *Descender plus bas,* as one of his remote literary ancestors remarked, *pour monter plus hautement.*[1] And the force is always intellectual. All five of our novelists are representative men in the lofty Emersonian sense, as we have already noted: persons who spell out, by word or by deed, what is elsewhere only implicit or potential in the body of their time; and among them, Camus is the representative man of thought and letters. Among them, that is, Camus is the most emphatically concerned with mind, and with its recorded history: although his Gallic lucidity is strangely enlivened by a rashness native to the Algeria where he was born in 1913. The combination in him of the austere and the immoderate (reminiscent of another passionate logician from the same province, Augustine of Tagaste and Hippo) lends an added pace and intensity to both his negative and his positive excursions. It also, one must admit, lends an air of elusiveness to his arguments. Camus was trained in philosophy, and briefly, during his young manhood, he taught philosophy in Oran; yet his meanings seem often to recede mockingly before us, shimmering but indistinct; and academic philosophers spend aimless hours exposing his baffling inconsistencies. Camus's thought is observably crowded with contradictions, for he is given to an excess of statement, a triumph of rhetoric over rigor; and he indulges himself in flat and reckless formulas the reverse of which may often be quite equally true. An example, from *The Myth of Sisyphus:* "What distinguishes the modern sensibility from the classic is that the latter was nourished by moral problems, the former by metaphysical problems." If "classic" can mean Plato and Aristotle—rather than Cicero and Seneca—the comment can be turned about; it is improbable that any age, especially the time-intoxicated twentieth century, will recover the unspoiled metaphysical insistence, the primary and controlling concern with the nature of reality, that characterized the Greeks.

Still, the encounters in Camus's stories and plays *are* almost invariably philosophic disputes over questions of value; while his essays dramatize the unremitting contest between human reason and the objects it confronts. His mind moves steadily forward, even when it can do so only by a sort of restless squirming. But the squirming is always honest; and it is a sign of the role Camus plays best—the dedicated dramatist of the besieged intellect. So the indifference he started from was in fact clear-sighted: a sturdily developed quality of mind, not a Moravian failure of sentiment. And he was able to get beyond indifference when his native rashness managed to transform his severe intellectual findings into the sense of compassion. That is why, in the present context, Camus stands not only for mind, but for the compassionate mind, although, as it may perhaps appear, there is yet too much mind in him for the compassion to do its full work in creating or restoring a believable image of man.

If Camus is the most philosophical, he is also the most cultivated—that is, the most literary and even the most bookish—of our novelists; he participates in the world of books to a degree a good deal beyond the occasional faddism of Moravia. Camus's writings are dense with reflections of other and earlier novelists, playwrights, poets, essayists, and philosophers (he would make an ideal victim of that favorite undertaking of the American graduate student: the hunt for sources); and where the reflections are not explicit, further affinities none the less suggest themselves. There is in him a sizable amount of the dark wit, the long vision and the intensive dialectics of Pascal (he has been called "a Pascal without Christ"); and he plainly writes in the tradition of Montaigne and those stylish French moral essayists known as the precursors of Nietzsche; while Nietzsche himself is the writer Camus has most unequivocally commended. His fictional heroes have been compared to those of Stendhal; and Martha in his play *Cross-Purposes* has been taken as the histrionic sister of both Greek Electra and the heroines of neo-classic French tragedy. He is beholden to André Gide for certain narrative techniques and to Kafka and, even more, to Ernest Hemingway for matters of narrative style. It is probable that several passages from the Marquis de Sade were in his head when he was writing the play *Caligula;* and his moral and metaphysical posture seems to owe much to Dostoevski and Melville. And though he has "signed off" more than once from the existentialist movement,[2] he has been greatly affected by the premises and by the thrust toward reality and experience of both major groups in it: Kierkegaard, Jaspers, and Chestov on the one hand, Heidegger, Sartre, and their antireligious colleagues on the other.

Yet out of all these elements there emerges, not the intellectual Heavy Dragoon one might have expected, but a strongly outlined individual personality with a sharply individual moral vision. That vision, as it has been unfolded for us since Camus's early book *Noces* (1939), has been energized by a pair of relentless quarrels: first, a quarrel with God and with any sort of consolatory supernaturalism; second, and more recently, a quarrel with history and the quicksands of historicism: in the name of human freedom, human suffering, human reason, and human solidarity. This is why, as Joseph Frank has remarked, Albert Camus, still more than Jean-Paul Sartre, is "the spokesman for the most serious part of the younger generation in France . . . his voice has a gravity, a moral weight, a human vibration, which Sartre, for all his brilliance, is never able to attain. Camus, one feels, is primarily interested in human beings." [3] And this also is why Camus, even while his ultimate meanings continue to recede so tantalizingly before us, is so widely and vigorously discussed by critics and commentators, and why he is crucial to our search for the contemporary human image. As one of the main characters says about the protagonist of *Caligula,* "He forces you to think. He forces the whole world to think."

What Camus has forced us to think about is the very warrant for continued human existence and the possible resources of the human spirit in a universe that appears no longer to make sense: a universe from which God has silently withdrawn; a universe in which, as Caligula says with bitter amazement, "men die and they are not happy"; a universe unspeakably indifferent to the natural aspirations of men. In his first few books, Camus used and abused the word "absurd" to identify such a universe (and also, confusingly, to identify the kind of person who learns how to get along with it, as well as the work of art that faithfully mirrors it). The special contemporary meaning of this word was first established by André Malraux, the intellectual hero of Camus's youth: in Malraux's *Le Tentation de l'Occident* (1926), a character is made to say, "At the center of European man, dominating the great moments of his life, there lies an essential absurdity." As Camus has elaborated on the word, and made it more complex, it has drawn to itself suggestions from the Latin words to which it is related: *absurdus*, which means harsh or grating and the root word *surdus*, which means deaf. An absurd universe is a tuneless universe—a universe that is tone-deaf (the universal representative in *Cross-Purposes* is, fittingly, a deaf and harsh-voiced old servant). It is a universe crowned by a deaf heaven that the individual, like the lover in Shakespeare's sonnet, troubles with his bootless cries. Shakespeare, indeed, foresaw as a frightful possibility the condition Camus has described as actual:

> Take but degree away, untune that string,
> And hark! what discord follows; each thing meets
> In mere oppugnancy . . .
> Force should be right; or rather, right and wrong—
> Between whose endless jar justice resides—
> Should lose their names, and so should justice too.[4]

For Camus, that discord has already followed; right and wrong have lost their ancient names, as the ancient order that named them has crumbled; and the task, as he has seen it, is not to restore but to create anew.

His initial indifference was his mind's way of matching the indifference it perceived as the first feature of the universe: so as not to be "swallowed up," like Conrad's Decoud (in *Nostromo*), "in the vast indifference of things." Everything started from that perception, for it led at once to a refusal that turned into an affirmation. He refused—as against the statement that once aroused such comfortable mirth in Thomas Carlyle [5]—to "accept" an absurd universe. He affectionately repudiated those who, like Kierkegaard and Franz Kafka, did finally accept the universe in a blind leap of faith beyond the limits of scandalized reason. His taste, as he has said, is for the vanquished: for man, as a being doomed to defeat; and in affirming the dignity of man, what he affirmed above all was the tragedy of human dignity. Through the strenuous confrontation of a discordant reality, he wrote in *The Myth of Sisyphus*, "tenderness, creativity, action, human nobility will take their place again in this insensate world. Man will rediscover at last the wine of the absurd and the bread of indifference out of which his greatness will be nourished." The bread and wine of Albert Camus, stripped as they are of all theological implication, are not the bread and wine that gave Ignazio Silone the title for his richest novel. But for Camus no less than for Silone, the symbols announce both a personal *and* an artistic conversion; and they foretell a communion.

THE FORGOTTEN MARRIAGE

In the opening pages of *The Myth of Sisyphus*, Camus introduced the image of man that by then had become fixed in his consciousness and which his novel *The Stranger* was simultaneously presenting in narrative terms: "In a universe suddenly emptied of illusion and light, man feels himself a stranger. His exile is irremediable, since he is deprived of the memories of a lost home country or the hope of a promised land." Yet Camus had in fact once known a kind of paradise and had poignantly traced the loss of it. It was the strange, sad, hazy paradise explored in the little volume of essays about Algeria and Tuscany called *Noces*. Camus's own Eden had, in that book, taken the form of a marriage, a "loving alliance" between man and the earth he inhabits. "Ah," wrote Camus, "I would gladly be converted to it, were it not already my religion."

It was the religion of the exalted present, with its sacred mystery of the human body and its worship of perishable beauty. Into *that* religion, Camus needed no conversion; he had been born into it, as an Algerian; [6] as a young man, then in his twenties, he had only to celebrate it. The need for conversion came later, after the vision of a "loving alliance" had been replaced by the bleak conviction of an irrevocable divorce. But even in that chilly, death-centered later moment, the vision continued, only half forgotten, to exert a force. It glimmers through the darkness of Camus's plays *Cross-Purposes* and *Caligula* and provides much of their protagonists' motivation, both as "the memory of a lost home country" and as "the hope of

a promised land." Caligula is driven to commit murder by the
memory; Martha, in *Cross-Purposes*, by the hope.

The incantatory language of *Noces* comprises a sadly exultant
hymn to life: that is, to a life surrounded by death, and by a death
beyond which there is an enormity of nothing.[7] Most of the themes
that would characterize Camus make their appearance in these four
essays: the devotion to an exclusively earthly experience—"the field
of the possible," as he would later call it; the stealthy approach of
death and the passionate revolt against the meek acceptance of the
obligation to die; the absence of a future and hence the flat dismissal
of illusory hope—for hope is precisely the emotion grounded in a
conception of the future. Even "the absurd" slips in, almost unno-
ticed in the salute to living. But the theme turns up in an exotic
perspective, colored by a restrained and meditative joy. A steady
current of sadness arises from the unresented loss of hope; yet from
it, the young Camus insists, happiness may be born.

> What is happiness except the simple accord between a being and
> the existence he leads? And what accord can more legitimately
> unite man to life except the double awareness of his desire to endure
> and his destiny of death? One learns from that at least to count on
> nothing and to consider the present as the only truth which is given
> us.

Out of that sense of things, Camus added, "the spirit finds its reason
in the body."

But the "accord" celebrated in *Noces*—represented by the marriage of sea and sky in the eternal Algerian summer, re-enacted by
the marriage of male and female flesh—is visualized as something on
the verge of dissolution. If there is a motion in this book, it is a
motion from the atmosphere of the essays on the Algerian countryside to that of the concluding reflections on Tuscany. The Algiers
of *Noces* is the country of the young: "indifferent to spirit . . .
[with] the cult, the admiration of the body"; the country tenderly
quitted by Yeats in "Sailing to Byzantium."[8] It was a country
where the Algerians lived like children in a perpetual high noon:
"a people without a past, without tradition . . . plunged entirely into
its present . . . without myths, without consolation." For myths,
Camus then believed, are merely consolatory inventions of man,
devices for hiding the grim truth about reality; but "the only

truth . . . is the body," along with the fact that the body will shortly rot away. A man who grasps those simple truths needs no consolation; he is relieved at once of the hope of heaven and the fear of hell. Unburdened by hope, the Algerian appeared as genuinely innocent: for the only sin, Camus argued, is a blindness to the beauty of this life in the foolish hope of another. To the hard-skinned innocent of Algiers, the very notion of hell could be no more than the subject of an occasional childlike joke.

Later, contemplating Fiesole and Florence in his own peculiar manner, Camus was able to find a Tuscan confirmation of his Algerian view of life. The prose of the final essay in *Noces* is full of enchantment, but the countryside it describes is oddly crepuscular, the atmosphere notably subdued—as contrasted with the actuality one normally experiences in central Italy. The Italy of the French is always a country one has never known; it fails to resist the transforming power of the Gallic glance; and in *Noces*, it is a never-never land seen through a glass darkly. Detecting Algeria everywhere, Camus even managed to detect a "common resonance" between the Franciscan monks at Fiesole and the betrothed young sun-bathers along the beach at Algiers. It was the resonance, or consonance, of their shared absorption in the immediacy of their physical surroundings. Camus attributed such an absorption to the figures on the canvases of the Tuscan masters; the attitudes of both the divine and the saintly persons suggested to Camus an exclusive involvement in the instant of their experience as depicted, whether the experience was agony or ecstasy. Giotto and Piero seemed to him "novelists of the body," announcing in line and color that "the body is ignorant of hope . . . [and] knows only the beat of its own blood." The very intensity of Camus's limited perspective thus succeeded in cutting the images he looked at clean in half.

But his own innocence, which was then radical, received a jolt from the epiphanies of death he also observed in abundance in Tuscany. The inscriptions over the buried dead in the cloister of Santissima Annunziata—"joy is a pilgrim on earth," for example—gradually provoked in him an impulse of rebellion. It is that frowning resistance that concludes *Noces*, for like *The Stranger* and the first two plays *Noces* ends in an outburst of passion and perception, of self-discovery and revolt. "That joy, indifferent and absorbed like a pilgrim upon the earth, was something I had to follow step by step," Camus told himself. "And for the rest, I said no. I said no with all my strength." He was saying no not so much to the fact of death as to the human docility—to him, indeed, the human dishonesty—before that fact. The one true honorable attitude, he suggested, was disdain grounded in hatred. And that was the exact notion carried by the epigraph he affixed to *Noces*, a quotation from Stendhal's Italian chronicle, *The Duchess of Palliano*, an image of pride and courage in the face of certain, immediate, and violent death: "The executioner strangled Cardinal Caraffa with a silk cord which broke; it was necessary to try a second time. The Cardinal regarded the executioner without deigning to pronounce a word."

THE LONG DIVORCE: *The Stranger* AND *The Myth of Sisyphus*

That picture of man—as a being condemned to death—dominates both *The Stranger* and *The Myth of Sisyphus*, which appeared a few months apart in 1942. The hero of *The Stranger* is literally condemned to death—for murder—by a court of law; the author of *The Myth* begins with the premise that all men are by nature condemned to death (are mortal), and looks to the inferences that follow. The two plays produced in 1944 and 1945 elaborate dramatically on the same idea: every prosperous traveler who stops at the provincial inn of *Cross-Purposes* signs his death warrant when he signs the register; and Caligula's chief diversion, the characteristic expression of his power, is to sentence rich and noble Romans to be executed. The Camus of this period had converted Montaigne's sensible meditation on death as an interesting and inevitable fact into a pugnacious confrontation of death as a kind of intolerable penalty. Man was not only born to die; he was condemned to die; and Rachel Bespaloff was quite right to entitle her long essay on Camus "The World of the Condemned Man." [9] "In the eyes of the man who is condemned to die and who refuses the consolation of the supernatural"—so Miss Bespaloff formulates the question raised—"what is the value which can sustain itself?"

Provisional answers would be offered in *The Plague* and *The Rebel*, but in the earlier writings Camus was concerned primarily with exposing the reality and the urgency of the question. It is

precisely the question propounded from the outset of *The Myth;*
it is something that is arrived at belatedly through the action of *The
Stranger. The Myth* deals with the release from purpose and obligation, the "divine irresponsibility," of man as condemned; but though
that very irresponsibility has all along been the protagonist's defining attribute in *The Stranger,* it is acknowledged and defended only
in the climax of the novel. What Camus calls "supernatural consolation"—a phrase that betrays its own animus—is ruled out emphatically throughout the essay; but only in the novel's final scene
is any such consolation suggested, and only then is it ceremoniously
rejected. In short, although both these books are dialogues with
death, and although Sartre was right to interpret the essay as a
"philosophic translation" of *The Stranger,*[10] the books are related in
a way that says much about the distinction between philosophy and
fiction, between dialectic and drama, between the motion of the
mind and the motion of dramatized experience. It should be emphasized here that, although Camus's fiction sometimes has too
markedly philosophical a manner and though it seems a trifle
stiff and too firmly controlled by a structure of ideas, none the less
he has usually conceived of his subject first in the narrative terms
of characters and action, and only later and secondly has he translated them into the terms of philosophy.

   The Stranger and *The Myth* belong to each other and are as inter-
dependent as *The Plague* and *The Rebel,* Camus's second sequence
of story and essay. As a matter of fact, all Camus's books belong to
each other. He has correctly placed himself among those writers
"whose works" (as he told an interviewer in 1952) "forms a whole
in which each one is illuminated by the others." It is just this mutual
illumination, this continuing and expanding countercommentary,
that provides the character of Camus's movement forward. It has
been doubted that there *is* any movement forward in Camus; some
critics have seen only an endlessly repeated tension. But the evolution few should fail to discover is one Camus, in a vehement open
letter to *Les Temps Modernes* (1952), claimed as self-evident:
"[the] evolution from *The Stranger* to *The Plague* is in the sense
of solidarity and participation." But it takes place through a series
of shifting perspectives on the same original image of man and his

condition, as though direct and steady advance were denied by the hard and tangled truth of things: and this is why one is tempted to talk about all of Camus's books at once. Meursault in *The Stranger* is the Algerian innocent of *Noces* inspected from a new angle; and so is Sisyphus; so are Martha and Caligula. The tangled truth, Camus suggests, can be honestly rendered only by a mobile pattern of perspectives.

The immediate perspective of *The Stranger* is the realized sense of the absurd; the hidden perspective is death itself as the basis of absurdity. But let me remind the reader of the slender plot of the novel, in language as fitting as may be to the spare concision of the plot itself. The stranger is a young man named Meursault, a petty clerk in an Algerian business house. He has sent his mother to a home for the aged. She dies. He goes to the country and attends her funeral. He feels no grief over her death, and he pretends to feel none. Back in Algiers, he takes to sleeping with a girl named Marie. Through another acquaintance, Raymond, he gets involved with some Arab hoodlums. He and Raymond and their two girl friends go to the beach on a hot day. They encounter one of the Arabs. The Arab becomes obnoxious and threatening. Meursault shoots him. He is arrested, interrogated, and tried. The court and the spectators are offended by Meursault's indifference toward the murder, the death of his mother, or anything else. He is condemned to be guillotined. The chaplain visits him and talks about repentance and redemption.[11] In the one outburst of his life, Meursault repudiates religious belief and passionately defends his own way of life:

> From the depth of my future, during the whole of this absurd life which I had lived, a dark breeze had been blowing in toward me across the years yet to come and this breeze leveled out on its way everything during those no more real years I had lived. What difference did the death of others make to me, or the love of a mother, what difference did his god make, the lives one chose, the destinies one elected: since a single destiny would elect me myself and the thousands of privileged persons who, like him, called themselves my brother.

He feels liberated at last in the floodlight of his discovery; he is happy, he has been happy. He opens his heart "to the tender indifference of the world." His only remaining desire—so the book ends—is that there will be many spectators at his execution and that they will receive him with cries of hatred.

Meursault tells his own story. Camus maintained later, during his debate with Sartre in *Les Temps Modernes*, that though *The Stranger* was written in the first person, it was "an exercise in objectivity and detachment," just as *The Plague*, written in the third person, was intended as the personal confession of Dr. Rieux. The sterile monotone of the narrative voice in *The Stranger*, confiding everything and somehow explaining nothing, makes for a fascinatingly repellent effect. It is not a new device. Henry James, who tried all devices, also experimented with this one; and the taciturn narrator who records surfaces but who interprets only through the set of his shoulders is the stock in trade of the American school of violence (and its European derivative), its well-worn legacy from Ernest Hemingway. But it was more probably from André Gide, and especially from his *The Immoralist*, that Camus (as Rachel Bespaloff has suggested) learned how to use the first person "to express the most intimate experience with the maximum detachment." What results is a disturbing blend of the cozy and the clammy: a blend close to the central meaning of the novel—what it is about, what it wants to bring into being. For the aim of *The Stranger* is to realize the exact sensation of absurdity. Meursault is what Camus would presently define in *The Myth of Sisyphus* as an absurd man: that is, a man whose indifference matches the indifference of the universe; a man with the instinct of the unreason in the heart of things; who has long since substituted quantity for quality in every human context; who sees, without any sense of the pain of loss, no blood relation whatever between himself and the earth he inhabits. It is Meursault's destiny, like that of many another tragic hero, to suffer toward the discovery of his own identity: to take upon himself, knowingly at the last, the burden of humanity.

Detachment, indifference, the absence of causal relations, a present unflanked by a remembered past or a hoped-for future: all of that belongs to the configuration of absurdity as a human attribute; and all of it marks the narrative style of *The Stranger*. The unremitting skill with which it does so makes Camus's first novel, in my judgment, his most successful literary achievement to date (with the possible exception of the artistically incommensurable play, *Calig-*

ula). *The Plague* takes in more of life and has a more intrusively satisfactory moral content; but it appeals perhaps more strongly to the ethical than to the aesthetic sense.[12] There is, on the contrary, an almost exasperating perfection about the plan and the execution of *The Stranger*. It has the air of a tour de force; its magic is occasionally only the magic of the skilled illusionist. But it seems to be invulnerable: what is happening in it is happening at every instant; and its sustained sterility turns out to be surprisingly fertile—the book grows differently in different minds, but it never fails to grow.

The atmosphere that greets us at once compares tellingly with the confessional fervor of *Noces*. Here is the opening sentence of the latter, from the first essay, "Nuptials at Tipasa":

> In the spring, Tipasa is inhabited by the gods, and the gods talk in the sunlight and the odor of absinthe, the sea plated with silver, the sky an unbleached blue, the ruins covered with flowers and huge bubbles of light amid the heaps of stones.

Here is the beginning of *The Stranger:*

> Today my mother died. Or perhaps yesterday. I don't know. I received a telegram from the Home: "Mother deceased. Burial tomorrow. Sincere condolences." That tells me nothing. Perhaps it was yesterday.

The staccato quality of those sentences reaches through style to one of the novel's underlying principles: the degree to which things normally related—*attached* to each other—have become staccato. Here, for instance, is verbally enacted the fragmentation of time. In the absurd vision, the sense of before and after—which Kant once found embedded in the mind's structure—has vanished. There is no real yesterday as distinguished from tomorrow, and events pulsate dimly in a permanent present. Nor is there any discernible causal relation: the concept of cause no longer pushes perceptions into a usuable order; Meursault's favorite conjunction is the colorless "and"—never "since," "because," or "therefore." [13] The experience he recounts emerges timelessly and inexplicably out of nothing—"by a sort of respiratory spasm," as Sartre has finely noted. It emerges, too, out of the silence that pervades the novel's opening pages: as Meursault cuts people short or does not reply; as silences last too long —"the silence of these people was telling on my nerves."

Meanwhile, in the enigmatic world that rises from that silence, the trivial—lighting a cigarette, catching a bus—is as important and as unimportant as the serious—murder, sex, religion. All gestures and events have an equal weight in this valueless environment: that is, very little weight at all. Before the shooting, Meursault wonders whether to stay on the beach, where the catastrophe shortly occurs, or whether to join his companions: "To stay, or to make a move—it came to much the same." Confronting the Arab, it crosses Meursault's mind that one might fire or not fire: "and it would be absolutely the same thing." Smoking, writing, friendship, love, marriage, a career, God: before each of these, choice dissolves as illusory and pointless. "So now you're my pal," Raymond says. "I said, 'yes.' It was all the same to me, and he seemed set on it." "[Marie] asked me if I loved her. I answered that the question didn't mean anything, but I supposed that I didn't. She seemed sad." (There, it can be noted, is a good example of the congealing lack of asserted connection: between the man's reply and the girl's sadness.) "Marie came to look for me and asked me if I wanted to marry her. I said that it was all the same to me and that we could do it if she wanted to." His employer offers him a better position in Paris, adding that life there should be agreeable to him. "I said yes, but that actually it was all the same to me." The chaplain wants to know whether Meursault is sure he does not believe in God. "I said I didn't feel the need to worry about it; the question seemed to me unimportant." Meursault, in fact, is convicted more for his indifference—especially his indifference about his mother's death—than for the murder he committed. His indifference is an insult, a rebuke to the world that must judge him.

And it is, of course, the unimportance and the sameness of actions that are justified in the climax by the vision of death, the dark breeze blowing in toward Meursault from the years to come, equalizing everything on its way. Death is the discovered perspective of the novel: the story's beginning, its middle, and its end. *The Stranger* opens with the death and burial of the mother, and it closes on the eve of Meursault's public execution—for a murder committed at the arithmetic center of the book. We are even given a preview of that execution, in the memory of a similar event the father had once witnessed and reported on, which had fascinated and nauseated his father. In *The Stranger*, death has not yet gathered itself into a single tidal wave of destruction, as it will do in *The Plague*. It reveals itself only at sundry times and in sundry places, and it is just the omnipresence of death that the hero must come to understand. That is the substance of his tragic perception, akin to the perception of the interplay of fate and freedom that often rounded out a Greek tragedy.

For willfully stunted though it is, and with everything said in a casual undertone, *The Stranger* does represent one of the modes of tragedy: tragedy, that is, as the critique of tragedy. The traditional rhythm of tragedy—to borrow the useful terms of Francis Fergusson [14]—moves from a *purpose* (do something about the Theban plague; revenge the killing of the former king) through a *passion* (the suffering of the hero, as conflict arises from the pursuit of his purpose) to a *perception* (the wisdom begotten of suffering). *The Stranger* is in some sense less a version of than a comment on that inherited pattern: a critique of it, almost a parody. For *The Stranger* moves from carefully realized purposelessness through a prolonged absence of passion to the perception that makes them both right and appropriate. It is, in short, the absurd mimesis of the tragic. Nor are other ancient tragic elements missing from the tale. In *The Stranger*, the Algerian earthiness of *Noces* has gone dry and joyless, under a heat that beats down inexorably like fate or the gods; the gods who talked in the sunlight at Tipasa now press upon Meursault, mute, alien, and hostile, and perhaps determine the disastrous pull of his trigger-finger.[15] And as the early chapters of the novel unfold—as we follow the sterile circularity of Meursault's daily life, waking up, going to the office, being busy, coming back, smoking, eating, and sitting about—we see an elusive reflection of Sisyphus and his own endlessly recurring toil, pushing his burden daily up the hill, watching it roll back, and returning to begin the job again.

Meursault, the central figure in this critique of tragedy, is thus a surrogate for the tragic hero. He is not, however, a surrogate for his creator, Albert Camus. Camus has properly denied that his fiction is to any dependable extent autobiographical. Meursault stands for a possibility of vision: the innocent, time-free character of *Noces* looked at from the side of death. Nothing has changed but the angle of inspection. Meursault is passive, negative—just as his favorite conjunction is "and," his favorite adjective, perhaps his favorite word is "no." [16] Yet a fair portrait of him would require the double negative: he is not unkind, not unthoughtful, not uncourageous. He retains his deep responsiveness to the sights and sounds and smells of physical nature: phenomena that punctuate the book at its beginning, middle, and end. He can and does inspire love; and one witness is able to say about him, persuasively, that he is a man. Within the peculiar possibility of vision that he represents, Meursault is in fact Man, attuned in his very being to the tunelessness of the universe.

It is not easy for the majority of American readers to understand, much less to sympathize with Camus's deep preoccupation with death, so alien is it to the public and official (as against a part of the private and actual) national temperament. The public impulse in America, when faced with a work of Camus, is to inquire into the causes for the psychological abnormality allegedly there depicted: to ask how Meursault, for example, or perhaps even Camus himself got so maladjusted in a generally satisfying world.[17] The European reader, remembering that both *The Stranger* and *The Myth of Sisyphus* were written during the Second World War and the occupation of France, for the most part finds their involvement with death almost inevitable. For death, cruelty, humiliation, violent aberrations of justice, and a searing contempt for human dignity have been the norms of contemporary experience for many Europeans; murder, Camus has said still more flatly, is the determining phenomenon of the past four or five decades. But Camus's steady concern with death is more than a natural reaction to the atrocious events of the twentieth century. It has the status of a philosophic position and it relates him to a lengthy intellectual and literary tradition—especially the nineteenth century Russian tradition (which he much admires) with its frequent sense of the emptiness of life because of the inevitability of death. That feeling, and the traditions it engendered, has (with a few exceptions) never made much headway in America; but recent European literature is inexplicable without it. In the writing of Malraux, to cite only a single example, "an obsession with death" (the key phrase and the crucial motivation in his novel, *The Royal Way*) is the note struck early and late and always. Beyond both the public history and the cultural traditions, it might be added, there is in Camus's case a personal basis for his death consciousness: the tuberculosis that afflicted him in his thirties. Tuberculosis is a disease peculiarly capable of heightening one's sensitivity to dissolution and death.[18] But it is not, after all, Camus's *sensitivity* to death that is truly impressive. It is rather his tenacious confrontation of death as the only way of getting at an honest and even a positive estimate of life. *Descender plus bas pour monter plus hautement.*

And so, although *The Myth of Sisyphus*, which followed the publication of *The Stranger*, may be accurately described as an essay on suicide, it is anything but a desperate or despondent book. It is so little "morbid," in the somewhat blurry Anglo-American meaning of that word, that it creates the very terms for dismissing morbidity. Where *Noces* began in the Algerian sunlight and a mood of nuptial joy only to end with funeral inscriptions and the dramatic citation of the stoical condemned man, *The Myth* begins with the vision of absurdity and the ubiquity of death in a godless universe—only to end on a note of prolonged and passionate revolt and a motto, out of Pindar, that urges the soul not to aspire to immortal life, "but exhaust the field of the possible."

Its first focus is the question whether there are cogent reasons for a man to go on living, given the maddening absurdity of the universe; or whether, like Cato, a man ought not, more wisely, to kill himself. "There is only one truly philosophic problem," Camus begins abruptly (perhaps remembering Novalis, the German romantic poet, who called it the one true philosophic gesture [19]), "and that is suicide." For self-annihilation provides in our day the grim context in which the ancient and perennial philosophic problem trenchantly raises itself: the nature and value of human existence. So Camus believes; and to judge from the other novelists we are considering, his formulation is correct. Ignazio Silone, in fact—though he says characteristically that suicide is one of the many things he cannot understand—has pointed to suicide as the representative phenomenon of contemporary Western culture. In "The Choice of Companions" (1953), he remarked:

> The number of writers in various countries who have voluntarily abandoned themselves to death in recent decades has reached a figure

without example in preceding epochs. It seems to me that the majority of those episodes, though externally very different, have a common base: what Nietzsche called the nihilism of the modern age. Whenever I happen to reflect upon the most significant expressions of the loss of direction, of ennui and disgust, my thought goes not so much to the books of Heidegger, of Jaspers, of Sartre, as to the suicides of Essenin, of Majekowsky, of Ernst Toller, of Kurth Tucholsky, of Stefan Zweig, of Klaus Mann, of Drieu La Rochelle, of F. O. Matthiessen, of Cesare Pavese, and of so many others only less well known.

. . . Beyond the exterior circumstances invoked at the moment to explain the desperate end of each of those men of talent (persecution, exile, isolation, misery, sickness, abnormality), one need only study what they themselves wrote before dying, or confided to friends, to discover in the last analysis an identical confession of anguish and desperation in face of the energy required to go on living, and a sense of the futility thereof.

Suicide, we should observe, is a recurring event in the literature of our time, as well as in the history of its writers. Mino, in Moravia's *The Woman of Rome*, shoots himself, and Astarita arranges to be shot; suicide is meditated by a range of Moravia's dispirited protagonists. Camus's *Cross-Purposes* ends with the self-slaughter of mother and daughter, and *The Plague* virtually begins with the inept attempt of Cottard, the dishonest wine-dealer. Minor characters in Silone's novels hang or dynamite themselves: Teofilo in *Fontamara*, Uliva in *Bread and Wine*. Quentin Compson goes somnambulistically to his death by water at the conclusion of his long interior monologue in Faulkner's *The Sound and the Fury;* and Eunice, the mother of Tomasina in "The Bear," slips more silently into the creek on Christmas day—"griefless, ceremonial, in formal and succinct repudiation of grief and despair"—when she discovers her daughter's incest; the suicides of priest and general flank the execution of the corporal toward the end of *A Fable*. Graham Greene, who flirted repeatedly with suicide during his bored childhood, has invested the theme with a mounting dramatic horror and fascination, drawn from Catholic doctrine on the subject; in *The Heart of the Matter*, and in his two plays, *The Living Room* and *The Potting Shed*, real or attempted suicide is the pivot of the action.

During most of the seventeenth and eighteenth centuries, suicide was at most an occasional and hushed-up aberration, hardly a topic for speculation or drama. Out of sight, so to say, since the sixteenth century, it reappeared as a central and urgent possibility in the nineteenth century, along with Nietzsche's announcement of the death of God and amidst the varieties of intellectual and political nihilism. Kirillov and Stavrogin, the oddly paired suicides in Dostoevski's *The Possessed*, are the most striking early illustrations in fiction of the trend that led the young Thomas Masaryk in his first publication (about 1880), to name suicide as the most revealing symptom of the European cultural condition.[20] The twentieth century was ushered in, as regards English fiction, by the suicidal protagonists of Joseph Conrad—Winnie Verloc in *The Secret Agent*, for example; Heyst and Jones in *Victory;* and more representative still, Martin Decoud in *Nostromo*, who finds in solitude that his very being is slipping away from him and who thereupon plunges willfully into the vast and watery indifference of things. Since Conrad, the novel in all languages has found in suicide one of the most revealing gestures of the modern world and of modern man.

Different external pressures force the various figures of contemporary fiction—Mino, Quentin Compson, and the others—toward their self-appointed deaths, but there is a common basis to all of them: a basis common, that is, to the purpose and the dramatic imagination of their creators. It is not the sense of "ennui and disgust" that Silone perceives as common in the suicides of authors. It is, quite the contrary, an agonized sense of life. In a time characterized by the "bias toward death," no novelist who aims to show that time its form and pressure can evade the fact of death, the feeling of darkness, the impulse to self-destruction. But Camus and Silone, along with Moravia and Faulkner and Greene, continue to dramatize the bias toward death in order to manifest more potently the counterforce of their own bias toward life. Like Malraux's Perken in *The Royal Way*, they all of them "think about death in order, not to die, but to live"; for like a novelist greater than all of them—Henry James—they know that "the poet essentially *can't* be concerned with the act of dying." They have dug through the darkness to discover the only optimism—and it is of course a profoundly tragic optimism—that modern experience can warrant and on which modern art can ground itself. Mino's intoxication with death, accordingly, has the purpose of heightening our sense of Adriana's gift for life; Silone's suicides point up the mutilated durability of his heroes; Quentin Compson is one of a fragmented trio—with Benjy and Jason—whose narrative function is to throw into relief the humble assent to existence embodied at last by the Negro woman, Dilsey. And the effect of the ninety-page rumination on suicide in *The Myth of Sisyphus* is to lend extraordinary vibration to the argument's conclusion: "Thus, by the play of conscience alone, I transform what had been an invitation to death into a rule of life—and I reject suicide."

Camus rejected suicide because he felt it would have been cheating in a game predicated on honesty, clarity, and endurance. The "absurd" is the feel of the relationship between two disparate entities: between the world and the individual conscience, the reasonless universe and the reason of man, the fact of duality and the unquenchable desire for unity. It is a relationship of unrelatable things; it is a divorce—but a divorce that depends upon the continuing presence of the two parties to it.[21] The absurd condition, unlike Eurydice, is something that disappears if you do *not* look at it. The absurd not only is what you confront; it *is* only and purely in the act of confrontation, and it endures in the current of the protest against it. Suicide would not solve the problem, it would only dissolve it; suicide would destroy the condition that exists in acknowledgment and refusal. The absurd, therefore, far from inviting the individual to quit this life, requires of him on his honor that he hang on to it; it becomes a rule, a principle of living.

But if the first focus of *The Myth of Sisyphus* is the question of suicide, the book's final intention is to carve out that "field of the possible" to which its motto refers; and Camus is hardest of all on those of our time, or of any time, who have not been faithful to the vision of the possible. It alone is the home of what Camus calls the absurd man: the man, that is, who is not absurd at all, but who is a kind of sage, with the special sagacity appropriate to an absurd situation. The absurd man will choose knowingly what Meursault in *The Stranger* chose instinctively; he will choose time and history, against God and the eternal (Camus's battle with history would develop later, along with a growing conviction about the shared essence of human nature); he will commit himself to human reason, and will acknowledge the limits of reason while hating and rebelling against those limits. Under no circumstances will the absurd man be cajoled into any effort to "transcend" the realm and the rules of reason; for to do so is to betray the possible and to vanish straight into the mouth of the enemy. To do so, in fact, is to commit another form of suicide: and a much more serious and scandalous form than to take one's merely physical quietus with the bare bodkin. This is what Camus calls "philosophic suicide," and the longest section of *The Myth* is a polemic against it.

Camus attacks, in that section, the whole tradition of those who, following Tertullian, have submitted to an enigmatic transcendent authority precisely because it *is* enigmatic; who have seen in the nonrational something infinitely grander than the rational, something the latter is bound to worship; and who have conspired to utter the phrase that, for Camus, is the ultimate defamation of the human spirit—*credo quia absurdum*. In the name of a passionate, almost a fanatical rationalism, Camus lumps together Kierkegaard, Chestov, Jaspers, and Husserl, as commonly betraying human reason by their "ferocious hopefulness." Faced with absurdity, Camus observes, these men do not say: "Absurd!" they say: "God!" Having learned so much from them about the human condition, Camus felt the more dismayed at the inferences they conclude with. The absurd, as they themselves had taught him, is a "divorce between the spirit which desires and the world which deceives, between my nostalgia for unity and this scattered universe; it is the contradiction which binds them. But Kierkegaard suppresses my nostalgia, and Husserl reassembles the universe. That," Camus adds in a sort of desperate gaiety, "is not what I had expected to hear." In an appendix, Camus puts the name of Franz Kafka on the list of the splendid disloyal. Camus has often been linked with Kierkegaard and Kafka as sharing a vision of things; the three names, strung together alliteratively, have made up a fashionable catch phrase; but Camus himself rejects the other two in favor of Nietzsche—for Nietzsche stubbornly refused the comfort of the supernatural. Yet when Kafka so steadily denied any "moral grandeur" to God, or even any coherence, "it was only," Camus writes accusingly, "in order to throw himself the more readily into God's arms." So Camus reads the endings of both *The Trial* and *The Castle*, as expressions of acquiescence to a hostile or a prankish supreme power.

He both revered and banished Kafka, as Socrates both revered and banished all poets for their insidious seduction of the human psyche. For the passion in Camus was all, at this stage of his mind's journey, in the service of his reason. A motion beyond reason, or a motion other than the rational, could only—he then felt—be in contempt of reason. It was what he called "the leap."

The key image in the discourse on *philosophic* suicide and the one most flatly objected to is that of "the leap." Camus no doubt got his use of it from Nietzsche's address to the "afterworldly" in *Thus Spake Zarathustra:* "Thus I speak to the afterworldly. . . . Weariness that wants to reach the ultimate with one leap, one fatal leap, a poor ignorant weariness that does not want to want any more: this created all gods and afterworlds." [22] But the source is not very important, for the figure has been invoked in all ages as obviously suitable to describe the jump of the spirit when sprung loose from the restraints of an exhausted logic. To reach for two chronological extremes, we may find it in Plato's Seventh Letter, in the account of the mind's surge beyond dialectic and myth toward the perception of the true ideas ("a spark leaps in the soul"), and in Graham Greene's *The End of the Affair*, where Greene (via his narrator) relates the capacity to "leap" and the achievement of sainthood. "We could all be saints by leaping as you leapt," Bendrix says resentfully to the dead Sarah Miles, "by shutting the eyes and leaping once and for all; if *you* are a saint, it's not so difficult to be a saint. It's something He can demand of any of us—leap! But I won't leap."

Camus—who, in *The Myth*, opposes the absurd man's ethic of quantity to the saint's ethic of quality—will not leap either; though a vigilant Christian reader might surmise that the chances of his leaping some day or other are not much less than those shadowed forth sullenly by Greene's narrator-hero, Maurice Bendrix. Camus has always had a painfully ambiguous involvement with sainthood. But for the time being, he postponed that question in order to get on with his more immediately urgent quarrel with God.[23] The quarrel was necessary if Camus was to clear away all the obstacles that hid one's honest view of the possible. But it was an odd sort of quarrel, and marked by some pretty inaccurate firing; for the only fragment of Christianity seemingly perceptible to Camus, as to most others today who share his general convictions, is an extreme, an unmodulated other-worldliness (or afterworldliness): that aspect—and it was by no means the determining aspect—of medieval Christianity that became the core of early Protestantism and of its doctrinaire antagonism to the natural and human. The God whom Camus, following Nietzsche, has declared dead was a God who in fact had not been alive very long; he had been created in the polemics of Martin Luther.[24]

On the positive side, and after all the denials and refusals and rebellions, Camus proposed "a sterile and conquering lucidity and an obstinate denial of all supernatural consolation"; and he looked forward to a bleak utopia—an "absurd world . . . peopled by men who think clearly and hope no longer." It is the mythical Sisyphus who provides Camus with his dramatic image for these qualities. *The Myth of Sisyphus* concludes with a poetic celebration of the legendary hero—Sisyphus, the cunning King of Corinth; Sisyphus, who even dared to chain up Death itself; Sisyphus, whose eternal punishment for that impiety and for others was to roll a huge stone to the top of a hill in Hades, to see it roll back down again, and to begin the toil endlessly anew. Powerless and rebellious, never pausing in his proud eternal quarrel with God, Sisyphus becomes for Camus a symbol of authentic human greatness. "The struggle toward the summit itself is enough to fill the heart of man. We must imagine that Sisyphus was happy." Like Meursault in *The Stranger*, but driven by the force of his active intellect, Sisyphus moves forever on his intolerable round: drawing thus from the wine of the absurd and the bread of indifference a greatness constantly renourished.

THE DRAMATIC ART

Caligula: I have taken on the stupid and incomprehensible visage of the gods. . . .
Scipio: And that is blasphemy, Caius.
Caligula: No, Scipio, it is the dramatic art!

Caligula, III, ii

One of the three chief models for the absurd man in *The Myth of Sisyphus* is the professional actor (the others are the conqueror and Don Juan). "Theirs," Camus wrote about actors, "is an absurd destiny," and a destiny, he added, "which can seduce and attract a clear-seeing heart." An actor may play the part, let us say, of Sigismond; but when the curtain rings down, Sigismond vanishes—and "two hours later, one sees him dining out." The actor commits himself fully to miming the emotional content of the limited present, and he emerges unscathed; this is the very profile of knowing absurdity, for the intense futureless present—as Camus had remarked in *Noces*, gazing with admiration at the Tuscan canvases—is the true field of the absurd: a being, primarily a body, that "knows only the beat of its own blood."

Beyond that, the existentialist sense of life, which Camus at this time shared with Sartre and Heidegger, is itself fundamentally dramatic; it thrives on confrontations and encounters; it turns on the unavoidable human collision, and smells emphatically of the buskin. Camus's involvement with the theater, with acting and actors, is therefore altogether fitting; and one is not surprised to learn that he himself is an accomplished actor and that he was a member of a theatrical troupe for several years. That was during his student days, when he used to perform in provincial theaters for two weeks at a time to earn money to pay for his courses in philosophy: a pleasantly symbolic alternation between the philosophic and the dramatic. (His favorite role, incidentally, was that of Ivan in a French version of *The Brothers Karamazov*.) The experience has been a constant source of metaphors in his essays; and it has made a solid basis for his plays.

Camus has written four plays (and sponsored or adapted others—most recently, Faulkner's *Requiem for a Nun*); of these, the two that primarily concern us are *Cross-Purposes*, produced in 1944, and *Caligula*, an earlier composition which was not produced, however, until 1945. They complete the first sizable portion of Camus's achievement, and the first example of the creative pattern he has since repeated: an inter-related series of novel, essay and plays. *Cross-Purposes* shows a notable correspondence with *The Stranger*, and *Caligula* with *The Myth of Sisyphus*. A similar design would appear in a later moment, when to *The Plague* and *The Rebel* Camus added the third and fourth of his plays—*L'Etat de Siege*, the allegorical treatment of an epidemic; and *Les Justes*, dealing with the historical Russian rebels of 1905.

Camus's first two dramatic efforts differ considerably in structure and scope. *Cross-Purposes* presents five bourgeois characters over twenty-four hours in nineteen scenes; *Caligula* gives us two dozen members of the Roman nobility and the imperial household over four years in forty-five scenes. Yet these plays manipulate the same motifs; they are those of the novel and the essay that preceded them. The perspective has shifted once again, and with it the style; Camus is probably unrivaled in contemporary literature as a master of the variety of style. (He has yet, in any serious degree, to repeat himself, and would perhaps be betraying his own conception of the literary art if he should do so.) But here, in fresh dramatic guise, we encounter again the familiar nostalgia for a lost intimacy with nature; and here, too, is the expression of indifference and the now desperately unsatisfying substitution of quantity for quality. Man reappears as a stranger, but now a stranger who is a close relation— a brother or son or lover—but who is no longer recognizable; and his condemnation to death is plotted shrewdly before our eyes. Both plays inquire dramatically into the moral and legal justification for murder: the starting point, some years later, for *The Rebel*. The questions arise within a universe characterized at the end of *Cross-Purposes* by the word "No!" and at the beginning and the end of *Caligula* by the word "Nothing!" But what is emphasized in these plays is the condition of individual solitude as affected by a violently urgent will to power: a solitude absolute and inconsolable; the solitude that at once maddened and exalted Melville's Ahab, and the power that served to pierce and explain it—"and Ahab stands alone among the millions of the peopled earth, nor gods nor men his neighbors! Cold, cold—I shiver!" In the evolution toward solidarity that Camus has demonstrated in his work, he reached, in *Cross-Purposes* and *Caligula*, that final depth of the vision of isolation where the force of compassion could at last announce itself. *Descender plus bas pour monter plus hautement.*

Cross-Purposes offers the ancient and oft-told tale of the son who returns home after twenty years abroad, does not reveal himself to his mother and sister, and is murdered by them during the night— as many wealthy and solitary travelers have previously been murdered by the two women—for his money, his identity being shatteringly discovered the following morning. This is another of

those fables that have appealed to Camus as tight images of human
experience: an image, in this case, of man as unrecognized and
destroyed by those closest to him and whom he has come from afar
to save. The story had already turned up, briefly, in *The Stranger*,
in a newspaper clipping Meursault found stuck under his prison
mattress. He read it over and over, reflecting that "On the one hand,
it was implausible. On the other, it was natural. Anyhow," he
concluded, "I thought the traveler deserved what he got. One
shouldn't play such tricks." In Camus's theatrical version, the
trickery of Jan, the son, earns his death by drugging and drowning,
and leads to the suicide of his mother and presumably his sister,
and to a state of horrified shock that almost turns the wits of his
wife, Maria.

But Jan's play acting is a mode of innocence. He is the Algerian
innocent of *Noces* pulled out of his natural orbit and sent north to
the play's unspecified setting, which sounds like Czechoslovakia,
but is, more importantly, a symbolic "Europe" as against a symbolic
"southern Mediterranean"—the world of divorce dreaming with pain
of a former marriage. It is his innocent evocation of the sun and
sea and sky of his adopted country that so torments Jan's sister,
Martha: "He talked to me about countries I am longing for," she
tells her mother, after the deed, "and by touching me, he armed
me against him. So it is that innocence is recompensed." Yet his
simple innocence might have been, it is suggested, the source of the
women's salvation. "Let's leave him alone tonight," the mother
pleads, wearied of a sudden by the endless murders for profit which
never seem profitable enough. "Let's give ourselves this reprieve.
Perhaps it is by him we will be saved."

> *Martha:* We have nothing to do with salvation—that language is
> ridiculous. All you can hope for, by working tonight, is the right
> to sleep afterwards.
> *Mother:* That is what I call being saved: to keep the hope of sleep-
> ing.

Cross-Purposes, here and elsewhere, seems constantly to echo—
or rather, seems constantly and delusively *about* to echo—the language of Christianity and especially of the New Testament. A
passage from the Fourth Gospel comes insistently to one's mind:
"And the light shineth in darkness; and the darkness comprehended

it not. . . . He was in the world and the world was made by him, and the world knew him not. He came unto his own, and his own received him not." The very names of the characters are mercurial clues: Martha, Maria (Mary), Jan (John). And indeed the son, while just managing to escape an imitation of Christ, appears not less tantalizingly as a near imitation of that other John, the Baptist, who "was not that Light, but was sent to bear witness of that Light." For Jan's chief function is to bear fatal witness—in a Europe that Martha calls autumnal and Maria, the wife, calls sad— to the sunlight of the Algiers he has left behind. In his own mind, Jan is neither Jesus nor John, but yet another New Testament figure, the Prodigal Son; and he broods on the way in which the old story had somehow gone wrong— "I expected the feast of the prodigal, and they gave me a glass of beer which they charged me for." Martha's later outcry to her mother seems almost consciously to echo the complaint of the prodigal's stay-at-home brother: "Everything life can give man has been given to him. . . . He has known other places, the sea, free human beings. But I, I remained here."

Those echoes refuse to come together into an unmistakable whole. The play remains a fable, an abstract of human destiny, unspoiled by a definable thesis. Implicit none the less is the first instance of what would grow, in Camus's later writings, into a profound and radical transformation of Christian doctrine and the Christian vision. The tactic is that of ironic deviation. As Moravia converted the ethical and poetic into the sourly erotic, so Camus converted the religious and the aspiring into the human and the hopeless—both men pushing through the available conventions and illusions to get at what seemed to them a more truthful picture of man. In *Cross-Purposes*, the mocking faint reminders of the New Testament serve only to intensify the anguish and despair of the final revelation—the total impossibility of divine intervention. The presence of hints about Jesus and John merely adds to the icy coldness of the absence of God; and the play's action moves inexorably to its close.

It is a remarkably tidy little action, rising evenly from the conversational murmurs of the opening scene—murmurs vibrating oddly like an ancient inherited ritual: "He'll come back." "Did he say so?" "Yes." "Alone?" "I don't know"—to the patterned exchange of lamentation and insight, the *kommos*, at the end, when the rhythms become Greek in their hard, sliced-off severity. The design is, indeed, classical, though the passionate exercise of reason throughout the play is more nearly neoclassical. But its rhythm, like that of *The Stranger*, follows the rhythm we have noticed above as characteristic of Greek tragedy. It begins with a hidden conflict of purposes (hence the aptness of the English title [25]): that of the son, to restudy his family in secret and then to rescue them, economically and otherwise; and that of the sister, abetted by the mother, to kill the rich visitor and so, with his money, to escape from dismal Europe to the sunny land she had dreamed of. The action proceeds through the murder, the revelation of identity, and the ensuing anguish; and it concludes with the various perceptions by which all three women, mother and sister and wife, are seized and destroyed.

For the mother, it is the perception of the reality of maternal love: a love so real that she must depart to join her newly found son in death at the bottom of the river. It was the mother who had carried the burden of the theme of indifference in *Cross-Purposes;* indifference is her most frequently mentioned attribute, and she contemplates the murder of Jan as Meursault had contemplated shooting the Arab: "When I understood that everything had already begun, I accepted the idea that one could go on, and that after all it didn't make much difference." Now her spontaneous grief is a kind of minimal rebirth, and suicide will be her first conscious exercise of will in half a lifetime. "This proves," she tells her daughter calmly, "that on this earth where nothing is assured, we do have our certainties. . . . The love of a mother for a son is now my own certainty." For Martha, on the other hand, the mother love that she had assumed as certain is now seen as a dire illusion; and the wisdom her suffering leads her to is just the apprehension of solitude—her own and that of every other individual on the face of the earth. This is the true order of things; this is the glaring truth that Martha, in her last gesture, forces the grief-crazed Maria to face up to next morning, when the wife arrives to seek her husband:

> *Martha:* . . . I cannot die and leave you with the idea that you are right, that love is not vain and this is an accident. It is now that we are in the true order of things. I must persuade you of that.

Maria: What order?
Martha: The order in which no one is ever recognized.

And for Maria herself, the final awareness is that of nothingness: no help, no pity, no solace. The curtain comes down on Maria kneeling before the deaf and nearly mute servant—that ominous presence who has not spoken ten words during the play, but who brought Jan the tea that would drug him.

> *Maria* (with a cry): Oh! My God! I cannot live in this desert. It is you I will speak to and I will find the words. (She falls on her knees.) It is to you that I must turn. Have pity on me, turn toward me! Hear me, Lord, give me your hand! Have pity on those who love and are separated.
> *Servant* (in a dry firm voice): Did you call me?
> *Maria* (turning to him): Oh! I don't know! But help me, I need someone to help me. Have pity on me, help me!
> *Servant* (in the same voice): No!

Caligula, which has to do with the young Roman emperor (AD 37-41) who followed Tiberius and preceded Claudius, belongs to what Berthold Brecht has called the epic theater. It is built on a series of rapid and agitated episodes, against a vast and crowded background. Like the American epic, *Moby-Dick,* which it continuously resembles, *Caligula* explores the nature of supreme power, of authority united with titanic spirit; and it dramatizes the effort of power to "break through the masks" and to arrive at the invisible spheres (as Melville put it) that lie, however frightfully, beneath the visible spheres of love, the comfortable deceptions of life. Like *Moby-Dick* also, *Caligula* employs many varieties of theatrical behavior to carry its action forward along many parallel paths: monologue and dialogue, prayers, celebrations, banquets, public contests, conspiratorial meetings, and metaphysical disputes. It achieves thereby a good deal of the mythic quality achieved by Melville, which both writers admired in ancient drama, with its choral songs, dances, prayers and patterned arguments. There is, in *Caligula,* a persistent concern with *la raison,* that almost untranslatable but characteristically French ideal of the logical basis and reasonable control of human conduct. But despite that concern, *Caligula,* pursuing as it does the multiple diverse rhythms of human action, trancends the more narrowly rationalistic (that is, neoclassical) strain of *Cross-Purposes*. What results, in my opinion, is Camus's most exciting and suggestive work.

What results also is a sort of sadistic theatrical version of the picaresque novel. Caligula is a tormented *pícaro*—a rogue beyond all roguery who yearns to be a saint. Through his imperial power and his frenzied, unswervable logic, Caligula manages to arrive at a majestic image of the diabolic, yet at every step in his unspeakable career he gives the impression of being only a step away from holiness: *corruptio optimi pessima* is the formula horribly developed in this play. By all odds the most monstrous of Camus's creations, Caligula is in an almost equal degree the most unforgettable and the most human.

The play opens at that instant (historically vouched for in the gossipy pages of Suetonius' *Lives of the Caesars*) when the twenty-five-year-old boy's sensibly benevolent reign is abruptly transformed into a reign of fantastic cruelty. The event producing the change is the death of Caligula's beloved sister Drusilla, with whom he has had incestuous relations. (Suetonius claims that Caligula commited incest with all his sisters and lived openly with Drusilla; at public dinners, he would distribute his sisters, naked, about the banquet hall.) Caligula has vanished for three days and nights; he returns as a man reborn into absurdity. He dedicates himself to publicizing the nihilism of a universe in which "men die and they are not happy"; and he initiates a series of experimental assaults upon the property, the wives and children and the very lives of Rome's leading patricians. What Ishmael says of Ahab, cauterized no less by his encounter with the whale and after a similar three-day rite of absence, can be said of Camus's Caligula: "Not one jot of his great natural intellect had perished. . . . His special lunacy stormed his general sanity, and carried it." At the end of the play (following history), Caligula is assassinated by a group led by the tribune Cherea. It is a fitting end, for Cherea is the one man—along with one woman, the Emperor's mistress, Caesonia—able almost completely to understand him.

Even more than Meursault and Sisyphus, Caligula is the full embodiment of Camus's "absurd man." After Caligula, Camus's representative hero begins to take on other and opposite attributes, but the emperor unites within himself the three roles mentioned in

The Myth as models of absurdity. He is always acting (like the historic Caligula who, according to Suetonius, was "passionately devoted to the theatrical arts," probably had a perverse affair with the pantomimist Mnestor, and used to wander at night disguised in a wig and robe). When, in a methodically obscene ceremony, he imitates the gods, he tells Scipio that his performance is not blasphemy but the dramatic art. He is constantly striking postures and practicing grimaces (again, like the original) before a mirror. He is, in addition, a conqueror, by temperament as well as by office; and though he prides himself on avoiding foreign wars, his goal is something larger—the unconditional surrender of the human mind. And finally, he is an existentialist Don Juan, a person who substitutes quantity for quality in relations of love, winning a succession of sexual victories, all equally valuable and valueless, with their arithmetical sum the only consideration.

Into the hands of this youth, who is accurately called an idealist by Cherea and a child by Caesonia, Camus places absolute power; and what follows is a laboratory test of the absurd hypothesis, a controlled inquiry into the chemistry of nihilism. "Now at last I understand the usefulness of power," Caligula announces; "it gives the impossible a chance." His career is a fiery hunt after the impossible, driven by a logic that assures him that life is empty and love is an impostor. Murder, rape, large-scale thievery, infanticide: he tries them all, and at no point does he come up against anything that resists him by asserting its inviolable worth; at no point does he stimulate what he longs to stimulate—a revolt against himself, an authentic sign of value and conviction. Before he strangles Mereia, the informer, he begs Mereia to confess to being a revolutionary: but Mereia, Caligula realizes sadly, is only a coward.

Behind the frenetic action of *Caligula*, there lurks what Mario Praz, in another connection,[26] has called "the shadow of the divine Marquis"—the Marquis de Sade; and it is partly by means of that shadow that Camus accomplishes his radical shift of values. It is not, here, the Sade of popular and distorted repute; nor is it altogether the Sade of history and of his own writings. It is the Sade of the contemporary intellectuals, especially French intellectuals. This is the man celebrated in *The Rebel* for exemplifying the condition of "metaphysical revolt," and whose grandiose beastliness is alleged to be the gestures of innocence. This is the rebel whose pedagogic conscience will not suffer any lingering hang-over of conventional morality or religious feeling to remain in the hearts of his pupils. Martha's harsh annihilation of Maria's piety in *Cross-Purposes* is a distinct echo of the eloquent Marquis; and several fragments of Sade's *120 Days of Sodom* contribute to both the behavior and the instructional discourses of Caligula. They are present in the Emperor's conduct with the wife of one of the nobles, whom, pursuing a technique familiar to *Sadistes*, he seduces jeeringly in the presence of her husband; they are present, too, in Caligula's taunting of the helpless Mucius, whose son he has killed, and in the oath he administers to his aging mistress, Caesonia—striking a huge gong to punctuate each merciless item in it. "You will be cruel," orders Caligula. "Cruel," replies Caesonia, weeping. "Cold and implacable." "Implacable." "You too will suffer." "Yes, Caligula, but I am going mad."

The peak of the play's nihilistic ritual and of the sadistic element is the remarkable prayer of the Emperor in the third act. Assuming the role of Venus, Caligula requires of his prostrate nobles that they repeat after him:

> Instruct us in the truth of this world which is not to have any truth. . . . Grant us the strength to live in the height of this unequaled truth. . . . Overwhelm us with thy gifts, spread across our faces thy impartial cruelty, thy objective hatred; open before our eyes thy hands full of flowers and of murders. . . . Give us thy passions without object, thy griefs deprived of reason, thy joys without future. . . . And thou, so empty and so burning, inhuman and yet so earthly, make us drunk with the wine of thy equivalence and press us forever to thy dark and mordant heart.

The prayer summarizes Caligula's creed; but the moment of its utterance crystallizes the entire play. For the theater-loving Emperor enacts by poetry and gesture what he elsewhere states as a philosophical principle; and what the whole drama, as the work of a human imagination under a particular pressure, implicitly represents: the notion of art as a necessary blasphemy. That notion is a corollary to the doctrine of the absurd. By dragging down the language of religion and by turning it about in a systematically blasphemous manner, art in our time (so the play *Caligula* suggests) can itself share in the necessary rebellion against a remote, delusive divinity: necessary, that is, if man is to reaffirm his gravely threatened dignity. This is why the behavior that to the less farseeing Scipio is merely sacrilege is the essence of the dramatic art to the formidably absurd Caligula; and why the dramatic art is the greatest of all arts. "The error of these men," says the Emperor, speaking of his Roman nobles, "is that they do not believe enough in the theater." It is said thoughtfully and almost without irony—certainly without sarcasm; for it is Caligula's belief that all men are actors, in the sense that all men wear masks and are deceivers; in a world of carefully contrived false appearances, the only thing left to believe in and to respect is the theater itself. The interchange between Caligula and Scipio is, according to Camus, the serious center of the play.[27]

But along with the sadism are qualities of humor and nostalgia, of recognizable courage and delicacy of perception: both in the play and in its hero. There are passages of high comedy, though perhaps of a somewhat ghastly hue; and Caligula is an often poignant figure, with a poignancy toughened by intellect. He surprises Scipio by putting into words the latter's dream of a life rooted in a lyrical marriage with nature: that union so precious to Camus, and the loss of which (in the loss of his sister) was the start of what Cherea describes as Caligula's "inhuman lyricism." The central *agon*, indeed, is between Caligula and the decent, rational, rebellious Cherea; for he alone understands the real threat posed by the Emperor—not the "little humiliations" he visits upon the patricians, but "a great idea whose victory would mean the end of the world." It is the idea of nothingness, of the worthlessness of reason; and Cherea fears it because it cannot be refuted (the one thing reason cannot demonstrate is its own value), but only opposed by action. "Here is what frightens me," Cherea says. "To lose one's life is a little thing, and I will have the courage when necessary. But to see the sense of this life dissipated, to see our reason for existence disappear: that is what is insupportable. A man cannot live without reason."

In the play's most moving scene (III, vi), the two antagonists are subtly drawn toward each other; as Ahab and Starbuck—a man whose great courage, like Cherea's, cannot withstand "those more terrific, because more spiritual terrors"—are drawn to one another in a parallel scene in *Moby-Dick*. "Cherea," asks the Emperor, wistfully and cunningly, "do you think that two men whose soul and pride are equal can at least once in their lives talk together from their hearts?" But the communication breaks down, in the face of a radical difference that both acknowledge.

> *Caligula:* Then you must believe in some superior idea.
> *Cherea:* I believe that some actions are more beautiful than others.
> *Caligula:* I believe that all actions are equivalent.
> *Cherea:* I know you do, Caius, and that is why I do not hate you.
> But you are disturbing, and therefore you must disappear.

The play closes, as do so many of Camus's writings, on the protagonist's outburst of defiant absurdity. Total and irrevocable solitude is Caligula's tragic perception—a perception made concrete by his strangulation of Caesonia, the only human being who loves him without question or resentment. His absolute power and his absolute freedom ensure his absolute aloneness—"I alone am free." It is at the instant of that pronouncement that the conspirators break in and stab him to death. The revolt succeeds, but Caligula's grand idea is not perhaps destroyed after all. His last words, and the last words of the play, are: "I am still alive!"

The Compassionate "No": *The Plague* AND *The Rebel*

Most of Camus's writings are implicit in any one of them, and later books are often elaborations of metaphors or anecdotes introduced casually in earlier ones. The plot of *Cross-Purposes* had appeared, via a newspaper clipping, in *The Stranger*—and the theme of Camus's second novel, *The Plague*, was articulated as metaphor by the Emperor Caligula. "My reign so far has been too happy," he remarks meditatively to the attendant and terrified nobles (IV, ii). "Neither universal plague, nor a cruel religion, not even a coup d'état. . . . Well then, *I* will replace the plague." In *The Plague* (1947), the process of replacement is reversed; the force of destruction becomes inhuman. The deadly epidemic has, in fact, long been a favorite image for Camus of the life-denying impulses of our century—as telling for him as the earthquake has been for Ignazio Silone. The difference between the images is a difference both of artistic temperament and of approach to a common problem; and it is spelled out by one of the characters in *The Plague*. "If this were only an earthquake! One great shock, and that's all there is to it. . . . You can count the dead and living, and the whole business is over. But this beastly disease! Even those who don't have it carry it in their hearts." Silone concentrates on the swift and convulsive disintegrations, and on the business of building anew which, at least, an earthquake makes possible. Camus visualizes modern experience as a long, monotonous struggle against the unending invasion of a mysterious and inexterminable enemy. *The Plague* is his most impressive narrative statement of that view of life.

The personified plague was itself the hero of *Caligula:* or better, the antihero. But in *The Plague* (despite its title) the focus has shifted from Caligula to Cherea, from the disease to the energies of resistance. Dr. Bernard Rieux, whose journal of the plague season is the source of the story, exemplifies these energies, as a more capable, a more selfless and indomitable Cherea—a better rebel.[28] To what extent Rieux's efforts, or all the medical efforts combined, are responsible for the plague's eventual disappearance, no one can say: that is central to the book's riddling point. But the efforts are strenuous, courageous, and skillful; and they are grounded in a tenacious theory of compassion. For by the late nineteen-forties, Camus had inched his way to and had settled upon his own truncated precept of charity—leaving the Lord to take care of Himself, and being content with loving one's neighbor. In *The Rebel*, Camus's charitable precept took the form of a sort of Cartesian proposition: "I resist, therefore we are." Like many of his formulas, this one, too, could be reversed without damage: what is important is the felt interdependence between individual rebellion and human solidarity ("I" and "we") as the only basis of genuine existence. "That was the new knowledge," as Auden has said in his poetic salute to the aging Melville; "His terror had to blow itself quite out/ To let him see it."

Both *The Plague* and its discursive counterpart, *The Rebel*, reveal Camus's gradual conversion from the solitude, nihilism, and absurdity explored in all the works clustering around *The Stranger* toward a sense of participation, as the only salvageable value and the one trustworthy meaning. "Toward" is the right word; for Camus will not be hurried, and he will not betray his own awareness of treachery by coming nicely to rest on his spiritual journey. A phrase that turns up toward the end of *The Rebel* continues to characterize him: *"Lutte, toujours"*—a constant struggle; and we may expect from him further unfoldings of the soul's lapses and deceitfulness, further warnings against the snares of the universe: only now, the most dangerous of them may be the complacency of positive belief. But insofar as it *has* been accomplished, Camus's conversion suggests a form of secular redemption. The latter phrase, too, is deliberate; for what Camus tentatively arrived at was just what imaginative and thoughtful men had been arriving at for three-quarters of a century, and what was best expressed by the elder Henry James in the title of his last book: *Society the Redeemed Form of Man* (1879). The elder James's career—from an arrant early individualism to a virtual annihilation of the spirit (or "vastation" as he tended to call it) to a rebirth into human fellowship—is suggestively similar to that of Albert Camus, but the pattern is discoverable everywhere. The generation of writers prior to that of Camus and Silone—the generation of Joyce and Mann and Proust—customarily ended its search in the private and personal city of art, where the artist is the only citizen; but Camus and his contemporaries have, so to speak, gone back to the age of their grandfathers and have insisted again upon the life of participation in the city of man. That same insistence is part of the design, for example, worked out by Conrad, between the systole of an icy skepticism and the diastole of a faith in human love, in secret sharing. And the entire movement is, I venture, carried by the thirty-page tale of Stephen Crane, "The Open Boat," with its double discovery, first, of the remote indifference of the universal power ("she was indifferent, flatly indifferent") and of the absurdity of life ("the whole affair was absurd"); second, of the one irreducible value remaining—"the subtle brotherhood of men . . . established on the seas."

Society, in some provisional and thinned-out meaning of the word, has become the redeemed form of Camus's representative man, though in a manner more austere and restrained than it had been for the elder James, or for Conrad and Crane. Having decided in *The Myth of Sisyphus* that being was after all more honorable than non-being, Camus went on to decide that being *with* is the only firm basis for being. This was the communion foretold and the conversion announced in the symbols of bread and wine, the indifferent and the absurd: from which everything, Camus had once bravely predicted, would eventually start.

It was *The Plague* that introduced Camus to a large American audience, when the Stuart Gilbert translation was published here in 1948; *The Stranger*, though translated earlier, was slower to attract attention. *The Plague* was rather extravagantly received by American critics, and its allegory worried almost out of existence. It would perhaps have been more readily and simply understood if it had been examined in the context of the other works (had they been available); for those works, to repeat Camus's remark, "form a whole in which each one is illuminated by the other." One ought, none the less, to meet Camus first through an imaginative work, like *The Plague*, rather than through a speculative work; for one should encounter at once his fundamentally dramatic view of life as an unceasing contest between the spirit that rebels and the universe that seeks to thwart or engulf it. And beyond that, the writing of a novel itself—according to Camus—is an act of rebellion.

Art, Camus said in *The Rebel*, is "a demand for unity and a rejection of the world. But it rejects the world on account of what it lacks and in the name of what it sometimes can be. Rebellion may be observed here in its pure state." The analogy is worked from the other direction: "In every rebellion is to be found the metaphysical demand for unity, the impossibility of capturing it and the construction of a substitute universe. Rebellion from this point of view is a fabricator of universes. This also defines art." Of all literary forms, moreover, the novel is the closest in kind to other instances (metaphysical and historical) of the rebellious act: "The novel is born simultaneously with the spirit of rebellion and expresses, on the aesthetic plane, the same ambition."

The assertions are put forward with all the precarious brilliance that typifies Camus; but they manage to suggest a good deal about the contemporary theory and practice of fiction. They help to explain the sense we have, in reading the best of second generation writing, that the contemporary novel is not only an imitation of life or (in James's phrase) a direct impression of life—it is an assault upon life, an effort to change it or reconstruct it. The notion of art as rebellion could have unfortunate results; it could produce over-strained or simply boring work, and no doubt on lower levels it has. But in the cases examined in this book, it has, on the contrary, produced a body of decidedly original and distinguished fiction—and precisely because the nature of the rebellion urged is in the name of humanity and toward the recovery of a more truly *human* human image; for the human image is the stuff of art. The tussle with life in the modern world which characterizes the fiction of Camus and the others is—since it is for the sake of man—a tussle for the sake of art. The very meaning of "to stylize," Malraux argues in *Les Noyers de L'Altenburg*, is to "humanize"; so that when he defines art as "a rectification of the universe," he means exactly (so he continues) that it is "a humanization of the universe." For this idea as for others, Camus is plainly indebted to Malraux; but with his customary intensity, Camus has not so much made or repeated the point, he has pushed it sideways and exposed it as something startling. Compare E. M. Forster's soft-spoken statement of the same thing, in *Two Cheers for Democracy:* "Viewed realistically, the past is really a series of *dis*orders. . . . [Art] is the one orderly product which our muddling race has produced. . . . It follows that the artist will tend to be an outsider in the society to which he was born." But perhaps it is not the same thing; Camus's intensity succeeds both in transforming its object and revitalizing it; and while Forster has long since declared sadly that it is no longer possible to write fiction, Camus continues to compose novels that are profoundly impressive in themselves and a splendid stimulus to the creative imagination of others. Among them, *The Plague* is the finest example of what he intends by the assertion that the novel expresses the spirit of rebellion.

The universe fabricated by Camus in *The Plague* is called Oran. The rebellion he describes is that of a number of Oran's citizens against the devastations of a plague and the moral corruption a plague brings with it. But the rebellion the book *enacts*, as an artistic work of defiant unity, is against whatever it is which we take the plague to represent. Literally, it seems to be the bubonic plague, and the story deals with its arrival, its mysterious nature and its history (studied in a quasi-scientific manner systematically blurred by a chilly lyricism), and with the self-watchful reactions to

it by a variety of characters. Among these presumptively condemned men is Rambert, a visiting journalist, trapped inside the
quarantined city, who renounces his chance to escape and instead
joins the resistance. There is Cottard, an anxiety-ridden swindler
who finds a new freedom in the besieged prison of Oran. There is
Grand, a petty functionary, who continues methodically on his
rounds, weeps silently over his wife's infidelity, and spends hours
polishing the first sentence of a projected novel ("On a beautiful
morning in May, a slender Amazon, mounted on a stately chestnut
mare, was riding along the flowery paths of the Bois de Boulogne"—
that, and a dozen alternatives for every word). And centrally there
is Tarrou, an enigmatic wanderer of no stated vocation except that
high vocation New Englanders used to call "seeking"; he is a seeker
after truth and moral purpose. And there is Dr. Rieux, the hero of
a Gallic Hemingway, a man whose whole being is engaged in doing
the job he knows best with all the skill at his command. Tarrou
dies, along with hordes of other residents in the city; Rieux unac-
countably survives, while his wife dies in a distant nursing home;
and the plague finally diminishes and stops altogether.

Those are elements of the literal story; but Camus makes it
clear, both by a prefatory quotation from Daniel Defoe and by a
steady austerity of language which keeps the novel midway between
the concrete and the abstract, that his story is an allegory. The
plague is, perhaps, whatever we think it is: that is, whatever the
reader happens to regard as the ultimate opposition to the human
will; for it is all the modes and sources of death, looked at from the
viewpoint of a glowering humanism. (If, like Keats, we happen to
be half in love with easeful death, *The Plague* will make little sense
to us.) It is evil itself, as Erich Fromm has somewhere defined it:
"All evil strivings are against life"; a definition, I take it, and not
merely an observation. And in this respect, we can distinguish two
identities for the plague, related as closely as may be to the two areas
of revolt that (along with that of art) Camus has indicated: the
historical and the metaphysical.

It is an image of a specific human condition, resembling more the
blight that afflicted the Thebes of Oedipus or the modern wasteland of T. S. Eliot than, for example, the more purely physical
plagues through which the heroes of Manzoni and Giono have

made their way. As such, it is a symbol of modern war: especially the Second World War in Europe, which, for the warriors, was singularly undramatic with its slow attritions, its piecemeal destruction, its occupations and military prisons and concentration camps. Antoine St-Exupéry, too, saw war as a kind of plague: "War is not an adventure," he wrote from his own experience; "war is a sickness, like typhus." And Faulkner, in *A Fable*, picks up the same figure to make a different point. "War," says the British dispatchrider, "is a fever the purpose of which is to rid the body of fever." Himself a gallant member of the French resistance, Camus, in his second novel, is bent on dramatizing the kinds of resistance that man may offer in our time to a world of war and of slavery. He had declared in advance the underlying theme of *The Plague* in a letter written during the occupation to a hypothetical German friend: [29] "Man is perishable. Perhaps; but let us go on resisting even as we perish. And if nothingness is what is reserved for us, at least let us not behave as though it were justified." That is the motto implicit in the conduct of Rieux, Tarrou and the others.

But in the incorrigibly metaphysical vision of Camus, the plague becomes a force that transcends history. It is in fact, I venture, a startling image of divine grace, seen humanistically as a mystery and a disaster: an immitigable power, infinitely stronger than man and infinitely unjust, or rather nonjust; a force always ready to pounce, but pouncing nonrationally, on this person instead of that, then rather than now. This is the conception of grace we regularly meet in the bizarre Christianity Camus usually portrays: a grace that— contrary to the best tradition—destroys the natural order for the sake of saving it, but never operates so as to enlarge, heighten, or perfect it. Paneloux, the clerical caricature in *The Plague*, preaches two sermons, in the second of which he helplessly accepts the horrors besetting his parish precisely because they will not yield to human understanding; he makes that "leap" of faith, and enjoins his congregation to make it, that Camus in *The Myth of Sisyphus* excoriated as a suicidal intellectual betrayal. In this peculiar framework, the plague cannot be explained or bargained with or pushed back; it can only be sacrificed to. It takes on the character of a Caligula with wings and a tail: a dragon, a devouring Moloch, to whom the young are sacrificed at intervals until the beast is sated and withdraws—to return, no doubt, for another ritual in another year.

Ignazio Silone has spoken of a childhood experience with the Italian state's legal machinery, and of his distinct impression that the state was looked on by its servants not as a political institution but as a fearful being above or outside of political actuality: a sort of monstrous demigod to be assuaged, to whom a few peasant women should be thrown in the tremulous hope that it might then depart for a while. There is a high degree of quizzical comedy in Silone's report; but Camus, in *The Plague*, offers a similar image in more tight-lipped tones. The doctors of Oran labor to invent new serums; perhaps they help, perhaps they do not; no one can be sure. The plague continues to devour its prey—"comfortably installed in its paroxysm and bringing to its daily murders the precision and regularity of a good functionary"—and then, inexplicably, it declines and disappears. The dreadful visit of the god comes to its end.

This reading of *The Plague* is reinforced by the argument of *The Rebel* (1951). For *The Rebel*, a somewhat loose-jointed history of human revolt, is nothing other—or so it seems to me—than St. Augustine's *City of God* written backwards. It is an effort to disentangle across the centuries the nobly human from the oppressively sacred. Against St. Augustine's secret history of divine grace, Camus proposes the more compelling but almost equally secret history of human rebellion. "There are only two universes for a human spirit," Camus writes; "that of the sacred (or in Christian language, of grace)"—the parenthesis is Camus's—"and that of revolt." *Civitas Dei* and *L'Homme Révolté* divided the pair between them. The great moments in Camus's history, therefore, are not the Creation and the Fall (as they were for St. Augustine), or the heroics of the prophets and the birth of the Redeemer. They are the revealing instances of revolt in ancient myth and in recorded fact: the heroics of men as otherwise incompatible as Cain and Ivan Karamazov, Lucretius and the Marquis de Sade. And if there is a Redeemer in this rebellious gallery, it is the legendary Prometheus—the being who defied the gods for the sake of mankind, who brought the gift of light to men and who was punished hideously and endlessly for doing so.

Camus's own title for the entire block of his work that includes

The Rebel and *The Plague* (along with two plays) is "The Myth of Prometheus"; as his title for the earlier block, including *The Stranger* and others, is "The Myth of Sisyphus." (The moment he is now engaged with, which began with *The Fall*, is called "The Myth of Judgment." Camus appears to have in mind a fivefold scheme of work, each to be labeled "the myth" of something; but his creative energy, in practice, is not as budgeted in advance as that scheme might suggest.) The Promethean brand of heroism is representative exactly because Prometheus—like the other lesser heroes in their widely different ways—challenged the power and the very sense of divine mystery. He strove to substitute the kingdom of earthly justice for the kingdom of grace.

Though it evidently gave him more personal difficulty than any other work (the decision to write it, Camus has remarked, was a singularly painful and lonely one), *The Rebel* does not seem to me Camus's most successful or persuasive book. But it is a major achievement in what I have been calling conversion: that is, artistic conversion, the replacement—through the techniques of language—of one set of values by another; the artistic process that reflects in writing the *personal* and actual conversion of the writer. Those baffling echoes of the New Testament that ironically underscored the godless atmosphere of *Cross-Purposes* have grown here to sonorous reminders of one of the masterpieces of Christian theology: but serving, in the modern manner, only to convey the author's radical deviation from the model being echoed.[30] The achievement is the more impressive since now Camus is deviating toward something and not merely away from something. He aims at transforming our perception and our estimate of both sacred and profane history, in the name of his newly discovered Third Force: the inviolable nature of man. Human nature, Camus now insists, *is* a kind of essence, distinct from the worlds both of time and of eternity, and common to all individual men. And that nature is what must be exerted with a constantly rejuvenated power against both those worlds as currently defined: against the excessive value claimed for history by the Marxists; and even more, against the curious value placed on suffering, in the interests of an eternal reward, by some theologians.

The rebellion Camus bespeaks is, in short, a double rebellion:

against a heartless God, and against a soulless history. In his novel, the two enemies are fused into a single image of the plague; in *The Rebel*, the argument logically divides them, and proposes both a "metaphysical" and an "historical" revolt. Beyond them both is the necessary revolt against the excesses of revolt. No pages in *The Plague* are more acute than those observing the evils that revolt can engender. The revolt against God can dissolve into nihilism; but "what distinguishes me perhaps from the contemporary intelligentsia which is or until recently was purely nihilistic," Camus has contended,[31] "is that I believe in a truth and I believe in searching for it—I believe that the search is the truth." The revolt against social injustice, meanwhile, can congeal into totalitarianism; and Camus has distinguished himself equally from those of his contemporaries who have swallowed communism for the sake of alleged social welfare. The act of rebellion must go on forever—"*Lutte, toujours.*" But though the historical section of *The Rebel* is devoted to an admirable, if long-winded, analysis and repudiation of both fascism ("the irrational terror") and communism ("the rational terror"), there is a feeling all along that the real threat to human dignity is something deeper than either and more ancient. The real threat is not a political theory but a religious tradition; and the real hero is not the Russian revolutionist but Prometheus.

The murderous violence of our time, Camus suggests, is a sort of horrible imitation of God. That is the central idea both of *The Plague* and *The Rebel*, and it crystallized in the latter by a passage about the philosophic Roman poet, Lucretius:

> Lucretian man . . . becomes a revolutionary. While denying the gods as unworthy and criminal, he himself takes their place. He emerges from the entrenched camp and begins the first assaults upon divinity, in the name of human misery. In the antique universe, murder was inexplicable and inexpiable. Already with Lucretius, human murder is seen as only an answer to divine murder. And it is not by accident that the poem of Lucretius ends on a prodigious image of holy sanctuaries swollen with the accusing corpses of the plague.

The Plague is just such a prodigious and accusing image, elaborated into book-length narrative. And the Lucretian note is struck by Dr. Rieux, in moments when he seems to speak most distinctly for the author ("The closest to myself," Camus says, "is not Tarrou the saint, but Rieux the doctor"). Rieux, like Lucretius, rests his confidence on the knowable nature of things; and he too emerges to attack the gods in the name of human misery. It is wiser and safer, he argues, to bet on the nonexistence of God: that way, human beings may confront the dangers that beset them with all their powers, and will not be tempted to slothful dependence on divine intervention or afterworldly consolation. Rieux's wager, of course, reverses deliberately the famous bet of Blaise Pascal (who counseled in favor of assuming the existence of God), and it crowns the entire reversal of the Christian tradition. It also shapes the image of heroism in *The Plague* and *The Rebel*. Camus believes that *The Plague* was "more anti-Christian than my earlier [books]," and perhaps he is right. The blasphemy of *Caligula* is more rousing, but the plain reversals of *The Plague* are more thorough.

Heroism, in the upside-down universe of *The Plague*, is accordingly an achievement beyond traditional holiness. Its nature is declared in a dialogue between Tarrou and Rieux, with Paneloux's sermonizing "leaps" echoing faintly in the background. The two men are seated on a terrace on a summer evening, listening to the rumble of ambulances and smelling the salt ocean air.

> "In short," Tarrou said simply, "what interests me is to know how to become a saint."
> "But you do not believe in God."
> "Exactly. How to be a saint without God: that is the only concrete problem I understand today."
>
> "Perhaps," replied the doctor, "but you know, I feel more solidarity with the vanquished than with the saints. I haven't the taste for heroism and sainthood. What interests me is how to be a man."
> "Yes, we are looking for the same thing, but I am less ambitious."
> Rieux thought Tarrou was joking, and looked across at him. But in the vague light that came from the sky, he saw only a sad and serious face.

With this dialogue, we approach the special heroic image that has been so pervasive elsewhere in contemporary fiction that I have taken it for the title of this book. Paradoxes cluster here, for though Camus may feel himself closer to Rieux than to Tarrou, the image he is projecting is in fact a composite of the two men and their ambitions. A distinction is drawn between the ideal of sainthood and the ideal of compassion ("solidarity with the vanquished"); but there is a clear implication that the ideal of compassion and the ambition to be a man *are* the ingredients of the one really authentic mode of sainthood in the contemporary world. What is absent from Camus's image at this point is, of course, any hint of the picaresque as an alloy of the saintly: any hint of the roguish element that characterizes Silone's Pietro Spina (as we shall see) and Greene's Mexican priest—and which characterizes Camus's earlier invention, Caligula, and his later invention, Jean-Baptiste Clamence in *The Fall*. Caligula and Clamence seem to me, I must acknowledge, more notable and more appealing artistic creations than Tarrou and Dr. Rieux; for all the latters' dedication to becoming a man there is too little in them of the sinful burden of human nature for them finally to succeed. They are less representative of human nature than is Clamence, for example; and insofar, they are less representative of contemporary fiction. They share with Faulkner's Isaac McCaslin the artistic weakness of too unmodulated a moral strength.

But Tarrou and Rieux do reflect—and *The Plague* mirrors—a conviction of the present age: a conviction about the division, even the incompatibility, between the religious impulse and human sympathy. Camus was obliged, for his own development, to emphasize that division, and to make clear his personal stand on the side of the human. Only by saying "No!" to the official pieties of the age could Camus sustain and enlarge that compassion he had come to believe in as the redeemed condition of man.

THE DISTANCE BETWEEN: *The Fall*

The first article of Camus's slender humanistic creed thus became compassion. Not yet companionship: not yet the sharing of bread that symbolizes the sharing of every sort of genuine nourishment; not yet that sharing that is in fact nourishment. It is the *suffering* of mankind that seized the mind and imagination of Camus; and so it is the suffering that he enjoins us to share (for that, of course, is what both compassion and sympathy etymologically mean—*suffering with*). The epigraph of the French edition of *The Rebel*—

deleted in the English translation—announces the theme: "And openly, I dedicated myself to the grave and suffering earth; and often, in the sacred night, I promised to love it, with its heavy burden of fatality, faithfully and without fear, and to scorn none of its enigmas." The words are Hölderlin's, and the speaker is Empedocles—the ancient hero who plunged into the troubled depths of volcanic Etna to partake of its disturbances, leaving only his sandals behind; but the voice is that of Camus. It speaks again, in the same emotional octave, in *The Rebel's* concluding lines:

> At the noon of thought, the rebel thus refuses divinity in order to participate in the common struggles and common destiny. We shall choose Ithaca, the faithful earth, the audacious and frugal thought, the lucid action, the generosity of the man who knows. In the light, the world remains our first and our last love. Our brothers breathe under the same sky; justice is living. Then it is that the strange joy is born which helps us to live and to die and which we shall henceforth refuse to postpone until a later time. On the grieving earth, *that* is the tireless thorn, the bitter nourishment, the harsh wind from the sea, the ancient and the new dawn.

The lyrical vocabulary of *Noces*, Camus's first book, emerges again after more than a decade, and now under the sign of rebellion. What has been added to the Algerian vision is the emphasis upon compassion for "our brothers," the emphasis on participation, on generosity and justice. In choosing Ithaca, like Odysseus (who rejected immortality and a goddess in favor of home and an aging wife), Camus chose the bitter nourishment of the earthly sorrows of man.

The Plague is an effort to realize both the sorrows and the action of choice. It is thus highlighted, on the side of resistance, by the rare occasions when Rieux can actually feel himself *into* the pain or the grief of another human being. The pain of a plague-stricken child: "Alone, the child was battling with all his strength. Rieux, who was taking his pulse from time to time . . . felt the child's agitation mingle with the tumult of his own blood. He confused himself with the tormented child and tried to sustain it with all his still undiminished force. But, united for a moment, the pulsation of their two hearts became disunited, the child escaped him, and his effort went down into emptiness." The grief of the elderly functionary, Grand, whom Rieux watches one day from a distance, leaning against a shop window, weeping silently over the absence and infidelity of his wife:

> Tears streamed down without interruption over the face of the old functionary. And these tears overwhelmed Rieux because he understood them and felt them, too, in the hollow of his throat. He, too, was remembering the unhappy man's betrothal, in front of a shop at Christmas, and Jeanne turned to him to say that she was happy. From the depths of distant years, at the very heart of this folly, the fresh voice of Jeanne was coming to Grand, that was sure. Rieux knew what the weeping old man was thinking at that moment.

Rieux exists because he takes his stand against the sources of human misery. But he is truly alive only in those precious instants when his being is vitalized by active membership in the common nature of mankind—a nature always discovered by Camus in the condition of suffering.

In passages like these, Rieux arrives briefly at a state of awareness, in the enriched meaning given that word by the influential Jewish writer, Martin Buber.[32] Buber's thought is drenched in the direct immediacy of experience, and the main theme of much of his writing is the human relation—but that relation so intensified that it becomes a channel for the relation between man and God. He is thus so close to the movement of contemporary fiction (with its almost obsessive interest in the human encounter) as to seem its philosophic spokesman. Camus acknowledges a profound respect for Buber, as does Ignazio Silone. And Camus is even willing to say that, for himself, "the sacred" is just that presence felt in the silence during a moment of genuine awareness.[33] He would accept—or at least in *The Plague* he has dramatized—the distinction Buber draws between awareness, on the one hand, and two other ways in which one man can perceive another. There is observation, which is detached and scientific (the relation between Moravia's characters is often that of pure observation); and there is "looking on"—the attitude of the artist, idle but absorptive. Only in what Buber calls the condition of being aware is even a transitory moment of communion accomplished: when the man perceived becomes not an "it," a scientific object, but a "thou," a human relative so to speak; and when he says something to the man perceiving. The saying need not be aloud. It need not even be conscious. "The man himself in his relation to me," Buber argues, "has nothing to do with what is said.

He has no relation to me, he has indeed not noticed me at all." So it is with the weeping Grand and the aware Dr. Rieux, the former not even noticing the latter but saying something to him none the less, a fragile and unknowing "thou," supplying Rieux with the fullest sense of being he has ever experienced.

But the moment is transitory, and, as in the case of the dying child, seems to end on a note of failure. The distance between Grand and Rieux, one feels, is after all too great. Buber has insisted that distance is a necessary prerequisite to relationship; what is aimed at is a communion of distinct and separate persons and not a mere blurring of individuals. It is possible for human beings to move too close to one another, either in fact or fiction: such, I will suggest, is the case with the characters in Steinbeck's *The Grapes of Wrath.* But Camus portrays the opposite, because (needless to say) that has been his impression of life. The physical distance separating Rieux and Grand stands for an abyss between souls; compassion undeniably exerts itself, but the impulse falls after a few seconds into the emptiness. And the explanation may be implicit in Camus's next novel, *The Fall.* For with that book he has revolted again, and this time against an illusory generosity, an unsoundly based solidarity with the wretched. Almost worse than the absence of communion, Camus seems to be saying in *The Fall*, is the parody of communion rooted in a pride of communion. The worst is the corruption of the best.

With *The Fall*, Camus appears to be departing anew upon a long cycle like the one that carried him from the marital joy of *Noces* through the long divorce of *The Stranger* and *The Myth* to the provisional affirmations of *The Plague* and *The Rebel.* Against those latter, too, Camus feels compelled to revolt, and perhaps against their consequences for him personally. *The Fall*, that is, may on one level represent a rebellion against the position of moral eminence readers throughout the Western world had forced him into. "I hate self-satisfied virtue," Camus has told an interviewer.[34] "I hate the despicable morality of the world, and I hate it because, just like cynicism, it ends by depriving man of hope and preventing him from assuming responsibility for his own life with all its terrible burden of crimes and grandeur." The whole basis of the contemporary novelistic image of a "picaresque saint" is in that statement; and *The Fall* is, among other things, a narrative version of the reasons behind it. It contains the implication (all Camus's works, we recall, comment on one another) that the characters in *The Plague* remain separated because they possess a virtue that could turn—though in them it has not yet turned—into sterile self-satisfaction. A man can be corrupted by too much virtue, as well as by too much vice (the note will be expressed in different tonalities by Graham Greene); the best means of rejuvenation is a periodic return to the depths, to the reality of the human hell. The idea of *mésure*, of balance and the constant need to adjust the balance, is close to the center of Camus's thinking.

In *The Fall*, we detect not only a new rebellion, but a new Eden too, more dangerously deceptive than that of *Noces*. We hear of a new divorce between the individual and his world, and we come upon a new sense of absurdity, though that elusive word has now been pretty well dropped. We confront a new image of the absurd man, attuned in a new way to the universal tunelessness; and we descend to new and more startling grounds for solidarity. The setting of *The Fall* is Amsterdam and the Zuyder Zee, a setting even grayer and sadder than the sunless scene of *Cross-Purposes*. The narrative consists of a monologue addressed to a visitor from Paris by a man who has taken the name of Jean-Baptiste Clamence. Clamence relates to his shadowy listener the adventures that have brought him (Clamence) from his lofty role in the Parisian world to the dark and foggy streets, the dingy bars and the bleak little room in Amsterdam where, under his new name, he practices the profession of "the judge-penitent."

His public and private life in France had once seemed to him to belong to a kind of earthly paradise. He had been a popular and successful lawyer, with a special talent for defending the wretched and unlucky; he had been an exemplary citizen who made a point of helping the blind across city streets and giving up his place to "deserving persons" in tramcars. "I freely held sway, bathed in a light as of Eden. Indeed, wasn't that Eden, *cher monsieur:* no intermediary between life and me? Such was my life." [35] And such had been the Algerian life in *Noces*, where happiness was once defined as "the simple accord between a being and the existence he leads." The fall from this later Eden was initiated by the sound of laughter, echoes of derision from unidentifiable sources, that Clamence began to hear in the air about him as he made his way proudly through

Paris. One particular incident helps to change Clamence's whole belief about himself—when he ignores the desperate call for help of a drowning woman. It thereafter begins to grow upon him that, far from being a character of high virtue with a large fund of human compassion, he is only a fraud. In his retrospective account of himself, he rehearses the same qualities that Camus used to define absurdity in *The Myth of Sisyphus*. He had been play acting all along; his career had been a farce of conquest (Napoleonic allusions ironically color Clamence's confession); he had been a self-admiring Don Juan, enumerating his erotic adventures and loving no one.

Clamence's fall consists, indeed, in acknowledging his own lifelong absurdity, and that of many others. The first symptom of recognition had been a series of bizarre public outbursts of inverted honesty, along with an experiment in groveling debauchery: reminiscent of Stavrogin in *The Possessed*, during his nose-tweaking phase and his hours of depravity. The next step was the departure from Paris, the arrival in Holland, and the assumption of the new name and the new profession. The name, be it noted, is heavily allegorical: John the Baptist (Jean-Baptiste), crying *(clamans)* in the wilderness of the modern world, yet preparing the way for no conceivable Lord. Now he earns the right to pass judgment on others only by the constant act of penance for himself: the judge-penitent.

Literary analogies, as always, cluster about Camus's hero. Beyond Stavrogin and John the Baptist, we detect shadings of the Ancient Mariner, seizing remorselessly upon any available stranger and turning him gray with his story; of Milton's Lucifer; of Shakespeare's Timon of Athens; and above all, of Dostoevski's underground man, probing through more radical lies to more radical truths, the seeds in turn of new spitefulness and ironic malice. The hell of Amsterdam is Dantesque to a degree made emphatic by numerous details; yet its atmosphere is really closer to the underground, the shadowy corners of Dostoevski. For in *The Fall*, the weight of Dostoevski is more immense than ever on the conscience of Camus. But it is somehow a liberating weight, and nothing oppressive. For what is striking about *The Fall* is the encouraging sign it gives that Camus is still a rebel: that he is still in motion, that he has moved onward, now, to a critique of all the false forms of just those qualities he had been recently extolling. The values of generosity and a concern for the helpless have, the book suggests, dangerously triumphed. We are all comfortably communal and jostle each other to assist the blind—this, too, must now be exposed. And in the course of doing so, Camus, through his narrator, gropes toward a new basis for solidarity with his fellows: to what might be called the fellowship of those ashamed, the democracy of the guilty.

The fellowship is large enough to include the entire human race; the democracy is universal—such is the novel's implication. Both Clamence and Camus would subscribe to the title of a recent French film: *We Are All Murderers*. The technique for suggesting that sombre solidarity is a cunning progression in the terms by which Clamence addresses his listener: from *monsieur* to *cher monsieur*, and thence to *mon cher compatriote, mon cher ami* and finally *cher maître*. The suggestion is artfully planted that Clamence is talking to no one but himself; but this suggestion in turn dissolves into the disconcerting realization that he is talking to no one in particular because he is talking to everyone in the world at once. At least one French critic violently rejected the insinuation in *The Fall* that Clamence speaks for and to all of us; to which a critic in Italy replied that we must not succumb to moral panic.

The title of *The Fall* is itself ironic, and it contains unexpected traditional echoes. For Clamence experiences what, in the Christian tradition, has been called a "fortunate fall." That phrase is intended to suggest, within the Christian framework, that the fall of Adam (that is, the fall of man) proved to be fortunate for mankind since it made necessary the entrance into human history of God as man; it made necessary the Incarnation. Modern literature, however, has often exploited a humanistic equivalent of the religious idea; and has suggested that the fall from innocence or virtue can have a fortunate effect upon an individual, that it can educate, enrich and humanize him.[36] Such, so far as we can make out in the Dutch fog and amid the interwoven ambiguities of the novel, is the effect of his fall upon Clamence. It is as though Dr. Rieux had fallen; and, for Clamence himself, the experience is at the same time a kind of "rise" —he is at least a much fuller human being, and a more real one.

Correspondingly, *The Fall* seems to me a fuller work of art, and more real than its predecessor, *The Plague;* I believe it to join with *The Stranger* and *Caligula* as the most accomplished of Camus's writings so far. For with *The Fall*, Camus has recovered the sense of impurity that was somewhat ominously lacking in *The Plague:* the sense, that is, of the vigorous impurity of human nature, "with all its terrible burden of crimes and grandeur"; and the sense that it is the business of the artist to render that impurity with all justice. He has recovered too, some of the humor that had been missing in his work since *Caligula;* and by returning to both the impure and the comic, Camus has moved still closer to a persuasive image of man in the contemporary world. *The Fall* is less comforting than *The Plague* and *The Rebel;* but in undermining to some degree the hopeful assertions of those latter two books, *The Fall* is not itself an exercise in negation. "I am tired of criticism, denigration, and meanness—in short, of nihilism," Camus remarked in the interview already mentioned. "We must condemn what deserves condemnation. . . . But what deserves to be praised should be exalted at length." And in *The Fall* there are hints of light, as there are hints of hope: carried by periodic references to the doves that circle promisingly in the gray Dutch sky. "The doves wait up there all year round. They wheel about the earth, look down and would like to come down." "Look, the doves are gathering up there." "It must be the doves, surely. They finally make up their mind to come down, the little dears." Irony invades those references, too; but the descent of the dove in its traditional meaning does seem to be hinted at—in however secular and skeptical a manner.

It remains a hint which must not be exaggerated. "The only certainty that remains to us," Camus still insists, "is the naked suffering that is common to all of us and that mingles its roots with those of stubborn hope." Camus will not forget the suffering, and he will never abandon the hope. He has arrived, apparently and by way of all the intellectual and artistic and purely human exertions that we have been rehearsing, at the moment when he feels able to put the whole of his image of man into a single novel. Modern man with both his suffering and his hope, both his crimes and his grandeur, both his saintly aspiration and his roguish tendencies: this is the subject of the work Camus is now engaged upon, a work significantly titled *The First Man.* It will be the detailed story of how an individual becomes an adult: that is, how he becomes a man. About it, one may with certainty predict one thing, that it will be altogether honest. For Camus has been faithful to his own vision, and he has a rock to build upon.

CHAPTER 4

Ignazio Silone: The Politics of Charity

> The spiritual condition I have described allows
> of no boasting. . . . It resembles a camp of refu-
> gees in some no man's land, out in the open, exist-
> ing by chance. What do you expect refugees to
> do from morning to night? They spend the best
> part of their time telling each other their stories.
> The stories are not very entertaining, to be sure,
> but they tell them anyhow—mainly, to understand
> what has happened.
>
> Silone, "The Choice of Companions"

The Artist in Action

Lecturing before Italian audiences in the fall of 1953, Ignazio Silone
spoke of a certain "trustfulness" he could find within himself—an
assurance about the human spirit that, though not very large or very
joyous, was enough (he said) to make him consent to go on living.
It resembled the feeling he detected and honored in the recent work
of Albert Camus; and, rehearsing that work, Silone aligned himself
with Camus's effort to chart a way out of modern-day nihilism.
But his own sense of assurance, he felt, went deeper than anything
Camus could yet honestly show. It was "based on and moved by
something more than the compassion of Albert Camus. It is based

on the intimate certainty that we are free and responsible, and it is moved by an absolute need for an opening on to the intimate reality of others." Silone took as his image of the Frenchman's slender yet irreducible humanism the scene in *The Plague* (glanced at in the previous chapter), between the weeping functionary, Grand, and the commiserating awareness of Dr. Rieux. It was a wonderful moment, Silone said; but it did not, perhaps, contain enough for the needs of man. The two characters remained too far apart, both literally and psychically: a valid image of the distance between persons in our time, and hence a challenge rather than a fulfillment. The constant purpose of Silone has been to abolish that distance—to progress from compassion to companionship; to move forward from awareness to charity. And the road selected by destiny and his own temperament has been the treacherous road of politics.

Silone's trustfulness is Christian and it is grounded in love; but it is very human and extremely modest. He cannot, as he admits, use a stronger word. What he professes is not quite a faith, and definitely not Faith.[1] In Catholic Italy, Silone is endowed with a singularly Protestant mentality; he has a hearty disregard for hierarchies and dogmas, and it might be said that he sees life as justified by faith rather than by reason or by the observed actions of mankind. But in fact, Silone is less a Protestant Christian than a primitive Christian. He resembles most of all some member of the earliest Christian community—during the earliest years, indeed during the earliest days of Christianity, before the shock of the Crucifixion had worn off or the meaning of the Resurrection had sunk in. "In the sacred history of man on earth, it is still, alas, Good Friday," he wrote in 1944. Some deep conviction is at work in him, as it must have been in those primitive Christians; but it is not yet fully articulated. It has not yet found the whole of its persuasive form.

The form it has found is imaginative, and not polemical—artistic, and not speculative; that form is the chief subject of this chapter. And incomplete as the form is, never more than implicit, with the air of having been bruised at birth, it comprises for me, nevertheless, the most effective image of human experience that contemporary fiction has devised. It is to be looked for in the sequence of the five novels Silone has so far written: *Fontamara* (1930), *Bread and Wine* (1937), *The Seed Beneath the Snow* (1940), *A*

Handful of Blackberries (1952) and *The Secret of Luca* (1956).
But we have to begin by facing a question that would otherwise
nag us throughout the discussion: the question about whether Silone
is a novelist at all.

European critics, and some American critics as well, are fond of
remarking that Silone is not really a writer, but something else—
a sort of moral force, perhaps, exercising itself amidst the political
explosions of the age. Italian critics mean something disrespectful
by this, though it would seem a great thing to be a moral force,
very possibly a greater thing than to be a writer. One of the notions
of this book is that the moral force—I do not say moral preaching—
is what is finally important in a man's writing: even if one accepts
the dictum of Henry James that the moral content of a work of art
is simply the amount of felt life in it; and if one, as a consequence,
attends primarily to the art that makes the life intensely felt—that
manages and makes radiant the moral vigor within. But "the Silone
case," as Italian critics uncomfortably call it, tends to dissolve the
issue it typifies. His fiction illustrates exactly the peculiar business
that fiction has perforce been up to in his generation—the business of
disclosing in life itself new grounds for the very sense of life; and
the business of fashioning out of the ruins a more truthful and more
human (in that respect only, a more "positive") image of man than
the forlorn, essentially aesthetic, and often dehydrated images received from the previous generation. At the same time, Silone's
novels do nothing to extend the linguistic and structural experiments of that generation (Silone hardly seems to know them). His
work is built on old-fashioned simplicities, and the critic must guard
against a sophistication which would shatter itself on his grizzled
humor and prophetic force. For Silone suggests the degree to which
fiction, while pursuing its contemporary mission, can yet reveal a
traditional fictional concern with story and persons and a traditional
interest in entertainment.

As a matter of fact, Silone is always a writer—has always been a
writer; and it can be argued that he tends to settle political and
social issues by an appeal to the criteria of good fiction. The good
life, he seems to hint, is the one that makes a good story. He does
unquestionably embody a moral force. But it is a force that emerges
from a poetic appraisal of experience and moves toward a poetic

account of it: an account, that is, which discloses in experience, and with a certain measure of beauty, the characteristic movements of the soul. Perhaps the best way to identify Silone would be to call him an artist in action: rather than an artist, simply, and much rather than a "committed" artist. The difficulties under which Silone has had to write are the same difficulties that have beset Albert Camus, and they have been eloquently and accurately described by the latter in the interview I have quoted from earlier:

> Every writer tries to give form to the passions of his day: yesterday to love, today to the great passions for unity and freedom that are tearing the world apart. Yet today, just as yesterday, art attempts to snatch from death a living image of our passions and miseries. Perhaps the task is more difficult these days. . . . The contemporary artist risks losing touch with reality if he remains in his ivory tower, while if he gallops round and round the political arena he may lose his creative talent. It is between these extremes, however, that the difficult paths of true art open up. . . . The artist, though obliged to share in the tragedy of his times, must also keep his distance from it in order to look at it and give it form. This perpetual shuttling back and forth, this tension which becomes more and more dangerous to him, is the task of today's artist.

Silone, indeed, has done or has tried to do more than "shuttle back and forth" between the tragic actualities and the artistic images thereof. Even when caught up in the actualities (when arguing with a Soviet professor, for example, about the meaning of the Hungarian revolution), he seems to be searching and commenting upon their poetic shape. And in his writing, conversely, he always aims to discover the imitable life—the moral content—that may be redeemed from the swarming violence of modern history; he aims always to discover the *action* of action. He is, accordingly, an artist in action; and his fiction is his own particular answer to one of the great literary questions of this time: whether the novel can still dramatize the intrusion into life of history, without being itself destroyed; whether power, in its present peculiarly aggressive and ubiquitous forms, can be controlled in a work of art. Silone thinks it can be, if at the same time it be transmuted by charity; art and charity go forward together.

The question must at least be confronted if literature is to carry out its venerable assignment, which is not to withdraw into the shallows of adolescent anguish or into the remoter atmosphere of the city of art, but to show, or try to show, the age and body of the time its form and pressure. There is no doubt that our immediate circumstances make that assignment unduly severe; we live in a moment more suitable for analysis, lamentation and criticism. But Silone has the perilous advantage of knowing the pressure of his time at first hand; he himself contributed to it not a little. He knew the fatal abstractions that power so promptly assumes ("politics," "history," and the like)—knew them while still they were quickening into life and could be seized upon by anecdote. So he brings to his writing an intimate acquaintance with just those matters with which fiction must deal or perish.

The same can be said, of course, about André Malraux, and in a more limited manner of George Orwell and Arthur Koestler. But it is not easy to go on adding names to the list. And Silone's experience has been, if anything, more central and representative (I do not say more exciting or admirable) than that of Malraux and the others; or, what is precisely the same thing, he has somehow made it seem so. In the Emersonian meaning I have been attaching to the word, the representative *experience* in contemporary Europe has been the personal experience of Ignazio Silone—in its rhythm, in the succession of its allegiances, in the mood and form of the personal conversions it has included. Silone's career is his first allegory, and it should be glossed in some detail as a prologue to the allegories he then went on to compose. The effort to understand it is part of our effort to understand ourselves, in the bitterness of our deepest honesty.

ROMAN REBEL AND MEDIEVAL SAINT

Representativeness was imposed on Silone. If he were to be anything, he was virtually required to be universal—or, anyhow, European, a familiar mask of the universal. He scarcely had the chance to be Italian. More than half of his life before 1945 was spent either in underground revolutionary politics, international in purpose and tone, or in exile in German-speaking Switzerland. And he was born and grew up in a section of Italy that had never been entirely Romanized to start with and had never since been very hospitable to the Italian temper and language. The section is called the Marse, after the Latin tribe that once inhabited it; it is a small fraction of that vast stretch of country in central Italy, east of Rome, known as the Abruzzo.[2]

Silone was born there in May, 1900, in the village of Pescina, on the slopes that lead eastward to the Maiella mountains and Sulmona, and look westward across the valley, past what used to be Lake Fucino, to Avezzano. The valley is itself a phenomenon in the Abruzzo, which is elsewhere a disorderly cluster of mountains: "The destiny of the men who live in this region," Silone observes, "has been decided principally by the mountains." They are the source and cause of the age-old Abruzzese tradition of resistance—a physical obstacle, in antiquity, to the unification of warring tribes; a barrier to conquest and cultivation by Rome; and the hard reason for the Abruzzo's insulation (as Silone goes on to say) "from the humanistic movement of the Renaissance, the Jacobinic influence of Napoleon's armies and even from the conspiracies for national unity." The Marse has thus been singularly aloof from the cultural forces that shaped the rest of Italy. Much the same can be said of Silone, whose style and attitude have been concocted out of an odd mixture of the stubbornly provincial and the broadly Continental, with only fragments of the recognizably Italian gathered in along the line.

His father, a small landowner or "peasant-proprietor," was the most restive member of a large family; after the floods of 1900, he even tried his luck, briefly, in Brazil. But Silone grew up in the huddled, impoverished maze of Pescina, in a dark stone hulk of a house crowding the angular slope of the village's principal street. His mother, a weaver, bore several children after Ignazio; only the youngest, Romolo—to whom *Fontamara*, for reasons to be noted, was dedicated—survived the earthquake of 1915. Silone went to school at the local diocesan seminary until he was fifteen, but what affected the boy, more than the Latin or the liturgy (though echoes of the latter are audible in his writing) was the experience of injustice in the Marsican community: a gentleman unleashing his dog on a peasant seamstress and later securing payment from court for damages to the dog; the cynical fraudulence of an election campaign. What impressed him was not only the viciousness and the deceit; it was equally the cautious hypocrisy with which others counseled against resistance. And he began to ask himself the question his novels so regularly intone: What can we do?

Like James Joyce, who in a number of unexpected ways provides a highly suggestive measure for him, Silone arrived at a clear answer only after meditating on and choosing an assumed name. The hero of *A Portrait of the Artist as a Young Man* acquires an identity and determines on a career when the name Joyce gives him discloses its meaning—Stephen Dedalus: "Now as never before his strange name seemed to him a prophecy." Silone's first identity came with the name he selected. For his family name was and is Tranquilli, and he was baptized Secondo.[3] He had to abandon Secondo Tranquilli for political reasons; and he replaced it with a variety of pseudonyms before settling on the name he has since made legal, Ignazio Silone. Its appeal was in its origin: Silone is an Italian version of the name of the Abruzzo's first distinguished rebel, Q. Pompaedius Silo. This was the man who commanded the Marsican infantry—the toughest fighters in the Empire, according to all reports, including those of Livy and Horace—in the revolt against Rome, in 90 B.C. The struggle was successful; it led to the Julian law and other statutes guaranteeing the franchise for all of Rome's allies, and the Marsicans were allies, not subjects. Pompaedius Silo's home, Marruvium, abutted the site of modern Pescina; and Silone felt justified in taking for himself the name of his ancestral neighbor. For Silone's revolt, too, had been toward a kind of enfranchisement —for all those landless and neglected people (the *cafoni*) who had no share in the economic and political life of their society.

Silone's adolescence came to its climax with a series of little gestures of rebellion, for which the devastating earthquake of 1915 gave the context and impetus. The quake occurred without warning at dawn on a day in January; fifty thousand people were killed in eight seconds, and the whole valley, from Pescina to Avezzano, lay in ruins from which it has never fully recovered. Nothing could have been more sudden or more total; and for Silone, it was an experience that in an instant touched the innermost nerve of his sense of existence. The earthquake erupts in his pages with the same quality of significance that Dostoevski found in his own experience of a last-minute reprieve from execution by a firing squad. And yet in the months that followed, the very scope of the destruction seemed to offer a kind of promise: a world had been destroyed; perhaps a better one might after all be built. "That was the start of my conviction," Silone has remarked, "that if ever the day comes when humanity is to remake itself, it will be . . . in a post-earthquake or post-war period." But Pescina, inevitably, began slowly and awkwardly to recreate a dreary image of its former self, with the state authorities imposing further taxes and fines on the homeless, and the representatives of private interests showing their familiar talent for productive dishonesty. Silone's urgent sense of the distance between the millennial possibility and the sordid fact hurried his maturity; and the following year, 1916, is remembered by him with a certain dark humor as the year of the three revolutions.

In the limited vocabulary of the Abruzzo, the slightest show of resistance against the most trivial authority is referred to as a "revolution." Silone's revolutions were against the local ecclesiastical power—a demonstration to protest the undignified removal of the bishop to Avezzano, after the earthquake; [4] against the unjust distribution of bread (completely unsuccessful); and, most memorable and comic of all, against the imprisonment of three soldiers. The latter, home on leave from the front, had committed some slight offense and were arrested by the *carabinieri*—those blockheaded but sometimes maligned keepers of the public peace. This appeared to Silone and his friends as a final monstrosity; and late that afternoon, they began to ring the big steeple bell—always the announcement of some grave or terrible event—and to blow on a dusty old trumpet, the same trumpet that provides a symbol for *A Handful of Blackberries*. A great crowd gathered noisily in the square— women and children, mostly, the men being at their work in the fields and vineyards. After firing on the crowd, the *carabinieri* escaped by the back door of the jail and fled for reinforcements; the soldiers went peaceably home. After a discussion between the boys over the advisability of creating socialism on the spot, that very night while the town was asleep and before the armored cars should appear, the revolutionists went home too.

Next day there was a mass arrest of half a dozen children and about two hundred and fifty women of all ages. The courthouse being too small for so many defendants, the trial was held in the bank. Sixteen-year-old Silone, after surveying the judge and attendant officials seated at a long desk in front of windows marked "Deposit," "Withdrawals," "Loans," and so on, stepped forward and made his first political speech. In the accents of an impassioned Marxism he had hardly begun to digest, he pointed to this intolerable proof that justice was controlled by finance capital. The judge was unmoved and simply ordered the women to come up, one by one, and explain their presence in the square at the time of the incident the day before. None of them could afford legal counsel, but a sympathetic lawyer happened to be standing nearby and the first woman, covered like the others in her black peasant's dress, asked him in a whisper what she should reply. "Why not say you were in the square posting a letter to your boy friend?" the lawyer suggested. She spoke up promptly: "I was mailing a letter to my *sposo*." [5] The next defendant, impressed by the efficacy of the formula, repeated it; she, too, was released. After the twentieth defendant had made the identical explanation, the judge begged the woman before him to think up another excuse. But the woman refused; the judge was only trying to trap her, and she wasn't so stupid as to be caught; "I was mailing a letter to my *sposo*." Two hundred and fifty women, some of them young, some ancient, some unmarried, some widowed, uttered one by one the magic phrase. All were released, except for a few who had been wounded by the shots of the *carabinieri*, and whose wounds were taken as evidence of their guilt. They were locked up for a few days.

It was full-blown folk comedy, but it led Silone to a revelation— and one more natural to an artist in action than to a half-baked Marxist, an aspiring social reformer. The trial was a revelation of the true nature of "the state," at least as its representatives seemed to conceive of it. There was no question of evidence or of legal procedure, so far as the boy could see; it was not a matter of serving the ends of justice, but rather of assuaging some mysterious entity referred to fearfully as "the state": something invisible yet palpable, hovering at the edges of the scene, a beast to be fed in the hope that it might then withdraw for a while. The women's faith in the magic syllables of liberation was matched by the court's ritual gestures toward the creature it served—and to whom it threw a half dozen of those same females as sacrificial human meat.

The following spring, Silone left Pescina. He went first to Avezzano, where he acted as secretary of the Abruzzese federation of farmers. Then he departed from the Abruzzo altogether, moved to Rome, and enlisted as a member of the Socialist Youth League. Against the image of the state as mythological beast, the question "What can we do?" was raised in vain; but collective political action might—so he hoped—provide an answer in the face of the living, the oppressive reality.

That particular answer was itself revolutionary—almost unheard of—for a person born and bred in the Abruzzo mountains. The mountains had fostered a tradition of resistance, but it was not at all a tradition of organized political revolt.[6] What the mountains contained was a much more secret, deep-lying tradition—a revolt of the spirit against the entire worldly shape of the human condition: the ancient dream of the Kingdom of God. "The politicians don't know about it, the clergy fear it," Silone wrote in 1953, "and perhaps only the saints know where to find it."

> Among those who suffer most, beneath the ashes of their skepticism, the ancient hope of the Kingdom of God on earth has never spent itself, the ancient dream of Joachim da Fiore, of the Spirituali, and Celestini. . . . On the other hand, much more arduous with us . . . has been the perception of the ways and means to a political revolution, *hinc et nunc*, the creation of a free and ordered society.

Silone's departure for Rome and his enlistment in the Socialist Youth League thus constituted for him, as an Abruzzese, a genuine and radical conversion—his first conversion, a conversion *to* the political. But we shall never understand either his career or his fiction if we forget that behind that first conversion there lay an impulse deeper than politics: namely, the inherited medieval dream of religious anarchy. His own " 'medieval' world," as he put it, "was shaken to its foundations as though by an earthquake"; but it was none the less *from* that medieval world that "in the last analysis the initial impulse of revolt derived." It was a buried impulse, unknown to the men of action and affairs, indistinctly feared by the officials of the Church. *"Perhaps only the saints know where to find it."*

If the saints in the Abruzzo know where to find that ancient dream, it is because they know where to look, which is among the poor people, on the mountains. For if, as Silone says, the mountains comprise the body of the Abruzzo, "to understand its internal

moral structure, one needs to know its saints and its poor people."
They go together. The Abruzzese saint is a sort of religious
proletarian hero, exploiting his poverty in the direction of holiness.
The mountains, which kept out humanism, helped breed sainthood
as the ultimate mode of resistance. And for Silone's people—the
substance of whose culture is religious—the lore of the local holy
man is far more influential than the formalized dogma of the Church
schools. Among those neighborhood heroes are some unexpected
figures, for the Abruzzese peasants (like the American Negroes)
enjoy telling each other biblical anecdotes in which the characters—
Herod and Pilate, for example, and Pilate's housemaid—turn out to
be residents of the immediate countryside.

The regional saintly folklore is reflected everywhere in Silone's
novels. He has adapted bits of Marsican hagiography—for instance,
the funny but touching and pointed life of Saint Berardo, the
farmer-saint, in *Fontamara*. And beyond that, he has extended
artistically the habit of localizing the New Testament: not by making Christ and Pilate talk in the native dialect, but by making his
characters who do so talk appear dimly to re-enact episodes from
the life of Christ (though never so explicitly as in Faulkner's *A
Fable*).

But the story that seems to have made the profoundest impression
on Silone, even more than that of the Passion, is the story of Pietro
da Morrone, greatest and poorest of the local heroes—the Bene-
dictine hermit who became Pope as Celestino V for a few grievous
months in 1294 and who was canonized in 1313. Celestino's story
is the tragedy of sainthood and renunciation, the comedy of antic
incompetence, the luminous disaster of the religious revolutionist;
and Silone, as though forever seeking to grasp its meaning, has written it again and again in his fiction. Pietro (also the name of
Silone's most memorable hero) was nearly eighty when he was
elected Pope. His life had been marked by extraordinary piety and
extreme asceticism, and by his eloquent urgings of a return to the
primitive austerity of the first Benedictines. From his cave on
Monte Morrone, Pietro drew to himself great numbers of people,
mostly peasants, who were fervently willing to share his rigorous,
God-intoxicated manner of life. In 1264, the disciples of Pietro were

officially approved as a legitimate congregation. The date was important, since it would be believed, in retrospect, that the founding of the order of *Celestini* (so they were later called) corresponded almost exactly with the date prophesied by Joachim da Fiore (died 1202) as ushering in the third and final stage of the history of the world—the era of the Holy Spirit, when law was to be succeeded once and for all by charity. A mighty wave of revolutionary excitement swept across the valley of the Marse and Monte Morrone and the Gran Maiella. Every hole on the mountainsides housed a hermit.[7] The movement represented, in Silone's view of it, the last great effort—within the Church—of radical religion.

In 1294, the cardinals in Rome, wrangling over the successor to Pope Nicholas IV, hit upon the notion of solving or at least postponing their intrigues by electing the monk Pietro da Morrone, of whose life and miracles and enormous following a great deal had been heard. It was a lunatic idea, but it was compounded as much of religious hope as it was of hard politics. A deputation climbed Monte Morrone and crawled toward Pietro's cell. The old man accepted his election in the conviction—hysterically shared by his congregation of fellow hermits and hermitesses—that he was the divinely chosen leader of the permanent restoration of primitive Christianity. Pietro was led away in triumph, his sackcloth replaced by pontifical robes; the King of Naples arrived in haste to hold the reins of his donkey; Pietro was invested as Celestino V and escorted south; and within a matter of days, the Papacy was reduced to an indescribable shambles. After five months of demonstrating that his piety was utterly inadequate to managing the complex affairs of state, the old man abdicated—the only Pope in history to do so.[8] He died a little later, his revolution a failure, his followers dismayed and scattered, he himself harried and pursued by the new Pope.

For many commentators, then and later, Celestino's story was one of folly and cowardice. Dante called him a quitter—that is, if Dante was in fact referring to Celestino when, amidst the trimmers in the vestibule of Hell, he "recognized the shadow of him who out of cowardice made the great refusal." [9] But according to Silone, Dante was motivated by a personal political disappointment:

The decision of the monk, placed as he was between two forms of life which appeared irreconcilable, between papacy and sainthood, can now be judged in a very different sense—as an act of Christian sincerity. Seen in that light, Saint Celestino V is certainly to be admired as the most Abruzzese of the saints. One cannot understand a certain facet of the Abruzzo without understanding him.

The historic truth of the Celestino affair is less important here than the shape it has taken in Silone's mind. And there it has a shape as tormenting and revealing as Ivan's story of Christ and the Grand Inquisitor in *The Brothers Karamazov:* the shape, that is, of the fundamental struggle between holiness and social realism. Silone's religious sense is, more than anything else, the product of his long meditation on the career of Pietro da Morrone. Its essence—its inner dialectic—is present in all Silone's novels, but almost the full substance can be detected in *Bread and Wine.* In Pietro Spina—fleeing to the mountains, pursued by the agents of worldly power, his mission a ludicrous disaster, his disciples scattered or dead or dying —we can recognize the shadow of him who made the great refusal. For Spina, too, had dreamed of the era when law (or political activity itself) would be replaced by charity; and his dream, too, foundered on reality. The dream, of course, is much older than the thirteenth century; it must be as old as the charitable impulse of man, and Silone might have encountered it in the epistles of St. Paul, with their emphatic movement from the age of the Mosaic law to the age of faith. But it was Silone's artistic fortune to discover that same ideal in dramatic and historic form in his own neighborhood; it came to him with the shock of immediacy, already supplied with a local habitation and a name, with the mark of truth upon it, its Abruzzese features clear and recognizable.

Moscow and the Retreat from Moscow

The essential paradox of Silone's career will now perhaps be evident. He was driven into the tough actualities of the political arena by a primarily religious and prophetic impulse. In order to imitate Celestino, he found himself forced to begin by imitating Silo—he became a Socialist because he wanted to become a saint;

and only belatedly and out of an odd fusion of the two roles did he draw a truly valid image of human conduct. The mission he understood himself to have taken on, when he departed for Avezzano and then for Rome in 1917, was the ancient mission of bringing some portion of justice and comfort into the lives of the very poor. But he wanted to take action *hinc et nunc* and through the new medium of politics toward that end.

"According to circumstances," he has said, "rebellion can lead to the Foreign Legion, to delinquency, to the movies, or perhaps to a monastery or to political extremism. What defined our rebellion was the choice of companions. Outside the Church, there were the *cafoni.*" The definition is crucial. There was a point in Silone's rebellion (as he himself has remarked) at which hate and love coincided: hatred of injustice, and love not merely of justice but of people. Love was the stronger emotion; and it may be said in advance that Silone survived the earthquake of his political experience exactly because he went into it primarily out of love rather than hatred. And since it was a love inseparable from the sheer fact of human existence, it was invulnerable to disappointment. All of that is implicit in the statement that what defined Silone's rebellion was the choice of companions. It was that *kind* of rebellion; and because it was that kind, it could renew itself in the sequel. For having chosen the *cafoni* with a view to action in 1917, Silone chose them again with a view to creativity in the early nineteen thirties, when he began to accomplish with the word what for a decade and a half he had failed to accomplish with the deed.

It was a peculiar choice on both occasions. The *cafoni* were not only the poor, the victimized, the exploited. They were the very bottom-most of Abruzzese society: and indeed not really *of* the society at all, but beneath it; not the dispossessed, but the never possessing, the landless and uncounted; the clowns and the criminals. The *cafoni* existed at a level below zero, as Michel Zampa explains in *Fontamara*, in his often-quoted description of the political and economic hierarchy in central Italy:

> At the head of it all is God, lord of Heaven.
> Then comes Prince Torlonia, lord of earth.
> Then comes the armed guard of Prince Torlonia.
> Then come the hounds of the armed guard of Prince Torlonia.

Then nobody else.
And still nobody else.
And still again, nobody else.
Then comes the *cafoni*.
And that completes the list.

("Where do you place the authorities?" asks the city agent; and the reply: "The authorities are divided between the third and fourth classes.") Berardo, the emerging hero of *Fontamara*, is a *cafone;* and so, more suggestively still, is Infante, the half-animal peasant, partly deaf and nearly mute, in both *Bread and Wine* and *The Seed Beneath the Snow;* so is the title figure in *The Secret of Luca*. With such hopelessly oppressed persons, communism will have nothing to do; it functions on higher levels. Only a religious radical with a quixotic streak would stoop to championing their scandalous cause.

Between 1917 and 1931, Ignazio Silone played out the singular role of the religious radical trying to make his love of men effective by the techniques of political revolution: a Celestino trying to be a Silo. The role turned out to be impossible—but it may have been necessary, for one of the chief forms taken by the religious aspiration in our century has been—has had to be—the political. What prevented the political form from achieving its purpose, in Silone's case, was the special version of it he accepted, when, in 1921, he gravitated out of the Socialist Youth League into the nightmare world of international communism. At that moment his first conversion became complete; for "joining the party of proletarian revolution," as he has remarked, "is not to be confounded with the simple inscription in a political party. For me, as for many others, it was a conversion, a total involvement. . . . Everything was put in question, everything became problematical—life, death, love, good, evil, truth changed their meaning or lost it entirely."

It was in the totality of his involvement, during those years, that Silone was so representative a man. For conversion of one kind or another—a profound shift of allegiance, with politics normally at one of the poles—has been a defining event in our epoch, when time has so repeatedly and relentlessly made ancient good uncouth. The principal conflict is not that between democracy and communism—in a larger perspective, that is a rather partial sort of conflict—it is the conflict between politics itself, any sort of politics, and the organizing power of religion or science or art or a variety of secular mythologies. *That* is precisely the conflict represented by Silone both in his career and in his fiction. And he may take a certain somber amusement today as that conflict renews itself in the generation after him, with the latter passing ardently again through a comparable illusion to a comparable disillusion and insight. Up until 1945, writes a young Italian critic, "Politics was everything: morality and revolution, hope and novelty of experience, conservation and poetry." [10] But now, the same writer adds, the problems of the day have moved beyond the possibility of political formulation and resolution. Silone has known that all along, in the deepest part of him; but for a long moment, he, too, thought he believed that politics was everything. It need only be added that, having once thought politics was everything, Silone does not now desperately assert that politics is nothing. He emerged from the disaster with that wisdom that is a sense of the right order of things, and in the right order of things politics continues to have an honorable place.

It is not our business to follow in detail Italian political history in the twentieth century. But the reader may be reminded that in January, 1921, in Livorno on the Ligurian coast, a stormy meeting of the Italian Socialist Party concluded with the formal birth of the Italian Communist Party. The left wing of the Socialists— led by Amadeo Bordiga, Antonio Gramsci, and a young law student named Palmiro Togliatti—marched dramatically out of the Goldoni Theater and reconvened at eleven in the morning at the San Marco Theater (Italian public affairs are always characterized strikingly by the theatrical) for the purpose "of discussing the constitution of the Communist Party of Italy, a section of the III [Communist] International," which itself had been established two years earlier. Accompanying the left-wingers was Secondo Tranquilli, not yet twenty-one, who had come to the Socialist Congress as a chief representative of the Socialist Youth Federation and who then bespoke the adherence of that federation to the newly formed segment of international communism. Silone's break with the Social Democrat tradition, accomplished that morning, would last until, in 1941, he became a Socialist once again—this time, a Socialist of his own very peculiar devising.[11] With the founding of the Communist

Party in Italy,[12] Silone was at once elected to the Central Committee of the new Youth Federation. And yet inside of a year, Silone was rebelling again—offering high-pitched resistance, in Moscow, even to the views of Leon Trotsky.

Silone was a member of the party for about a decade, and for most of that decade, he was pretty well favored by his colleagues; yet, in his later account of it, the experience was one of steady disillusion. Several processes were at work in him simultaneously. For one thing, he was busy learning the effective means of revolutionary action—the vocabulary, the techniques, the program of the international Communist movement. At the same time, he was steadily exposing to himself, by way of a more profound educational development, the ultimate irrelevance and the ironclad wrongheadedness of this particular mode of political action—the irrelevance, that is, to his chosen mission and his ancient dream. And all the while, he remained the Marsican, the Silonian rebel, the little revolutionary who rang the bells at Pescina to disturb the *carabinieri*. He remained impulsive, antic, and *révolté*—in Moscow, he suggested, to the terror of his friend, the young Russian Lazar Schatzky, that they set fire to the wooden mausoleum of Lenin, and wait to see what might happen.

He had the impatient feeling that the operations he was working to further were designed not to restore the poor and the oppressed to some sense of their own dignity but to amass more and more power for its own sake. The situation came to a head in Moscow, in 1927.

Six years is a long time in any kind of war. In the political wars of the nineteen twenties, between 1921 and 1927, it was long enough for a lifetime to end and to begin. During some of those years, Silone had been the editor of the newspaper *Lavoratore (Workman)* in Trieste, where his competence and eloquence had gained considerable favorable attention. He had been to Spain in 1923 and to France the following year on various assignments dealing with the first clusters of Italian political exiles. He had been jailed in both countries—and it was while he was meditating in a Spanish jail that he hit upon the name which was to stick, Ignazio Silone. He had been to Moscow again, where he had watched the insistence on unity crush the common humanity out of Communists from all countries. He had taken part in the struggles within Italian communism, between the fiercely energetic organizer Bordiga and the visionary genius Gramsci, whose dreams of a grand historic mission for the Italian peasantry merged in Silone's mind with the medieval Abruzzese prophecy and so left its mark on him forever. He had felt the impact of the Fascist movement, which gave that internal struggle its special intensity: [13] and he had seen antifascism loom as the central issue for Italian communism and divide it from other national branches. He had been imprisoned and had escaped arrest, had seen his co-workers, including his then friend Togliatti, arrested and released innumerable times.

Silone was at work in Trieste on the night of November 5, 1926, when the Fascist Council of Ministers met in Rome to pass what were to be known as the "exceptional laws": measures that outlawed every active political party in Italy, other than the Fascist Party, and drove communism and all other left-wing groups underground. Gramsci was arrested (he died in jail, twelve years later, after writing several volumes that have become part of the sacred literature of radicalism in Italy); Palmiro Togliatti was named head of the Italian section of the III International, and in Switzerland, moved to create a working underground in Italy. The most important units within Italy were the Central Committee and the Office of the Interior. In charge of the latter, with the mission of coordinating all clandestine activity, was Ignazio Silone.

For about a year, the work of both these internal headquarters was remarkably effective—the work of spreading word through Italy and into the neighboring countries that the victory of Mussolini was an ephemeral one and that communism was still very much alive; the work of holding the centers of revolutionary energy together and of providing the means of travel (passports, tickets, clothing, cover stories) for many scores of agents. But the weight of Fascist oppression grew too heavy. Whole groups, with their leaders, were rounded up almost nightly in the early weeks of 1928; and by the summer of that year, underground activity had dwindled to nothing.[14]

One of the reasons given out by Italian Communists for the defection of Silone (a defection that has never ceased to rankle and worry them) is his alleged discouragement over the final failure in 1928 of the clandestine efforts he helped to supervise. But Silone is more persuasive in claiming that his decisive disenchantment with international communism had occurred the year before—in May, 1927, when those efforts were at their most successful. If, even after that, Silone kept on in the Party (with the sort of desperate and bewildered loyalty that characterized even the most anti-Nazi German soldiers in the—to them—hideous spring of 1945) it was only at considerable psychological expense, for he could no longer feel convinced of the ends he was serving. In any case, in the first version of his autobiographical sketch—the one published in *Comunitá* in 1949, and printed in English in Richard Crossman's *The God That Failed*—Silone leaves the impression that the turning point for him occurred as a result of the Moscow Congress of 1927.

Silone went to Moscow from Milan via Berlin, where he met Togliatti by arrangement. They traveled on to Moscow in company. The congress was held against the background not only of the Fascist triumph in Italy, but still more momentously of the catastrophe of the Communist insurgents in Shanghai a month before that permitted the ambiguous victory of Chiang Kai-shek (the basis of André Malraux's *Man's Fate*). Trotsky, already deep in troubled waters, had written a document about the "problems of the Chinese revolution," and at a committee meeting that both Silone and Togliatti attended, a resolution was proposed condemning Trotsky and his followers for the "misleading implications" thereof. Silone commented that he, of course, could not vote on the resolution, since he had not yet read the document in question. He was assured by the presiding chairman, Ernst Thaelmann, that no one else had read it either. Silone was astonished. Stalin then said that it had been deemed imprudent to let the document out, since it dealt with affairs of state; however, if any member of the committee opposed it, the proposal would be withdrawn. Thereupon, a Bulgarian member, Kolaroff, was assigned the job of talking the recalcitrant Italians (Silone and Togliatti) around. At supper, Kolaroff argued amiably and shrewdly: "This has nothing to do with documents. It isn't a matter of getting at the historical truth of the Chinese revolution. It's simply a struggle for power here between two hostile and irreconcilable groups. You have to choose. For my part, I've chosen. I'm for the majority."

Silone, who enjoys amiable candor, enjoyed the speech very much. But he confessed that he was not in the least persuaded; and next day, speaking for Togliatti and himself, Silone repeated that he could not vote on the condemnation of Trotsky until he was permitted to read Trotsky's report on China. The French and Swiss representatives went along with them, and the proposal was then withdrawn. Thaelmann flew into a rage and demanded on the spot a full investigation (which was later initiated) into the policy of the Italian Communist Party. The position of the Italian delegates became even more precarious at the congress when they were seen seated near Trotsky and chatting with him and when Trotsky most revealingly (in the Stalinist view) ended a discourse with a sentence in Italian, punning on the name of one of his opponents, Béla Kun.[15] Silone's narrative of these episodes stirs with his irrepressible sense of humor, but his chief emotion, as he departed from Moscow, was one of profound depression. That emotion hardened into something like tragic understanding when he learned in Berlin, on his journey home, that the resolution had been rushed through after all. He called on Thaelmann to ask if that meant that the mysterious document had after all been released. No, replied Thaelmann coldly; but perhaps the affair would be instructive to Silone about the nature of Communist discipline.

Silone's autobiographical essay of 1949 concluded (after a peroration) with his reminiscences of the congress of 1927. Palmiro Togliatti—whom Silone had treated in an almost friendly tone—answered the essay at once with an adroitly reasoned and well-supported article in the Communist newspaper *Unitá*. In his precise and legalistic way, Togliatti made two points: (1) Silone could hardly accuse the Soviets of behaving tyrannically about the proposal of 1927, since Silone himself had quoted Stalin to the contrary; (2) Silone was lying when he implied (even if he did not exactly declare) that he had quit the Party of his own accord after the Moscow Congress. In fact, contended Togliatti, Silone had remained a member for four more years, until 1931—and then he did not quit, but was formally expelled. Silone, in his turn, answered Togliatti in a long postscript to his original essay. The exchange adds up to one of the few significant political debates of our time, deeply suggestive and representative, and incomparably more substantial than the somewhat similar debates Americans have had to listen to in recent years.

Togliatti and Silone were engaged, as so many Americans have been engaged, in probing backward to reconstruct the history of their generation—which sometimes can mean to rewrite it—in so far as that history has been touched by revolutionary politics. This is a task that depends ultimately not only on records but equally on the sense of man at work in it. Rancor, in this case, was at a minimum. Even Togliatti's conventional vilifications seem half-hearted; one detects a feeling of regret on both sides at the way things turned out, after the adventure they had been through together. And as a matter of fact, both men were right. Both men were telling a kind of truth. Only, the kinds of truth respected by the two antagonists were incommunicable one to the other. Togliatti's was the truth of scientific fact, the truth of what Proust calls "intellectual memory," the truth of law and of procedure (in one perspective, the truth that kills, though for all that it remains the truth). Silone's was the truth of the whole reconstituted feel of the experience, the truth of another kind of memory altogether, the truth of poetry as rightly understood, the truth of aspiration— of the way aspiration measures and so defines the recorded fact (in one perspective, the truth that, accompanied by grace, can conceivably save). Togliatti, the astute and clearheaded lawyer, is impervious to the real validity of metaphor. Silone, the spinner of parables and the apprentice saint, is careless of exact detail.

So Togliatti was quite right about the committee action on the 1927 proposal; but then, so was Silone. Stalin did say the proposal would be withdrawn if any member opposed it; and it was withdrawn; but it was quite certain to be passed anyhow, and it was passed the moment the congress broke up. Trotsky was doomed all along; the matter of timing was an affair of public relations. Tyranny, as Silone rightly believed, was smoothly at work in its familiar guise of an insistence upon legal democratic procedure.

The question of Silone's departure from the Communist Party is much more complicated. Silone himself was still trying to explain it to himself and to others, in the only way he knows how—which is the way of anecdote, not of archives—as late as 1953, in his novel *A Handful of Blackberries*. On this point also, however, Togliatti was telling the strict truth—that is, the truth of strictness. Silone *did* remain inside the Party until 1931, and he *was* formally expelled. For a year and a half after leaving Moscow, Silone was active in the Party, as active as circumstances permitted. It was the most strenuous and dangerous period of his life; in 1929, his always uncertain health broke under it, and he left Italy for France and a time of restful inaction (he would be away from Italy for fifteen years). He was still a Communist when he crossed over into Switzerland in 1930, and he even told Togliatti that year that he was anxious to continue as a Party member.

Why? For one thing, as Silone wrote in the postscript mentioned above, because the experience was slow to touch the spiritual quick of him. He was undergoing a critical inward process of disintegration and reintegration—that is, a conversion, his second personal conversion. But for the moment, he was inclined to think of his problem as being more immediate and superficial, more purely political. He saw it as a problem of accommodating revolutionary socialism with the peculiar local stresses of Russian communism. In the internecine warfare in Moscow, Silone could recognize the universal contradictions of modern society re-enacting themselves—the opposition between freedom and tyranny, the promotion of strikes to better the conditions of workers and the brutal suppression of strikes in the name of stabilizing the new economy. And he was tempted to identify the dialectic of communism, simplemindedly, with the distinction between the Russian brand and the brand observable in France and Italy. The temptation was increased on his return trip by the dedication and solidarity he witnessed in those two countries. He was ready to rebel against Russian highhandedness. But he did not yet see that this inevitably required rebellion against communism itself—involved the splendid lonely posture later described by Albert Camus as that of man in revolt, in revolt even against the original movement of revolt, when that movement passes into the frozen hell of totalitarianism.[16]

And so, during the long months of growing realization, Silone could not fully believe the signs of petrifaction and demoralization he saw building around him: the symptoms of corruptive capitulation to Russia even of French and Italian communism. He did not quite believe the news brought back from Moscow by a trusted friend, Angelo Tasca, that Stalin was destroying the agricultural system begun by Lenin, and was murdering or deporting to forced labor in Siberia some six or seven million peasants—the Russian cousins to those *cafoni* Silone had chosen as his companions in Italy, and for whom he descended into the hell represented by Moscow. He did not quite take in the flat condemnation by Moscow of the entire policy of the Italian Communists from 1924 onward. To have done so would have been to understand what it took him yet a little longer to understand: that what was occurring was not a quarrel over method, but a crisis of the spirit. If it took him a little longer, it was because, as Silone has said, a man is bound to a political party in proportion to the sacrifices it has cost him. And since communism exacts the most, it is the hardest to break away from. In Silone's case, it had required of him the abnegation for a decade and more of the first elements of his real being—his saintly aspirations, his mission for the *cafoni*, his primarily poetic resources.

It had also cost him his younger brother, Romolo, the only brother who had survived the earthquake of 1915—and this was a second and related reason for the slowness of Silone's retreat from Moscow. Romolo's story, violent and pathetic, illustrates again the singular intertwining of modern history and the career of the peasant-proprietor's son from Pescina.

On an afternoon in April, 1928, Romolo Tranquilli, then twenty-four years old, was arrested in the town of Como, on the edge of the lake, by the Fascist militia. Romolo was a young man interested mainly in sports and studies, a good Catholic with no serious political affiliations. He was against fascism because it made life harder and more miserable; also because the Fascists had chased him out of his home town, Pescina, on account of his brother's activities. It had occurred to Romolo to try to reach Switzerland to continue his studies in Zurich; and at the time of his arrest, he was on his way to a rendezvous in Como with a benefactor who was to supply him with a passport and money. A couple of days before, he had been held up by two *carabinieri*. Nervous because of his lack of proper papers, he had run away from them: so, when the Fascist militiamen took him, he supposed it must be related to the previous incident. Perhaps his benefactor had been seized also, while he himself was under arrest for traveling without documents. But now, to his complete bewilderment, he heard himself accused of being the ringleader in an attempt upon the life of King Victor Emmanuel III.

Romolo literally did not know what his captors were talking about. When, in his confusion, he was unable to answer, he was beaten unconscious; revived, and again beaten senseless. Romolo had not been reading the newspapers. The day before he arrived in Como, a bomb had exploded in the Piazza Giulio Cesare in Milan (twenty miles south of Como), just ten minutes before King Victor Emmanuel was due there to open an annual fair. A huge crowd had assembled for the event, and in the storm of flying metal and shattered glass, some sixty persons were killed, and scores more wounded. It seems clear now that the parties responsible were not political radicals indulging in simple terrorist action, but a group of fanatical Fascist *squadristi*, bent on assassinating the King so that their god, Benito Mussolini, could rule unchallenged in Italy. (There was still an overlapping or doubling of state functions, intolerable to the Fascists: the King's army, the Duce's militia; two separate secret services; two channels of diplomacy; and so forth.) But the Fascist authorities, averting their eyes from the manifest culprits, put it out that certain radical outlaws were guilty of the outrage. When word came down from Como that Romolo Tranquilli had been arrested, they were sure that they had their man. They informed the world in an official communiqué (with a sidelong leer at the King's laggard police) that the leader of the plot had been promptly discovered.

It was not hard for the Fascists to put two and two together, especially since the sum was arbitrary to begin with. Romolo was the younger brother of a famous archcriminal, Ignazio Silone. Silone had recently returned from Moscow, where he had conferred with Stalin, Bukharin, and the other leaders. The plot had obviously been hatched in Moscow, the planning of it delegated by Stalin to Silone, and the execution assigned by Silone to his brother, whom he had no doubt met in Zurich. A couple of other young men were picked up in the neighborhood of Milan, and the bag was complete. The Fascist tribunal was dissuaded only by the stubborn resistance of the King's not completely hoodwinked representatives from shooting the assassins on the spot.

A number of influential outsiders, stimulated by Silone, wired Mussolini guaranteeing Romolo's innocence. The pressure mounted in his favor. Since the affair was one of public relations rather than of justice and truth, Romolo and the others were finally convicted, not of attempted assassination, but simply of belonging to the Communist Party. To this crime, of which he was no less innocent, Romolo had in fact confessed—not because he could withstand no more punishment, but as an act of participation in his brother's suffering. "I tried to behave," Romolo wrote Silone from prison, "as I imagined you would have behaved in my place." Romolo was sentenced to twelve years' imprisonment. He served only four: brutal treatment and tuberculosis ended his life in 1932, in the penitentiary at Procida.

Symbolically, perhaps, Romolo had died earlier than 1932—died heroically under the name of Berardo in the novel *Fontamara*, which Silone composed in 1930 and dedicated to his sick, crippled, imprisoned brother (it was not published till after Romolo's death). Berardo's story is a dramatic foreshortening of Romolo's. Like Romolo, Berardo is a young man of no vital political interests who is arrested quite accidentally and who discovers, in prison, the reality of the conflict to which he hitherto had remained indifferent. In his moment of revelation, Berardo takes upon himself the role of the sacrificial scapegoat. He confesses to being what he is not at all: the Unknown Hand, the underground leader of the Marse. He is tortured to death by the Fascist guards, but the work of rebellion goes on. Silone was that underground leader, that unknown hand, in real life—if anyone was; and Berardo's gesture of identification in *Fontamara* vibrates with the expiatory pain of his creator.

Romolo's fate weighed heavily on Silone. He could not bring himself to move out of the Party to which Romolo, in his name, had falsely declared allegiance. To do so would have been (it may be said without irony) to have rendered false in essence a very good story, indeed a grand story—a recognizable tragic drama; and however smothered the perception, Silone always sized up life in poetic, in dramatic terms. But the pace of conversion was accelerating; not much further humiliation was necessary. In 1930, three of Silone's

friends—the three who had headed the other underground headquarters with Silone in Italy—were expelled from the Communist
Party for expressing criticism of Soviet policy.[17] Togliatti visited
Silone in Davos, Switzerland, to secure his approval of the expulsion.
Silone was depressed, weary, in poor health, reduced to a kind of
dark and silent immobility. He listened as his old colleague explained
matters. The present state of the International, Togliatti agreed, was
certainly unsatisfying; but it was not for them to attempt to modify
it. There were "objective historical conditions" that one had to
understand and submit to; and if the forms of proletarian revolution did not correspond to their own personal and private desires,
the worse for them. Besides, what was the alternative? This was
an effective thrust. What had happened to those who had broken
with the Party—how had they ended up? Silone knew they had
ended up in silence and suicide.

But for the first time, Silone had a fleeting intuition of what was
troubling him. And it was not, after all, a political matter; it was a
tug upon his spirit from some very different direction, some nearly
forgotten land—a place where objective historical conditions counted
less than the sense of individual dignity and the need for an
intimacy between man and man. The intuition rose and fell away
again. "I was like a man who has received a tremendous blow on
the head and who continues to stand upright, to walk, to talk and
gesticulate." He told Togliatti, in his stupor, that he was content
to remain a member of the Party. Togliatti went away satisfied;
but he was back a short time later, insisting on a written approval
by Silone of the expulsion of his three friends. While Silone
watched mutely, on a sunlit Swiss terrace, Togliatti sat down and
typed out a few lines, signed Silone's name to it, and took the
document away with him. Silone's self-disgust was close to maximum—almost enough to encompass the death that would make life
possible again.

The final incident involved a personal letter Silone wrote after
a brief interval to one of the three expellees. It was a letter that
criticized both Moscow *and* Trotsky; and a copy of it, with the remarks adverse to Trotsky carefully deleted, was published in Paris.
Silone was at once accused of playing a double game—approving
the expulsion and condemning it. A full recantation was demanded

by the Party authorities. This time Silone's silence had a negative force. He would do no more, he could do no more; he was finished. In a kind of sterile peace, he awaited the expulsion that speedily followed. The agony of the political death was over; the pain to come would be creative. What was the date upon which Silone ceased to be a Communist? This, anyhow, was the summer of 1931.

Letters in Exile: *Fontamara*.

"For me," Silone remarks, "writing has not been and could not be a serene aesthetic enjoyment, but rather the painful and solitary continuation of a struggle." Silone is perhaps unaware how few writers of talent (a quality somewhere defined as a violence in the soul) have found in creativity a serene aesthetic enjoyment. The ideal seems limited mainly to the school of latter-day Italian classicism—an ideal ironically invaded by Thomas Mann in *Death in Venice*.[18] But the *continuity* Silone insists upon between his overt political struggle and the internal artistic struggle that succeeded it is, of course, the first thing to remark about his fiction. The continuity is not simple. Silone's fiction does not merely reproduce history under a series of assumed names. Writing is part of his effort to understand and to make others understand: with the intention of moving forward, once understanding has been achieved. Silone had in particular to make sense to himself—in the only terms that really satisfy him, in dramatic terms—of his long-delayed departure from the Communist Party. This is the theme of almost everything he has written since *Fontamara*.

But it is not, after all, a political theme. And once Silone grasped that fact—as he did in *Bread and Wine*—he was well on his way to genuine understanding, and hence to further action. We can say quite literally that Silone was "saved" by the very endeavor he made, and by the means he chose—by the telling of stories. Formulas are nearly worthless in discussing Silone, since formulas are exactly what the political Silone had to break through and beyond (Spina in *Bread and Wine* is "seized with a great fear of abstractions"), but perhaps we can risk the following. In the early nineteen thirties, Silone was engaged in a tremendous conversion from politics to love. But that conversion was finally effected only by a corollary transition from politics to art. This was the road of Silone's salvation; and along that road, like an Abruzzese Saul of Tarsus, Silone died into life.

The phrase is used deliberately—and hence, all the more tentatively and guardedly—for salvation of any sort is something we can never begin to be sure about. But we have to do here with a question that at least mirrors theology. We have to do with an analogy of grace. Silone describes his departure from communism as the death of his youth (he is, it will be remembered, as old as the century, and hence thirty-one in 1931). For many another European intellectual, the same event was the death of everything else— of the soul and often, willfully, of the body as well. The God-that-failed was as devastating to a certain type of European as the God-that-was-withdrawn or the God-that-allegedly-withdrew seems to have been for the first generation of Protestants in the sixteenth century.[19] Now, as then, the immediate sign was a wave of suicides, including those listed by Silone in his lecture of 1953.[20] Silone maintains, with sardonic cheerfulness, that suicide is one of the things he cannot understand; but he has also described his emotions on the verge of his apostasy by comparing them with those of an acquaintance in Switzerland who longed to kill himself but hesitated because of the recriminations he was sure would follow.

In traditional Christian theology, suicide is a sin based on despair— despair based in turn upon the sense of utter separation from divine grace. The Catholic apologists of the sixteenth century argued with no little psychological acuteness that the outbreak of suicides among the newly created Protestants was the dire consequence of the Protestant doctrine of grace. For according to the older view, there were at least *two* modes or moments of grace: that which moved and directed a man in the regular conduct of his life; and that which, at the end, as the case might be, crowned all his grace-directed efforts. But in the truncated new doctrine, the first mode was withdrawn, and nothing remained but "saving grace"—a grace that withheld its support, to descend or not, without reason and without warning, to save only by destroying the natural man at a moment of its own incomprehensible choosing. Meanwhile, the daily routine of life was bereft of God's presence, and men were left to their own corrupted resources. For some temperaments such a life was meaningless (or, as we now say, absurd); and it could become desperate.

So it has been for comparable temperaments in the twentieth century, when the force that seemed to provide direction to their lives failed them completely. Silone's fortune has been to find a replacement for the infusion of daily grace once spuriously supplied by the Communist program. While a good many other renegades merely died, Silone managed somehow to die into life—a life grounded in the search for community, and that the invisible community of free and responsible men everywhere. This is Silone's real *Civitas Dei*, it was his beginning and has become his end. For Silone's way through the ruins of his time has led him back from the concept of unity to the ideal of community, from a party program to a poetic vision, from "the group" to the *polis*.[21] The energy that moved him was the energy of storytelling.

When someone asked him recently why he wrote fiction, Silone replied simply: to provide a little company *(offrire un po' di compagnia)*. The content or interior purpose of his fiction sometimes reflects that ulterior motive. His stories often have to do with individuals who succeed or fail in coming together, in being companionable, in putting themselves in touch with each other and with reality by the exchange of anecdotes. The relation between Silone and his readers is not very different from the relation in his novels between the character who reports on his trip to Rome or his brush with the authorities and the characters who listen in sympathy and wonder and then swap their adventures with him. Silone envisions life not only as anecdote but as a give-and-take of anecdote; and he would like his readers to respond with the fiction of their own experience, so that understanding might grow apace amid a grand chorus of narratives, a community of *romanzieri*. Even his autobiographical sketch began that way, with the scene—historically true—of half a dozen revolutionists, hiding out in a villa near Milan, telling one another their stories as a way of defining their political and moral philosophy. And his most compelling image for the situation in which he sees himself and other writers of like experience reflects the same idea. The condition of even the most "affirmative" of modern writers, he has said (in "The Choice of Companions"), is at the best a makeshift:

It resembles a camp of refugees in some no man's land, out in the open, existing by chance. What do you expect refugees to do from morning till night? They spend the best part of their time telling each other their stories. The stories are not very entertaining, to be sure, but they tell them anyhow—mainly, to understand what has happened.

But when Silone first began to write fiction, he had little of that ambition clear in his mind. His own recognition of his new role came not so much with the writing of *Fontamara,* but with the peculiar response to it. That response gave Silone his first glimmering of how much more he might conceivably accomplish with the word than he had ever been able to accomplish with the deed. He saw, too, what in fact it had been that he had been striving *to* accomplish with the deed; and he saw how tragically his purpose had been deformed by the political agency he had selected.

Silone went to Switzerland in 1930 and for six months lay hidden and sick in Locarno. He then moved to Davos, in the German-speaking part of the country, and spent the second half of the year there. It was in Davos that he composed *Fontamara.* Publication of the novel was held up for three years. Though Silone had written it primarily for an Italian audience, distribution of an anti-Fascist book was plainly impossible inside Fascist Italy. One imagines that he would have liked to send the book home, carrying a message like the one exiled Guido Cavalcanti entrusted to his poem centuries before:

> *Perch' i' non spero di tornar giammai*
> *Balatetta in Abruzzo . . .*

> Because I do not hope to return ever again,
> Little ballad, to Abruzzo . . .[22]

Excluded from his countrymen, Silone turned to the rest of the world, like St. Paul turning to the gentiles. But there was a question whether his provincial tale would be of any interest outside of Italy. Gaetano Salvemini, that embattled liberal, read the manuscript in Paris in 1931, and wrote Silone that no one could be expected to care what happened in a mountain village of the Abruzzo. Meanwhile, Nellie Sutro, a German woman of Silone's acquaintance, translated *Fontamara* into German. It was this translation that was finally brought out in Zurich, in 1933, two years after Silone had moved and settled there. It was published at the author's expense, with the backing of seven hundred private subscribers.

Copies of the German edition and of the Italian manuscript were carried literally all over the world, mostly by emigrants who passed through Zurich on their way to France, England, Canada, the United States, Australia. A Hungarian Jewess, Rosika Schwimmer, fought the book through several American publishers, while Silone received belated quarterly reports of some new American rejection. The American objection was usually the one indicated by Salvemini, but one firm (well known then and today) turned *Fontamara* down because it was unrealistic. In the introduction, this publisher observed, Silone says that three persons talked to him all one night, and the narrative that followed was the substance of their talk. This was unrealistic: the narrative would have required at least a couple of nights. A Dutchman, Barthold Fles, then appointed himself Silone's literary agent (and remained so until the relationship was broken off after a disagreement over some transactions connected with *The Seed Beneath the Snow* during the war). With the help of Fles, *Fontamara*, translated by Michael Wharf, was published in 1934 by Harrison Smith and Robert Haas. There would be no edition in Italy until 1949, nearly two decades after it was written.[23]

But if publication was slow and disorderly, the response to *Fontamara* was uncommonly swift. Letters to the exiled novelist began to arrive from all parts of the globe. And what struck Silone almost with the force of revelation was not so much the discriminating praise in high places (Leon Trotsky, for example, wrote that in *Fontamara* revolutionary passion was raised to the level of art); it was rather the note of intimate and personal comprehension, it was the urgent sharing of their own experiences, conveyed by scores of virtually anonymous individuals—unknown to each other and to Ignazio Silone—from the towns and farms and ranches of three continents. His correspondents realized at once that Silone had spoken to their condition, and they made haste to tell him so. And this was the more impressive to Silone since letters from readers to authors is relatively unheard of in Italy, where novelists have been traditionally regarded as paid entertainers, ornaments to the serious business of life.

Silone began only then to enlarge upon and to transform a little his ancient Abruzzese dream, and to dream now of an invisible, worldwide (or at least Western) community, a community underlying all others and composed of free, responsible and responsive spirits anywhere they might be found. It was to this community that he would hereafter direct his energies. But for the moment, the community appeared to exclude his own country, Italy. And so the Marsican, who by heredity and temperament and speech had never been much of an Italian anyhow, became in a special sense a man of the world. Silone's real *and* symbolic distance from Italy during those years is the first explanation of the paradox of his literary reputation ("the Silone case"): his considerable prestige abroad and the belated and grudging, if now increasing, acknowledgment of him in Italy. An Italian critic, Luigi Russo, remarked spitefully in 1950 that Silone's reputation "was formed abroad for reasons foreign to art and literature." The second half of the statement is belletristic nonsense; the first half is entirely true.

Fontamara is a story—told to Silone, allegedly, by a refugee family of *cafoni*—about the life and death of a village. Silone says in the introduction that Fontamara (which means "bitter fountain") is not mentioned on any map, but there is a grimy little section of Pescina, a single alley thick with dirt and children and opening on to the town pump, called Fontamara. However, the place Silone had in mind was not located in the valley, where there was a modicum of prosperity and civilization, nor even in the little villages dotted along the lower ridges of the encircling hills. Silone's Fontamara lies at the furthest outskirts of life—barren, isolated, almost inaccessible, like the mountain home of the Bundrens in Faulkner's *As I Lay Dying* (whose eccentric rhythms, both somber and comic, those of *Fontamara* resemble in several respects). It is nothing but a cluster of families, an immobilized tribe, huddled together far up toward Celestino's Maiella, a place where automobiles and tax-collectors arrive at their own risk and the priest comes once a year, if at all, on mule-back. This is the whole point of Fontamara's geographical location. It is as far away as one can get from the center of power and history; and the meaning of its catastrophe is—that this is not far enough.

The village suffers a series of invasions, and the villagers respond with a series of rebellions. The invasions are motivated at first by simple greed and narrow meanness; they progress to savage cruelty and conclude in total destruction. The rebellions increase from complaints and helpless curses to something like organized revolt. The ultimate disaster is traced back to the action of Fascist officials in diverting Fontamara's one tiny stream so that it will flow through the vineyard of a rich landowner in the valley. The already suspect Fontamarans (who had recently sent a government agent flying with gunshot in the seat of his pants) march down in a body to demonstrate beneath the landholder's window—with noisy, confused, childlike appeals. A compromise is arranged by "the people's friend," fat, alcoholic Don Circonstanza: the water will be divided evenly, three quarters to the landholder and three quarters of what remains to the villagers; and things quiet down. But after a good deal of earnest, puzzled discussion, the poor folk discover the nature of the fraud; and curses and demands start up anew. This time the official response is violent. Fascist militiamen arrive in force to investigate the village. Their investigation consists of looting the houses, bullying the men and raping the women.

While the political enlightenment of Fontamara is thus developing, a young *cafone* named Berardo goes off to Rome to look for a job that will pay him enough to marry the seamstress Elvira. He is promptly sent to jail for vagrancy. It is here that he learns of the death of Elvira—who succumbs to the shock of the brutal "investigation"—and here that he meets the leader of the anti-Fascist underground of the Abruzzo, the Unknown Hand. In order that the latter may go free to continue the fight against the power that had destroyed Elvira, Berardo confesses to being himself the Unknown Hand; and he is tortured to death. His friend and jailmate (one of the narrators of the story) sees him carried away by his legs and shoulders, "like Christ when they took Him down from the cross." The friend returns to Fontamara with messages from Berardo. The villagers, awakened at last to the necessity of organized resistance, are about to publish a revolutionary proclamation when Fascist troops arrive again, and in the massacre that follows, Fontamara dies. The end is a question: "What must we do? After all this suffering and all this fighting, all these tears and all this anguish, all this blood, all this hate, all this hopelessness, what must we do?"

The question is itself a kind of answer, and an important achievement—both by the villagers and by the novelist who created the village. For it was a sign of conscience; and Silone's task in *Fontamara* was very much like that of Stephen Dedalus as defined at the close of Joyce's *A Portrait of the Artist*—"to forge in the smithy of my soul"—and in exile—"the uncreated conscience of my race." In German-speaking Switzerland, Silone might have uttered that phrase with stricter accuracy and greater fervor. For the job of forging, in this case, was a good deal more difficult than it could have been for Joyce—the race was harder to identify, and its conscience was so deadeningly nonexistent. Silone's race, though he did not know it at the time, was the invisible community of free men. He chose to represent that race in *Fontamara*, before he had even discovered it, by his old companions, the *cafoni*.[24]

The choice presented Silone right away with a number of artistic problems; a part of the interest of *Fontamara* is the author's way of exploiting his difficulties. Language, for example. Like Joyce again, and again more arduously, Silone was forced to write in a language that for him was alien and acquired. Speaking as an Abruzzese, he said in the introduction: "The Italian language is a foreign language, a dead language, a language whose vocabulary and grammar have grown complex without remaining in touch with us." The Italian of the Abruzzo is limited and undiscriminating; it is unequipped to describe the gradations of life, it cannot express the distinctions and refinements by which experience becomes precise. It lacks words to suggest the charms and beauties of the earth; for the charms and beauties, like the refinements, do not exist amid the impoverished monotony of the Marse; in the dialect, Silone has noted, there is no word for nightingale.

But Italian proper, while it had grown rich and complex through the centuries, had also become seriously corrupted in the nineteen twenties by the rhetoric of Fascist officialdom. It had grown inflated and perverse; it had lost touch with moral and metaphysical reality. (In *Fontamara*, the villagers are puzzled by the word "refractory," which is so often applied to them; they decide that, along with most other strange official words, it means "has to pay.") It had suffered the decline that invariably sets in—that has set in recently in America—when public faces and voices intrude too ubiquitously in private

places. It was hardly capable of rendering a true drama of conscience; it was suited only for what Silone contemptuously called
"court literature"—writing that snuggled up to fascism in a wordy
betrayal of conscience.[25] So the linguistic limitations of the *cafoni*
had a certain negative value. Silone was able to return, as V. S. Pritchett has said about Verga, Silone's closest literary ancestor, to those
"original and despised sources which have often been fruitful to
novelists."

Seeking a language suggestive of modern man, mutilated by power
and struggling dumbly to understand, Silone thus began by writing
in a sort of *brutto stil nuovo*—Italian, to be sure, but Italian stripped
to the blunt predicates of the Abruzzo, cut to the bone of life. He
has greatly refined on it since; but one still senses in the inner spring
of Silone's style a tenacious resistance to the dangerous suavities of
conventional literary Italian.[26]

Beyond language, other familiar narrative resources were almost
equally limited or were altogether absent in the Abruzzo. Italy itself
has never had a very robust narrative tradition (it is generating one
in the present day). The Marse had no tradition at all—*Fontamara*
was the first novel of any merit to come out of that district. What
the Marse did have, first of all, was a passion for *talk*—"the inter-
minable litany of the poor," to quote Pritchett on Verga once more.
It had talk in the form of anecdote, and anecdote rising at its most
fervent and meaningful to fables about the saints. Here, from *Fontamara*, is part of an anecdotal sermon about San Berardo, the good
farmer who was the patron saint of white bread and who died of
starvation.

> When he appeared before the heavenly throne, the Lord, who
> knew him and wished him well, took him in His arms and said to
> him:
> "Whatever you desire lies at your disposal. Be not abashed in
> asking of me whatsoever you most desire."
> San Berardo was much moved by this offer.
> "I wonder if I might make a request," he said timidly.
> "Anything at all," answered the Lord encouragingly. "Here in
> heaven I am the one in charge. I can do as I like here. There's no
> Pope around here. And I mean to be good to you: whatsoever you
> ask of me shall be granted unto you."

But San Berardo did not dare express his wish. He was afraid that his immoderate desire would excite the anger of the Lord. Only after much insistence upon His part and after He gave him His word of honor that He would not go flying into a temper about it, San Berardo revealed what it was he was yearning for:
"Lord, a piece of white bread!"
The Lord kept His word of honor and did not lose His self-control over it. But He drew the saint into His arms and they wept one with another.

This anecdote also illustrates a second distinctive Marsican resource, and one supremely well managed by Silone—humor. It is a humor that is never wit (the humor of the cities) and rarely gaiety; it consists rather of an inexhaustible awareness of the droll and the grotesque in human conduct, even in suprahuman conduct. It is a childlike, Christian humor, akin to Jewish humor, springing from the sense of ultimate equality among all persons—the humor of the saints and the consolation of the peasants. Characteristically, it is often most alive in the description of pain, which it modifies by poignancy as it seems to look down on the event in a musing perspective of unchanging centuries. Humor is never missing from Silone's best pages. He recreates the local humor in the mouths of his characters and then circumscribes it with his own comic vision— a tragic vision turned gentle and faithful, a compelling sanity that measures the most hopeless failures within a dimension of wisdom. In such a dimension, even the sniveling cruelties of the Fascists are brushed by a kind of humorous sadness, as though visited by grace:

> The examination [by the Fascists of the Fontamarans] commenced.
> The first to be called was Teofilo the sacristan.
> "Who're you for?" the runt with the tricolored sash asked him.
> Teofilo seemed to come dropping down out of his clouds . . . [he] turned a frightened face towards us as if for suggestion, but none of us knew any more than he did.
> Teofilo continuing to give no sign of readiness, the runt turned to Handsome Filippo, who had a big registry in his hands, and commanded him:
> "Write beside his name: refractory."
> Teofilo passed on. The second to be called was Anacleto the tailor.

"Who're you for?" the paunch asked him.

Anacleto, who had had time to think it over, responded:

"I'm for Mary!"

"What Mary would that be?" Handsome Filippo asked him.

Anacleto reflected a bit, seemed to hesitate, and then answered:

"The Mary at Loreto."

"Write down: refractory," the little man ordered the laborer.

Each bewildered answer is more hopelessly unsatisfactory, as the episode proceeds, than the one before, until the whole group of villagers has been written down as refractory. *Fontamara* loops together an assortment of such anecdotes. The narrative consists of the alternating storytelling by a father, a mother, and a son. The rhythm achieved is emphatic and original: and a peculiar native rhythm is yet another resource Silone could draw upon. He has compared his method of narration to the rhythm of the loom—"an art of Fontamara . . . [which] we learned" (in his case, from his mother) "lying awake beside the loom." It is a matter of setting down one thing after another in a single direction and within a fixed, endlessly self-repeating design. In the rhythm of Silone's story, one can hear the steady sound of the treadles, the beat of the batten smoothing down the pattern after each throw of the shuttle: "Then nobody else. And still nobody else. And still again, nobody else." The wife describes the various techniques of urination at Don Carlo's party, with unabashed earthy curiosity:

> First to descend was Don Abbachio, fat and fuming. . . . He began to make water against a tree in the garden, steadying his head against the trunk. . . . Then the pharmacist came . . . and made water behind a pile of bricks. . . . Then there descended the old clerk from the town hall. . . . He went and relieved himself behind the house. . . . Then the lawyer Don Cuccavascio . . . then the lawyer Tarandella. . . .

Here is the extraordinarily effective account of the rape of Maria Grazia:

> Gripped by her legs and shoulders, she was thrown to the ground and there stripped of all she had on and held by four men with her arms apart and legs asunder, so that the fifth might stretch himself out upon her. Maria Grazia kept making a sound like the rattle of an animal with its throat cut. When the first man had used her, his place was taken by another and the torture began all over again.

And after the second, it was the turn of the third, and the torture commenced again. And after the third, it was the turn of the fourth, but the rattle in the throat of the woman had already grown so faint that it did not reach us any more. She gave up all resistance.

As the batten crashes back with ravisher after ravisher, the impression grows of something hideously patterned, fixed, inevitable.[27]

But Silone's narrative exploitation of the inevitable and recurring is related not only to his mother's loom, but also and equally to the pattern of life—monotonous and drearily circular—in the Marse: "For twenty years, the same sky, the same earth, the same rain, the same houses, the same feast days, the same food, the same poverty." The seasons revolve in unchanging persistence. It was precisely in the face of this monotony that Silone's political *and* his artistic ambitions intersected—in the desire to introduce some motion into the immobility of the Abruzzese, some distinctiveness into the sameness of character created amongst them by the seasonal sameness, and by poverty, fear, ignorance, and selfishness. The revolutionist in Silone wanted to beget men, the artist to create characters; and the companions he had chosen helped and resisted him in both respects. "What must we do?" is a cry with a double meaning. The *cafoni*, moreover, were not only all alike, they were all separated one from the other: separated but not individuated, alike in their selfish aloneness. The political Silone suggests at the end of *Fontamara* that the answer to the question is unity ("Organize!") But the artist was beginning to shape the better answer of community.

The final achievement of *Fontamara* is, against an array of nearly insuperable odds, the unmistakable creation of a character: a man: what Jews call a *mensch*, a concrete and sharply outlined embodiment of common humanity: Berardo, the sacrificial scapegoat. For two-thirds of the novel Fontamara is itself the hero, the village and the villagers taken en masse. There is no real differentiation possible or attempted between Ponzio Pilato, Michele Zompa, Antonia Zappa, and Venerdi Santo, or between Lisabette Limona, Maria Grazia, Giuditta Scarpone, and Marietta Sorcanera. Out of that welter of indistinguishable lumps, with their indistinguishable passions and illusions and stubbornness and folly, there emerges the utterly impoverished young innocent, Berardo, the lad with the uncreated but yet creatable conscience. He is first introduced as a person "who reasons like one who has nothing to lose." He is independent and indifferent, his loyalties wholly unengaged. But Berardo is quickened by love of Elvira the seamstress; and because of that love, by the ambition to make enough money to marry her. The ambition leads him to Rome, to prison, and finally to conscience. It is the death of Elvira that speeds his awakening, not only through the enlivening pain of loss, but through the awareness of what he loses her to—the savage, unavoidable force of political history. Elvira had witnessed, from the bell tower, the entire process of the multiple rape of Maria Grazia; she literally dies from horror. When he has learned about her death and its cause, and after a night-long talk in a jail with the Unknown Hand, Berardo presents himself to the authorities as the underground leader they are searching for.

Conscience, Silone suggests in *Fontamara*, is not in our time the child of history; it is born rather out of the battle against history. This is the splendid truth dramatized, not preached, in his first novel; and this is what most of his native critics have obstinately misunderstood. They continue to think of Silone as a kind of slovenly historian who happened to acquire a reputation abroad "for reasons foreign to art and literature" (items, it seems to be implied, that are less valued abroad). Silone has, to be sure, aimed at giving a direct impression of life, something the epigones of Croce believe themselves bound to oppose.[28] But Silone's aim is the traditional aim of literature—that of showing the body of the time its form and pressure. And the form or soul of the modern epoch, its essential plot, is the shape of the experience of political history. Or rather: it is the shape of individual experience during a period when political history affects all experience. Silone confronts history exactly so as not to be seized unawares by history, and devoured. For history nowadays is the dragon of conscience. And the reality progressively touched by Silone is just what history prevents us from knowing, unless we confront history and do battle.

This is why Silone never introduces us into the midst of the grand events, as Malraux has done in *Man's Fate;* or into the company of the great captains and the princes, as in *War and Peace.* Silone's purpose is to dramatize the clutch and challenge of modern political history by setting his scene on the outskirts of life, to show how the remotest corners of space and spirit are invaded and even annihilated by the political demonology of the time. He writes under the aegis, not of Tolstoy (much as he admires him), but of Manzoni; and like Manzoni's *I Promessi Sposi*, Silone's fiction tends to center on the adventures of countryfolk sprung loose from their natural center of earth and family and sent wandering by the political tornado. Silone does not give us history, which freezes under our glance; he gives us the impact of history; not the framed abstraction, but the vital pressure. And in the struggle to transcend history, the shape of humanity begins again to be visible.

Bread and Wine: THE PICARESQUE SAINT

Bread and Wine, first published in 1937, is the best of Silone's novels and possibly the best and probably the most representative novel of his generation. This time there was no serious delay in publication; but, like its predecessor, *Bread and Wine* appeared originally in a German translation, published by the Europa Press in Zurich. It has, in fact, never been printed in Italy, though there was an Italian "emigrant" edition by a Swiss house in 1938.[29] By that time, however, the novel had already been translated into Czech, Danish, Dutch, Polish, French, Spanish, and English. So once again, Silone communicated to the world in many of its languages, while remaining unread in his own country—the most literal image of the exiled artist that our unhappy time has managed to provide.

Bread and Wine has also been the most popular of Silone's novels,[30] though critics of a certain fastidiousness claim to prefer the artful simplicities of *Fontamara*. The latter does perhaps accomplish more completely what it sets out to accomplish. Yet the range of ambition and of achievement, too, is surely a good deal greater in *Bread and Wine*. Silone began—as he said in a prefatory note to the play *And He Hid Himself*, which was based on the novel—with the desire to represent "a certain contemporary society"; but he found himself "drawn by painful degrees to search into its structure." That search is part of the substance of *Bread and Wine*, as the artist's intent is acted upon by his hero, Pietro Spina, in the latter's puzzled wanderings, his involvement seriatim with many types and conditions of people. At the same time, the rhythm of the narrative is more varied and intense; the loom is assisted here by the lyre, and harmonies vibrate in *Bread and Wine* that give it a height and depth of suggestiveness not attempted by *Fontamara*.

The story centers on a young, well-to-do Marsican who has turned revolutionist and who has been living in exile in Belgium. It is 1935, the year of the war in Ethiopia (and the year before the book was written). Pietro Spina comes back to the Fucino Valley in disguise, on a lonely and self-appointed mission of political propaganda and organization. With the reluctant help of a former school friend, he is bundled off into the hills, to Pietrasecca, where he assumes the role of a priest and the name of Don Paolo Spada. The balance of the story is a series of encounters: with various peasants; with the local nobility, including Cristina Colamartini, a girl of conventional purity and religious inclinations; with another girl, Bianchina, a lass of affectionate and defenseless *im*purity; with his one-time teacher, the aging priest Don Benedetto, who is eventually poisoned; with the circle of revolutionists in Rome; with Fascist officials, including some renegade Socialists; and finally with a student named Luigi Murica, who is the equivalent of Berardo (and hence implicitly of Romolo Tranquilli) in *Bread and Wine*. Spina persuades Murica to go on with his conspiratorial activities, even after the boy has been arrested and tortured. The end is a triple disaster: the murder of Murica, the collapse of Spina's little campaign and his flight to the mountains, and the death of Cristina, who is set upon by wolves while in search of Spina.

At first glance, *Bread and Wine* is a bewilderingly haphazard novel, a collection of anecdotes held together loosely by the presence of a single character. It seems less a novel of journey than a mere chase—a stumbling tale that for all its many philosophic meditations seems about to descend to the pointless antics of cops-and-robbers. One is tempted to disregard the many characters and even the adventures of Pietro Spina, and to remember primarily the two or three vivid and funny moments that richly show forth the peasant nature and life: Sciatàp, the man who had returned from America with the one English phrase that stuck ("Shaddap!"), as he belabors his donkey; the peasants quarreling confusedly over a card game. *Bread and Wine* is indeed an episodic novel—the mode of literature that Aristotle, in the *Poetics*, dismissed as the worst because the most formless. Yet Silone's second novel does have an impressive measure of genuine form, once we discover where to look for it. It has a form that, admirable in itself, reveals at the same time certain major possibilities for the art of narrative today.

It belongs (whether Silone knows it or not) to the old-fashioned genre of the picaresque novel—the account of the rogue on his travels. In a time when, given the quality of laws and the tendencies of power, the heroic figure is almost bound to be in some manner lawless, the picaresque novel is especially well suited for the purposes of fiction. And in a time characterized so widely by the sense of "cosmic homelessness," [31] the image of the anxious journey—of life as a succession of provisional encounters—very naturally suggests itself to the watchful novelist. Greene's *The Power and the Glory* manipulates such an image; so do Camus's *Caligula*, Moravia's *The Woman of Rome*, and Faulkner's *Light in August*. All of them suggest how the picaresque can after all fulfill many of the traditional requirements of form—how it can be responsive to the current requirements of narrative literature; and none more effectively than *Bread and Wine*.

The single hero of *Bread and Wine* is at all moments, through all his encounters, undergoing a single experience: the experience of becoming a man. We shall see in a moment what kind of man he becomes—what constitutes manhood in Silone's moral universe. But it may be noticed at once that Spina, who looks to one character, part way through the book, like a baby, is referred to at the end simply as "the man." The story begins in April and ends in early winter, a period suggesting the span of human gestation—particularly that of Jesus. The nine-month rhythm, is, if anything, too much insisted on in a final scene, the funeral feast for the murdered Luigi Murica, when Murica's father—passing the bread and pouring the wine—observes how long it takes to make bread, how long for wine to ripen; and, the mother adds to herself, for a man to be made. Murica was conceived in August and born in April; Spina is introduced in April and symbolically reborn in the Christmas season.

Now the intimate relation between that central experience—"and He was made man"—and the nature of Spina's picaresque adventures is this: Humanity, in Silone's view of things, is a condition exactly opposite to that abstraction from human reality represented by the doctrinaire political activist. The first sign of manhood is a shedding of abstractions in an effort to press toward "an intimate opening on to the reality of others" (as Silone would later put it). In narrative terms, the shedding and the pressing become visualized as the quest for friendship. The motion in *Bread and Wine* is a grand and elementary motion from politics to love—from the recruiting of co-workers to the stimulation of friendship.[32] This is a movement from death to life. The successive encounters delineate and energize the movement as they progress meaningfully from the early meeting with Nunzio Sacca, a former friend who has compromised his conscience, through a political debate in Rome with the disillusioned revolutionist Uliva, to the achievement of intimacy and communion, beyond politics, with the tragically fated Luigi Murica in the climax.

And the whole drama, the whole motion, is crystallized wonderfully in the episode of the deaf-mute, Infante. *Bread and Wine* comes rushingly to life with this incident—vitality and something more, genius perhaps, gleam in the account of it. Spina, as the priest Don Paolo, has been making the rounds of Pietrasecca, trying to ignite some spark of political consciousness among the peasants (Chapter VI). But "these casual encounters left him dissatisfied": what he really wanted to do was "to establish relations between man and man," not to hold a public rally and make rousing speeches. To establish relations, to exchange genuine ideas, "two men must be alone together, talk softly and with many pauses." [33] Spina notices one young man who appears more responsive than the others— "barefooted, badly dressed, tall and thin"; with a wild look about him, but eyes as kind as a tame dog's. They smile at each other; Spina accosts him, and they walk away together to the man's hut. In the filth and stench of the stranger's miserable hovel, Spina begins to lecture on Soviet Russia, while his host prepares the evening meal.

The young man cut some corn bread, sliced two tomatoes and an onion, and offered them to the priest with a piece of bread. There were still traces of earth on his swollen, scarred hands. The knife he cut the bread with looked as if it were used for everything. Don Paolo shut his eyes and tried to swallow the bread.

"There is a land," he said, "a great land, in which the peasants of the country have joined with the workers of the city."

Meanwhile Matalena [keeper of the inn where Spina is lodged] had been going from house to house, searching for her lodger. At last she found him.

"Dinner has been ready for an hour," she said.

"I'm not hungry," Don Paolo said. "Go back to the inn, because my friend here and I have a lot to talk about yet."

"But haven't you noticed he's deaf and dumb and only understands signs?" Matalena asked.

The young man was sitting at the threshold of his hovel, beside the priest. Don Paolo looked him in the face, and saw that his eyes were slowly filling with tears.

"It doesn't matter. Go back to the inn. I'm not hungry," the priest said to Matalena.

The two men remained seated at the threshold of the hovel, alone; the one with the gift of speech was silent now, too. Every now and then the two looked at each other and smiled. Day had faded into evening, and now night came. Don Paolo coughed once or twice. The deaf-mute got up, fetched the blanket that covered his straw mattress, and carefully put it around his guest's shoulders. Then Don Paolo remembered that this man would have to get up early in the morning and go to work, so he arose, shook hands with him, and bade him good-night.

Later, the peasants at the inn tease the priest good-naturedly. "When I saw you talking with the deaf-mute, sir," says one of them, "I thought it was a miracle, but it was only a mistake." Spina replies: "It wasn't a miracle, and it wasn't a mistake." But in the comic and merciful theology of Ignazio Silone, what had taken place was not much less than a miracle. Both Pietro Spina and the novel he inhabits have perceived the nature of life itself, and have taken possession of it: life as companionship, the peaceful sharing between two persons of intimate human reality. Companionship happens in its literal meaning—the sharing of bread (com-panis: the sharing of ill-tasting corn bread this time), in its moral and psychological meaning of the common nourishment of the spirit, and in the religious meaning of Holy Communion. Companionship is achieved in a transcendence of words, those dangerous elements that are here rendered impossible by the physical limitations of the young peasant; and in a transcendence of tendentious political argument.[34] This passage, which grows richer in one's mind as one reflects upon it, seems to me the furthest thrust in contemporary fiction toward that special human relation which this fiction has so cherished.

With no less art—in its stubby rhythms and homely details—than
Camus brought to bear on the somewhat comparable scene in *The
Plague*, it moves beyond any passage from Camus in its presentation
of human sharing.

The speechless conversation between Spina and Infante is a
microcosm of the whole novel. The movement it briefly enacts
from the strained effort at a political relation to the achievement of
a radically human relation may be traced at length and in larger
letters in the sequence of two other significant encounters of Pietro
Spina. (We shall come upon another version of the same transition
in the highly symbolic battered trumpet in *A Handful of Blackberries*.) Spina goes to Rome to get in touch with the underground
activities there. He meets a man named Uliva, a once-ardent revolutionist now reduced to suicidal despair. Uliva's muscular intelligence
has penetrated to the deep futility of the conspiratorial mode of
political action; but the point about him is precisely that he has not
discovered any other possible mode of action. Spina is shocked
into insight by Uliva's swordlike bitterness; but—and the parallel
here with Silone's personal life is very marked—while Uliva's disenchantment leads to his self-destruction, Spina gradually dies into
life.

> Every revolution . . . started as a movement for liberation and
> finished as a tyranny [Uliva argues]. . . . The regenerating passion
> by which we were animated in the student group has become an
> ideology, a network of fixed ideas, a cobweb. . . . A Red inquisition
> will succeed the present inquisition, a Red censorship the present
> censorship. . . . Against a life which is dominated by pitiless laws
> the only weapon left to man's free will is non-life, the destruction
> of life, death, beautiful death.

(It may be remembered that these words were written in 1936.)
Uliva acts upon his own convictions; shortly thereafter he blows
himself up in his apartment; his wife and other lodgers in the
pensione are buried with him.

The political possibility seems to explode simultaneously, in *Bread
and Wine*, with the suicide of Uliva; and what remains of it dies
violently, not long afterward, with the killing by Fascist agents of
Spina's former teacher, the liberal old priest, Don Benedetto. "We
can no longer talk of politics like other people," Spina says now.

He says it to the student, Luigi Murica, in the last and most profound of all his encounters. Between Murica and Spina, an authentic friendship develops in the little time that is left them: partly because they have exchanged their anecdotes, their "confessions," the accounts of their individual experiences; partly because they are listening to each other and asking at last the right questions. "Politics have become something quite different for us," Spina insists; the question is no longer "What must we do?"—it is rather, he argues, "What is man? What is this human life?" These are the questions that provide a definition of revolt:

> It is not a matter of putting new formulas, new gestures, or shirts of a different color into circulation, but rather a matter of a new way of living. To use an old expression, it is a matter of conversion. It is a matter of becoming a new man. Perhaps it is sufficient to say that it is a matter of becoming a man, in the real sense of the word.

And the new way of living, the outline of manhood, is indicated by Murica, who puts the seal on the entire discussion: "The revolution . . . is a need of being no longer alone, one man against another; it is an attempt to stand together and to be afraid no longer; a need of brotherliness."

There, in the halting language of gradual insight, is the basic principle that all Silone's novels have labored to give birth to. Man in the modern world feels himself wolfish and deformed—because he is oppressed, because he is alone, because he is at odds with his fellow. But the rebellious No!—and this is Silone's principle—can be sustained only by the force of the assertion that lies beneath it: the assertion of love as the first attribute of the living human being. Between rebellion and companionship, there is a crucial and intimate involvement. To some extent, of course, that is the theme as well of Camus's *The Plague* and *The Rebel;* and we shall hear it sounded again by Silone—for example, in the figure of Lazzaro in *A Handful of Blackberries*, who in moments of crisis and oppression blows on his trumpet, not to announce meetings and call men to arms, but simply as "a way of calling out to each other, of being together, and giving each other courage."

"It is a matter of conversion . . . of becoming a new man." It remains for us to define the image of the new man in *Bread and*

Wine. To do so, we have so to speak to *locate* that image, for we find it in the midst of a series of tensions; we find it hovering precariously between two extremes. Similar tensions and similar extremes are exemplified in the narrative method, and in the role played in the novel by the women; and it is worth looking first at those other two items before attempting to specify Silonian manhood. The question of narrative method, for instance, is reflected in the course *of* the narrative; for Pietro Spina, who in so many ways represents Silone as a seeker and convert, represents him equally as an aspiring artist, looking for the effective means of expression and communication. He knows that his effort to explain social justice to the nunlike Cristina and to compose political essays for general distribution are both badly hampered by a tendency toward the abstract. Spina dreads abstractions and is drawn to them, and the dilemma both of the novelist and the revolutionist is described in Spina's remarks to Bianchina: "In no century have words been so perverted from their natural purpose of putting man in touch with man as they are to-day. To speak and to deceive . . . have become almost synonymous." But at the other extreme from the deceptive abstraction there was the scientific statement of immediate fact—concrete, no doubt, but lacking in suggestion, incapable of reaching to another's heart. "What must we do?"

Before he began writing the novel, Silone had found the solution that his hero arrives at only in the book's climax. Silone's solution was what determined his narrative method. And that method was something we observe time and again: first a concrete statement of immediate and particular reference, then a generalization, and finally an anecdote. Don Paolo, for instance, speaks against joining the *carabinieri*, because in Sulmona and Pratola, the *carabinieri* have been shooting the peasants. Sciatàp agrees. "To live at all well you've got to sell your soul," he generalizes; and he goes on to tell a local legend of a peasant tricking the devil in a bargain involving a human soul. Or again, a certain Don Genesio tells Spina that there are about thirty thousand mortgages in the Fucino basin. "We are a nation of debtors," he adds; and thereupon offers the story of a peasant who had mortgaged his liver to a Roman pathologist. "First by means of anecdotes, then by abstractions," says Hans Castorp about Settembrini's method of instruction in Mann's *The Magic*

Mountain; that's what makes Settembrini so much a humanist. In Silone's humanism, the same elements converge, though he orders them the other way round. For to Silone, the anecdote and not the abstraction is the climax of discourse. And so it is that Pietro Spina and Murica fail to touch when they exchange facts or the language of politics; but they become friends, they become whole, when they exchange their personal confessions. In that crowning episode, the artist and the revolutionist are one, as the agent of the abstract becomes the servant of love.

The tension reflected in language appears still more centrally, by analogy, in the relation between the two chief women of the novel: Cristina Colamartini, the other-worldy, and Bianchina Girasole, the all-too-human. The difference between the women represents a serious dilemma for Spina, as he suggests to Cristina in the course of trying to explain to her the necessary struggle for social justice.

> "We are in a country which is still primitive in many ways, a country in which there is great economic distress and still greater spiritual distress. If a peasant ever succeeds in overcoming his animal instincts, he becomes a Franciscan friar; if a girl ever succeeds in freeing herself from bondage to her own body, she becomes a nun. Do you not think that is the source of many evils? Do you not think that this divorce between a spirituality which retires into contemplation and a mass of people dominated by animal instincts is the source of all our ills?"

Cristina is on the side of excessive spirituality, as she drifts purely toward the convent, abstracted from the harsh immediacy of life; Bianchina—a girl of fragile virtue and direct emotions, who has an illegitimate child and is often a little the worse for drink—incarnates the physical bondage and the animal instinct. Spina is drawn to both of them. He finds Bianchina touchingly affectionate and physically desirable, with her graceful body and her breasts like ripe oranges; but Bianchina is partly right in her teasing suggestion that Spina is in love with a nun. The singular power of the novel's ending is supplied by the tension of the two women—and by its hideous resolution, as Cristina, who enters the struggle at last and departs in search of Spina, is destroyed by wolves in a mountain blizzard. She had always had, it is noted early in the story, a special respect, a special apprehension of wolves, after an encounter with one in childhood. And in a wolfish world, her trust in other-worldly justice renders her helpless—"In the unforeseen combat with the wolves," Silone wrote elsewhere, speaking of the fight against fascism, "only those . . . were saved who were . . . whole, real and entire men." Lured into that combat unprepared, Cristina is too partial, too unreal a person to be saved; but her death occurs in the moment when she is closest to being entirely alive.

The controlling tension in *Bread and Wine*, however, and the primary analogue for the book's representative action, is that between the religious and the political. It is here that the full shape reveals itself of the ancient tension in Silone's vision between the saint and the rebel, between Celestino and Silo; and it is of course symbolized throughout by the figure of the revolutionist disguised as a Catholic priest. But unlike the memorable hypocrite of Max Beerbohm, who wore the mask of goodness so long that he became good, Spina does *not* become the priest he pretends to be. The analogous tensions and contrasts that animate and inform *Bread and Wine* are fertile—they beget something new: a new style of communication, a new response to the challenges of power, a new image of heroism. Pietro Spina does not become a priest, but he absorbs a portion of the priestly role into his secular mission: especially since, in circumstances rich with irony and humor, he is trapped into performing a number of priestly duties. The irony lies in the fact that, like Silone himself, Spina had entered politics out of a religious aspiration.

> It was a religious impulse that led me into the revolutionary movement [he tells his old teacher, Don Benedetto], but once within the movement, I gradually rid my head of all religious prejudices. . . . Perhaps it was the religious education I received as a boy that made me a bad revolutionary, a revolutionary full of fears, uncertainties, complexities. On the other hand, should I ever have become a revolutionary without it? Should I ever have taken life seriously?

Much of Silone's career is crowded into that statement; the puzzle Silone represents for his former political colleagues is explained by it. It is the paradox of the ancient dream and the immediate action; of the follower of Pope Celestino V taking on the function of Pompaedius Silo. Celestino led him to Silo, but exerted a pull on his spirit just when he felt himself most Silonian. The force, indeed

the propriety of that paradox is what Don Benedetto articulates, in
other language, in his reply to Spina:

> It does not matter. In times of conspiratorial and secret struggle,
> the Lord is obliged to hide Himself and assume pseudonyms.[35] . . .
> Might not the ideal of social justice that animates the masses today
> be one of the pseudonyms the Lord is using to free Himself from
> the control of churches and banks?

Between the revolutionist disguised as a priest and the priest disguised as a revolutionist, there is little difference, Don Benedetto
suggests. Circumstances require the humanizing of the one, the
spiritual enlightenment of the other.

The conversion of Pietro Spina is thus enacted amidst a cluster
of tensions. And this is a suitable moment to distinguish again and
relate the two kinds of conversion to which I have been referring
throughout. Spina's conversion—from politics to companionship—is
after all an *artistic* event, the artistic achievement of Silone as the
author of the novel; but it reflects a *personal* conversion in Silone's
own life—and it makes that event understandable. It has been said
about St. Augustine that his entire theology was simply the meta-
physic of his own personal conversion to Christianity; in a much
more modest and humble fashion, almost the whole of Silone's fiction is the fiction of *his* experience, a fulfillment, in dramatic terms,
of the gradual transformation that began in Moscow and ended in
Switzerland. That experience led, in Silone's novels, to a radically
new image of heroism, neither traditionally religious nor recognizably political. For Pietro Spina assumes an image that is neither
priest nor politico, neither monk nor peasant, neither saint nor rebel
—but a curious wedding of each of those pairs. It is the image of
the picaresque saint.

The image emerges with special clarity at three distinct moments.
Almost the first allusion to Spina is a quotation by his teacher from
one of Spina's high school essays: "If the prospect of being displayed on altars after one's death, and being prayed to and worshipped by a lot of unknown people, mostly ugly old ladies, were
not very unpleasant, I should like to be a saint." Several chapters
later, Spina, as Don Paolo Spada, is talking with Bianchina, who
has been turned out of her house because of her illegitimate child.

Spina is seen—and the briefly sketched background is suggestive—"sitting under a fig tree. He was motionless and pale as a corpse. The tree was dead. It had been condemned to be cut down and thrown on the fire." The tree represents, perhaps, a dead country, withered and corrupted by injustice. But the eventual rebirth of Spina (his return to physical and moral health) and that of his country are faintly implied in the conversation that follows.

> Bianchina looked closely at his hands. There was no trace of stigmata. There was no trace of crucifixion. He was not Jesus. He was a saint, but not Jesus. Bianchina was disappointed and remained silent. After an interval she said:
> "My aunt Berenice has turned me out. She wouldn't have anything more to do with me."
> "Why?" the priest asked.
> "Because I am for liberty. My aunt is against liberty. You, as a saint, are against liberty, of course."
> Don Paolo interrupted.
> "I am not a saint and I am for liberty," he said.
> Bianchina seemed not to believe her ears.

The implication remains faint because of an alleged hostility between sainthood and a belief in liberty, and it exists primarily in the sweet humor of the exchange. It is only near the end of the novel that Spina perceives the possibility of a fusion of his childhood ambition ("I should like to be a saint") and the devotion to freedom he announces to Bianchina. "A new type of saint will be born," he writes in his parting message to Cristina; "a new type of martyr, a new type of man. I do not believe there is any other way of saving one's soul today." It is Spina who is being born—as a rebel saint; because of the world in which he lives and struggles, an outlaw saint.

The man who flees into the mountains at the close of *Bread and Wine* is the fullest embodiment we have yet met of the representative heroic figure of second generation fiction. If we accept Silone's hints and speak of Spina as a kind of contemporary saint, we must add that he is a saint just *because* he is a martyr; he is a saint just *because* he is a man. His sanctity is manifested not in a private communion with God, but in an urgent communion with his fellow men: in his dedication of himself to assuaging a little the human sufferings of his time. That dedication requires of him that he be forever a wanderer, forever pursued and pursuing. It requires of him that, in the view of that much of the world that oppresses and hurts, he appear as a rogue. And at the same time both art and humanity demand of his creator, Ignazio Silone, that he should present Pietro Spina not only as combatting the miseries of men but of sharing in them: of sharing, indeed, in their mixed and muddled humanity, their aspirations and their folly. If I may risk a final paradox about him, Spina has the makings of a tragic figure because he has some of the elements of a comic figure, in his amiable incompetence and his ridiculous errors of judgment. All these qualities and requirements have come together in Silone's persuasive profile of his hero as a picaresque saint.

TRIALS OF THE WORD

Bread and Wine combines humor and sadness in almost equal proportions, and these elements, fused, provide the steady flow of narrative one responds to even when the prose itself is at its most gnarled and awkward. Humor and sadness were also, one judges, the defining qualities of Silone's personality during the years in exile. It was a time of prolonged suspension, at least as regards external political activity, between the official departure from the Communist Party in 1931 and the return to political life as secretary of the Foreign Headquarters of the Italian Socialist Party a decade later. Silone's acquaintances in Zurich, in the little circle of refugee intellectuals (occasionally including Martin Buber) were struck by his pervasive sadness; but not all of them detected the humor in which it was rooted.

Arthur Koestler, for example, in his autobiographical volume *The Invisible Writing*,[36] describes Silone as "surrounded by a soft but impenetrable cloud of melancholy and depression." Silone, who (as Koestler remarks) was being increasingly bracketed with Koestler and Malraux in a triumvirate of ex-Communist Continental novelists, showed up occasionally in the so-called "Humam Circle" in Zurich to join in conversations about literature and history; and Koestler tried in vain to engage his interest. "I found him a kind but very reserved person," Koestler writes, "wrapped up in himself. . . . To my great disappointment, I was unable to find any real personal contact with him." To this Silone replies, with characteristic subterannean humor, that Koestler missed the sorrowful comedy of the situation—Koestler wanted to make contact on the grounds of Communist enthusiasms that Silone had never shared very deeply to begin with, and a total rejection of which had in any case been the most important event of his life.

A similar time-lag would affect Silone's relations with Koestler and others after the war as well; his constant motion *in advance* of the spiritual history of his time is central to the complexities of "the Silone case." In 1948, on a visit to Rome, Koestler again tried to make contact with Silone, now on grounds of enthusiastic and total anticommunism. But Silone has never been powerfully "anti" anything: "antifascism always got on my nerves," he has observed; "our problems are post-fascism, they are new problems." In a sense they were post-communism too; Communists and anti-Communists alike have been puzzled and annoyed by Silone's failure to participate in the struggle in conventional terms. And on this occasion, Koestler professes himself to have been utterly bewildered. Silone met Koestler and his wife in a restaurant for dinner, but "after addressing a few melancholy words of greeting to us, buried himself into a newspaper for the rest of the meal." [37] Koestler's recollection, Silone insists, is novelistic rather than historical (a comment that might validly and as a form of praise be made about many of Silone's recollections). He did not bury himself in a newspaper, Silone claims; he didn't even have a newspaper; the image is simply a dramatization or externalization of Silone's real attitude. Koestler was excited by the conviction that communism was the only problem of the day—and the only menace (he went about with a huge and silent bodyguard, according to Silone, and left him propped against the wall inside apartments and restaurants). Silone agreed that this was the fashionable view, but it was too easy: there were spiritual and psychological problems that went far beyond any political formulation of the matter; and as to politics, the essential problem in Italy was the monarchy rather than the Communists— and forthwith Silone buried himself in his metaphorical newspaper.

Behind the cloud of depression that did envelop Silone in the middle nineteen thirties, then, there lay hidden a sardonic appraisal of the historical situation, and a never-ending search into the question it raised: "What is man? What is this human life?" *The Seed Beneath the Snow* (1941) is Silone's most elaborate answer.[38] It is not a very good novel—and precisely because it reflects a time of prolonged suspension. It constructs the image of a world momentarily at rest, and there is thus not enough momentum in it, not enough interior action to give life and movement to the surface plot and the assembled characters. The rebirth announced in the title never gets itself accomplished; the kind of activity on which fiction depends is replaced by intensive, static brooding; and it is the only one of Silone's books that deals with death and dying rather than with life. But if it is not a good novel, it is in some respects Silone's most interesting *book*. For what it does offer is a rich survey of ultimate or anagogical possibilities—clues, that is, to the ultimate purpose, the mysterious design of the universe, of the intention of God and the nature of man—in a way perhaps suggested to Silone by *The Magic Mountain*. And such movement as it engenders turns on a sort of secret, never articulated pun, best rendered in English as "trials of the word": essays and assays in language and communication; and an exacted *imitatio dei*—a re-enactment of the trial (and martyrdom) of the Word made flesh.

The Seed Beneath the Snow is the sequel to the events recorded in *Bread and Wine*. The time is Lent. Pietro Spina comes back at last, though still in hiding, to his own town and his own home, after lying up for some weeks in a stable, with the self-interested help of Sciatàp, the formerly comic (if brutal) peasant who is now regrettably made into a mean-spirited scoundrel. Spina is protected by his grandmother, the doughty but confused old Donna Maria Vincenza, who exerts her energies toward securing a governmental pardon for her grandson's subversive conduct. The story that unfolds consists largely of long, often overlong, dialogues between various members of the town's society. And what gradually emerges from them is a radical distinction between two societies—a false society and a true one. On the one hand, the cluster of pompous, compromised, and corrupted men—leaders of "the high society" of Colle—with their equally pompous and corrupted wives: persons incapable of spontaneity, contemptuous of conscience, between whom no spark moves, by whom nothing is begotten; the real victims of Fascist suffocation. On the other hand, the community that slowly comes into being in a little hovel in the other side of town—owned by a *cafone* called Simone-la-faina (Simone the Polecat), one of Silone's most attractive and eccentric creations, and inhabited also by the huge lack-wit Infante, and eventually by Pietro Spina. These three are joined in spirit by Don Severino, the one member of the upper class who possesses a conscience (it is a tormented and desperate one), and Faustina, Severino's mistress, with whom Spina falls in love. The only external incidents of any importance are the abrupt departure of Spina from his grandmother's comfortable home to take up residence in Simone's hut, where he can look after Infante (who had visited him nightly, with animal affection, while Pietro was in hiding), and the murder by Infante of his father, who had returned from America after two decades of silence. Like Berardo in *Fontamara* (and like Andrew in Greene's *The Man Within*), Spina confesses to a crime he has not committed; and the conclusion finds him led away to prison and the scaffold, looking like a man who has suffered not a disaster but only some trifling accident—"like any other poor little fellow."

The themes that recur endlessly in the dialogues of both societies include language and eloquence, Christianity and the Church, and various kinds of human relations. In none of Silone's novels is the theme of companionship pursued so doggedly; but in *The Seed Beneath the Snow* the tendency is rather to insist upon it, to speculate at length about it, to inquire formally into its abstract nature, rather than to represent it. What in *Bread and Wine* had been a symbol of almost Blake-like purity—the scene in the deaf-mute's hut, for example—is elaborated here into a vast and generally inert allegory, as the ancedote is lost in the abstraction. "In those days, friendship still existed," sighs Don Coriolano, the most sympathetic of the stuffy set, talking about his schooldays with Spina's father (whose name, incidentally, is Ignazio). "Perhaps the old people in the neighborhood would understand [friendship]," says Severino, "but the boys and girls . . . innocent souls, would ask: 'Friendship? What's that?'"

This is the real revolution of our epoch [Severino tells Donna Maria] . . . the collapse of friendship. It is the most tremendous

of all revolutions. Instead of friendship today there are so-called
relationships, which last only as long as they are useful.[39]

All those characters who deplore the decline of friendship agree that
political history is the cause of it; and the revolution that almost
occurs toward the novel's end, the second or counterrevolution, is
a new wave of *amicizia*.

The counterrevolution dissolves into chaos, after great numbers
of persons all across the valley have taken to dropping in on former
friends for the sole purpose of being together. (One perhaps notices
here a modern Silonian version of the saintly hysteria that seized
the same neighborhood in the thirteenth century, under the leader-
ship of Pietro, the hermit of Morrone.) But it provides the context
for the intimate relations between Spina and Infante, and the chaste
love affair between Spina and Faustina. In a long and characteristically undramatic speech to his grandmother, Spina tries to explain the basic urgency he feels and its bearing on his affection for
Infante. In his stable hideout, he explains, he felt for the first time
in immediate relation with the reality of his surroundings—the stable,
the donkey, the mice, the hay, a broken lantern, and Infante himself.

> "Perhaps friendship isn't the best word to describe the sort of
> relationship which grew between me and the other objects in the
> refuge. Perhaps it would be more exact to say that I felt myself
> in company, in good and trusted company, that I had in short found
> companions. 'Company' was the first new word Infante learned
> from me. He already knew how to say bread, which he pronounced
> *paan;* and I explained to him with gestures that two people who
> ate the same bread became *cum-panis*, companions. . . . The next
> day Infante gave me a proof of his intelligence and of his complete
> agreement with my way of thinking, by pointing out several mice
> who were moving about in the hay looking for crumbs of bread—
> murmuring in my ear: *Cumpaani*. From that time on, he began to
> offer a piece of bread every day to the donkey, so that he too could
> take part in our company, and we could without lying call him
> companion too, as he well deserved."

This is the experience that supplies the constant aim of all of
Spina's searching, and that justifies his sacrificial gesture in the book's
denouement, when he lays down his life for his friend. At the time,
that final sacrifice is a conscious and deliberate imitation of Christ.
For the true and binding relation between men, according to *The*

Seed Beneath the Snow, is the one—and only the one—that reflects the original relation between Christ and humanity. It must be ready to conclude in a personal sacrifice, the determining attribute of which is that it is altogether gratuitous.

Christ appears in this novel as the supreme example of the gratuitous sacrifice.

> "On the high altar of your parish church [Don Severino tells the other irritated and uncomprehending guests at a social gathering], there are written words which indicate all by themselves the whole difference between Jesus and our own good Christian customs. *Oblatus est quia ipse voluit.* 'He sacrificed Himself because it pleased Him to do so.' No one, as it were, made him do it; nor, being a god, could he feel any impelling need to be talked about in the newspapers, nor was he seduced by the idea of becoming communal counselor of Jerusalem. His act was entirely gratuitous. From the point of view of common sense, Donna Palmira, Jesus must have become mad. And I warn you that the word madness, in referring to the cross, has been used by many saints. Is that any example to offer to the young people of your country?"

The interplay of the Christlike and the gratuitous and the lunatic and the saintly informs a good deal of *The Seed Beneath the Snow,* and creates one of its most suggestive patterns. Against it, there stands the hostile world of the sensible, the well established, the habituated; the world of planned compromise. The latter is a sort of pious prison, and the preposterous gesture of self-sacrifice appears as the supreme act of liberation; so that, in the final pages and as he is led off to prison and death, Spina seems (or is intended to seem) genuinely free.

The particular image of Christ that is mimed in *The Seed Beneath the Snow* is thus the not unfamiliar one of the clownish savior—another variation on the picaresque saint, and one that moves still closer to the figure of Myshkin, the idiot redeemer in Dostoevski's *The Idiot.* One measure of the difference between *The Seed Beneath the Snow* and its predecessor—and the superiority of *Bread and Wine*—is that in the earlier book, Spina *is* the antic saint in action: yearning, dedicated, harmful, foolish, and completely exposed to conversion; whereas, in the sequel, there is rather a speculative emphasis on those qualities, a somewhat laborious piecing together of a profile. At the same time, the image of Christ and hence of Spina's imitation of Him is impressively darkened in *The Seed Beneath the Snow* by a special quality that goes far to justify the static mood that pervades the book. It is the quality of dying.

"And there was darkness over all the land unto the ninth hour." The Lenten season during which the sparse events of *The Seed Beneath the Snow* enact themselves represents the three dark hours of Good Friday, the hours of the agony on the cross; and both are made to symbolize the darkened agony of Italy under fascism, of the modern world under its variety of crucifixions. Two moments in the novel underscore the point. In one of them, the grotesque Don Marcantonio, who dreams horribly of a fusion of Nazi and Fascist, discusses with the carpenter Eutimio the idea of attaching a *fascio* to a local cross. "But where will that leave the head of Our Lord?" asks Eutimio. "You forget," replies Marcantonio, "that Jesus is no longer on the cross." "But there are some who believe he still is," the carpenter says, "still on the cross, still in agony." And later, Spina and Faustina confront a shrine in the country, where the image of the dying contorted Christ is disturbingly realistic.

> "He is not dead yet," said Pietro. "Faustina, do you think that some day he will die?"
> "What a country," murmured Faustina to herself.

The country of *The Seed Beneath the Snow* is a country of seemingly permanent Good Friday—and its quality of prolonged suspension (even in the literal meaning of that word), of excruciatingly painful immobility, is just the quality Silone has managed to convey in his pages. The seed is imagined beneath the snow; it is known to be there and will someday emerge; but what we are made conscious of is the endless monotony of the snow.

It is, finally, just that sense of terrible prolongation that is established by the voluminous talk throughout the novel about the nature of human speech. Once again, and yet more radically, there appears a distinction between two worlds, two societies: or better, here, two universes of discourse—the universe of Fascist rhetoric, where truth has yielded altogether to sophistry, in a tidal wave of *bel parlare;* and the universe of Spina and Infante, where language is stripped to its minimal elements and to the point where once more it touches upon the reality of experience—where it serves as communication among companions. Spina and the deaf-mute (or, perhaps, partly deaf near-mute) inhabit in their filthy hovel that lost Eden dimly longed for by Michele in Moravia's *The Time of Indifference*—"a paradise where everything—gestures, words, feelings—would have a direct connection with the reality in which they had originated." Silone is here able to exploit the literal in the interests of the symbolic: to extend the realistic to arrive at the reality. Infante, like any man of limited intelligence learning the Italian language for the first time (for example, like some of the English and American soldiers in Italy during the Second World War), expresses himself solely in the infinitive forms of verbs. He cannot say, "*Faustina è partita*" (Faustina has gone); he can only say, "*Faustina partire*" (Faustina go).[40] But Spina finds this admirable—more precise, closer to truth, than the past indicative.

> With the infinitive, everything becomes present, everything is still unfolding. . . . With the infinitive, the past is forced to repeat itself in the present, the future to anticipate itself. It is an almost magical operation. "*Faustina partire*" is more moving, more powerful, and indeed more exact than "*Faustina è partita*."

The whole of *The Seed Beneath the Snow* is in the infinitive mood: that is what its mood of stasis means to reflect. And the stasis itself is grounded in the tragic reality that only the infinitive can accurately render. The career of Pietro Spina unfolds in a world best defined not by the phase "*Gesù è morto*," but by the phrase "*Gesù morire*." "In the sacred history of man on earth, it is still, alas, Good Friday."

It is no easier to date the effective termination of Silone's static mood than it is to date his departure from the Communist Party. In both cases, the evidence is almost entirely internal, invisible symptoms of the spirit. It is a fact, however, that in 1941, two years after the outbreak of the war and a decade after his formal expulsion, Silone began again to participate overtly in political activity as secretary of the Foreign Headquarters of the Italian Socialist Party, in Zurich. He functioned as editor and publisher of the weekly newspaper, *L'Avvenire dei lavoratori (The Future of the Workers);* and after the occupation of southern France, Silone's chief obligation was the dispatching of news—that is, of the truth about immediate events—to Italy. A year later he was arrested, on account of these mild and semiclandestine operations; he was interned and after a short time released. In 1944, Silone returned to Italy.

His journey home has been the subject of a good deal of fable-making. Like William Faulkner, but for rather different reasons, Silone has given out several romantic versions of his adventures; and the one that has stuck, in this case, is that—to quote from the personal data accompanying the Penguin edition of his most famous novel—he "disguised himself as a priest, like the hero of *Bread and Wine*, and made his way down from Switzerland through the German lines toward the Americans." Silone did make his way toward the Americans, but in the relative comfort of an airplane provided by American authorities in Switzerland—a nonstop flight to Naples. For diplomatic reasons (the war, it will be recalled, had still a year to run), Silone felt obliged to give what—in referring to Koestler—he calls a novelistic rather than an historical account of his "escape."

More important than the method of return was the identity of the man returning. Silone was once again prepared to be Silonian, and he was once again a Socialist. The conviction had dawned on him almost thirty years earlier, as we have already seen, that "if ever the day comes when humanity is to remake itself, it will be . . . in a post-earthquake or post-war period." He had plunged into political action by becoming a Socialist after the earthquake; now, following the tormented years of communism and the brooding years of suspension, he re-entered the Socialist Party as the post-war period was on the verge of beginning. Was he back where he started? "I can see you're tired, son, and disappointed," says Giuditta, the innkeeper's wife, to Rocco in *A Handful of Blackberries*. "You have the sadness of one who set out to go very far and ends up by finding himself where he began. Didn't they teach you at school that the world is round?"

THE POLITICS OF CHARITY

The question about Silone's development over the years is answered by the fact that it is Silone himself who has asked it. The world may be round, but Silone's ironic self-awareness makes it clear that his own journey has not been circular—though it may, perhaps, be regarded as a series of spirals. He brought to a second decade of intermittent political action not only a complex experience and a prolonged meditation thereupon.[41] He brought also a pretty well-defined vision of the real end of social effort, and a firmly grounded guess as to the relevance of politics for such an end. The end was charity, which has its own peculiar politics: a set of tactics that only occasionally, and almost by accident, intersect the tactics of the struggle for power. Silone's involvement with the latter is part of the confused history of Italian socialism after the second war, and its conclusion is best described in his own words: "In 1950, the Italian Socialist Party broke with the party of Saragat and emerged as the Italian Social Democrat Party. I remain inscribed in the latter without engaging in any activity, with the single exception of the election campaign of 1953. After that date, I've never set foot on any political scene, and I haven't even renewed my registration in the party—though I'm considered none the less a social Democrat of the left with a certain leaning toward the anarchists." [42]

It is scarcely worth while to attempt to work our way through the various splinterings and patchings of Italian socialism since 1945; chiefly because, splinter and patch as they would, Italian Socialists did not succeed in exerting any measurable force. And that, not because of incompetence (socialism probably contains more talent and brains than any other Italian political group), but because Italian politics itself was unable to exert much force. For a while, it seemed about to; but the political illusion dissolved with the fall of De Gasperi in 1953. Silone ran unsuccessfully for office in that unhappy campaign (as a representative of the Marse), but it was a mark of his pessimistic foresight that he had already turned back to fiction, and that his novel *A Handful of Blackberries*—in which the transformation of the political into the companionable is more artful and explicit than ever—appeared before the campaign had run its course.

These facts are worth noting, however, especially since they underscore Silone's visionary hope of transcending the pettifoggings of domestic intrigue in a thrust toward the more universal society to which he has always been dedicated. As a member of the

P.S.I.U.P. (Partito Socialista Italiano Unione Populare), Silone was editor of the periodical *Avanti!* and an elected deputy to the convention to draft a constitution for Italy in 1946; but in the very next year, he was a leading figure among a sizable number of persons who broke away from the P.S.I.U.P. in order to form a new movement carrying the name of Europa Socialista. Silone, the Abruzzese who has never been much of an Italian, felt more at home in this more Continental enterprise—and yet, a year later, he cooperated at the merger of Europa Socialista with other Socialistic bits and pieces in the formation of the Italian Socialist Union. The latter joined with Saragat's Socialist Party in 1949 and broke with it in 1950. What remains is the Social Democrat group to which Silone refers in his remarks quoted above.

In recent years, Silone's activities, apart from writing, have centered on the kind of program represented by Europa Socialista—have centered, that is, on and within the invisible Western community in which Silone so strongly believes. When he is not writing, Silone can most often be found in the local office of the International Committee on Cultural Freedom, or in attendance at some international cultural meeting in one of the capitals of Europe. Notes on his conduct at such meetings show up in the periodicals; and his conduct almost always serves to bring a touch of sanity and reality into the haze of illusion that customarily prevails. Stephen Spender, for example, reports with pleasure on Silone "blowing the gaff" at a gathering of the Société Européenne de la Culture in Venice, a couple of years ago. Assembled, among others, were Jean-Paul Sartre, Maurice Merleau-Ponty, Konstantin Fedin and others from Russia, Mario Ristic from Yugoslavia, and delegates from Poland and England. The theory was that all national interests were transcended, and that all members were working together in a common and ancient humanistic tradition. "After two days of looking across [the] round table (so wide, by the way, that it almost defeated its purpose by reminding one that the dividing world is also round)," writes Spender,[43] "Silone launched forth a speech dispelling every inhibiting ghost which, until then, had thickened the air. He challenged the right of the Russians to talk about the continuous development of Russian literature from Dostoevski and Tolstoy. 'I think the breaking of the Russian tradition has taken place. The tradition of the defence of the poor against the police is broken.' " [44]

Silone thus continues to speak out for his old companions, the poor and the never-possessing. He speaks out, too, for his new companions—the men of talent and sensibility, the writers and artists of the contemporary world, and especially of the world behind the Iron Curtain. In late 1956 and early 1957, he attempted to engage in a dialogue—through the pages of the excellent Roman review he has founded with Nicola Chiaramonte, *Tempo Presente*—with a leading Russian academician, one Ivan Anissimov. The attempt followed another international meeting, this time in Zurich; Silone meant to put to the test the earnest assurances made there of Soviet readiness to discuss all cultural issues. He sent a series of questions to Anissimov, asking about the literary consequences of the so-called post-Stalin "thaw," and querying the whereabouts or the facts about the deaths of a number of Soviet intellectuals. Anissimov replied evasively, and Silone pursued with still more searching questions: his title for the second installment of the exchange was "A Difficult Dialogue." To this, Anissimov answered that Silone was plainly out of his head and that his letter was full of intentional falsehoods, the marks of a vicious reactionary. Silone repeated some of his questions ("What is the fate of your colleagues in literary criticism and history"—naming thirty-five of them as examples); and published the final round under the title "An Impossible Dialogue." Silone could hardly have expected his questions to be answered; but the way in which he put them testifies both to the obdurate common sense which Spender had applauded, and the continuing strain in him of the impish Abruzzese rebel, the boy who rang the church bell and the young man who suggested setting fire to Lenin's tomb.

But of late, Silone has tended to express himself in the language of fiction. He has, it seems, become a novelist by profession: his two journeys, toward art and toward charity, have arrived simultaneously at their appointed destination. More than a decade of intermittent political effort separated *The Seed Beneath the Snow* from its successor, *A Handful of Blackberries,* but only about four years elapsed between the latter and *The Secret of Luca* (an unsatisfactory but accurate translation of the Italian title, incidentally).

And in the sequence from *A Handful of Blackberries* to *Luca*, we find eloquently recapitulated the whole curve of Silone's personal and fictional career, in a manner that is full of promise for his artistic future. *A Handful of Blackberries* is a successful re-enactment of the movement from politics to love; and *Luca* itself is entirely and simply a love story, though a most singular one. The transcendence of the political in *Luca* is accomplished in its earliest pages, when Andrea Cipriani, who has come back to his Abruzzese village of Cisterna dei Marsi on a vote-getting mission, quickly abandons that mission for the deeper purpose of probing into a local mystery grounded in a hopeless love affair between a *cafone* and a lady of high degree. Much that had been implicit and aspiring in the work of Silone—his fundamental concern with human beings and their "intimate reality," as against historical forces and abstract causes—emerges to take its solid and strangely colorful shape in *The Secret of Luca*. It is his most beautiful book, though its beauty lacks the complexity and variety of *Bread and Wine;* and the writing of it was made possible by the transcendence of the purely political achieved in the life and writings that preceded it.

In *A Handful of Blackberries*—the first of Silone's novels to be published in his native country and in Italian, before appearing elsewhere—Rocco de Donatis, another surrogate (like Spina and Cipriani) for his author, retraces the long and painful path from an essentially religious youthful impulse, through the association with the oppressed *cafoni*, to the political effort to assist them, and thence through the slow withdrawal from communism and to the discovered supremacy of love and friendship and integrity. "I see you coming and going," the majestic old rogue, Zaccaria, tells him. "Why do you keep retracing your steps? Have you lost something?" The questions reflect the questions with which Silone had been nagging himself; and the novel supplies their answer. Rocco, a young man of a once-wealthy but now down-at-the-heels landowning family, comes back to the Abruzzo as commander of a partisan band, and soon after the liberation he appears as the leading member of the local branch of the Communist Party. The second and longer section of the novel tells of his gradual break with communism, and the attendant suffering and bewilderment. The tale unfolds in a rather confusing fashion, for Silone has attempted the Faulknerian or Conradian method of circling over an event instead of charting its successive moments. The chronology is vague, but the circling is necessary and appropriate—we have here a precise image of the frustrated coming and going, the circling search for the lost or betrayed sense of dedication and possibility with which the whole adventure began. Like Pietro Spina, and presumably like Silone, Rocco "was born" (as his old friend, the priest Don Nicola, says about him) "with an evident vocation for the religious life. . . . But although he did not obey his vocation he has constantly demanded from secular life the absolute quality that he could have found only in a monastery. For this reason he is in a tragic, absurd situation." Rocco finds at least a portion of release in his love for Stella, a refugee Jewess, whom he eventually marries; and perhaps even more in his friendship for Lazzaro, an old peasant-farmer in whom Rocco sees something of the absolute quality he is seeking.

There is a good deal of rough-and-tumble in the book, too disorderly to be summarized, but including the excellent farce of Zaccaria, the tavernkeeper, declaring his tavern and his stretch of land to belong to Soviet Russia; the brutal shrewdness with which Stella is tricked into denouncing her lover to the Party; and an assortment of disappearances, mysteries, captures, and escapes. The essential action, however, lies in the movement of Rocco de Donatis between the two poles of politics and charity—as represented by Oscar, a cold but effective visiting Communist agent, and Lazzaro, the indomitable farmer. The contrast between them is symbolized, in a homely but impressive manner, in the contrast between the phonograph record of the Communist hymn, which was played so often that it now produces only strident and incomprehensible sounds—a hoarse, impersonal call to arms—and the ancient trumpet of Lazzaro, formerly a token of crisis and community, now lost or buried but expected someday to sound forth again. It is Oscar's intention to win the peasants to the Communist cause by persuading Lazzaro to blow the trumpet at a political rally. He approaches Lazzaro's friend Massimiliano with the suggestion:

> His voice was trembling with emotion. After a pause he went on: "If he agrees to call people together for a meeting, this very evening, with his trumpet, I'll explain in public why we are on his side."

"You don't understand a damn thing," grumbled Massimiliano, shrugging his shoulders. "Who told you that Lazzaro's trumpet was used to announce meetings?"

"What is it used for then?" asked Oscar in astonishment.

"Lazzaro isn't a town crier or a bell ringer," said Massimiliano indignantly. "He's a peasant. He has a plot of land. He belongs to the church and the countryside. Nothing else. He'd like to mind his own business. . . ."

"But when is the trumpet used, then?" insisted Oscar.

"When we really can't stand things any longer," cried Massimiliano, losing patience. "If there's something that's turning everyone's stomach, and yet everyone is keeping quiet because they're afraid. It's a way of calling out to each other, being together and giving each other courage."

The trumpet is also, it seems to me, an admirable symbol of Silone's fiction and the purpose of his storytelling. His writing is not a call to arms; it is a calling out to others throughout the invisible community, an effort to be with them a little; it is the kind of writing that, for the rest, minds its own business. In the figure of Lazzaro, we find a similar ambition. He is first seen returning to the valley after many years, approaching Massimiliano's stable, moving "out of the darkness and [coming] forward like a piece of rock breaking away from the mountain and taking human form and shape." Lazzaro is a creation of the hard resistant mountains (which have principally decided the destiny "of the men who live in this region," as we have heard Silone remark); and his great achievement, in that harsh environment, is to acquire a human form and shape. His humanity is powerfully infectious, because it seems so readily to communicate itself. Rocco and Don Nicola, toward the end of the book, watch Lazzaro at work in the fields.

He really was a fine old man, white-haired, strong, a little stooped. He went about his work as though performing some light-footed, rapt, harmonious dance. As he advanced, his whole body described a semicircle with each stroke of the scythe, in the alternate movement to and fro. . . .

"That calm of his is deceptive," said Rocco. "Don't have any illusions about it. His mere presence in the valley is enough to create a ferment."

"His calm does have something terrible in it," Don Nicola admitted.

"He has the calm of a cart loaded with sacks of wheat," Rocco said. "A cart loaded with sacks of wheat in a starving village. Wouldn't you say so?"

In the insistently humanistic theology of contemporary fiction Lazzaro too, accordingly, belongs on the roster of the saints: with that higher sainthood aimed at by Camus's Dr. Rieux, whose great ambition it was to become a man; and with the sanctity attributed to Pietro Spina just because he *was* a man, and a man willing to share of himself with his suffering fellows. Lazzaro is a much more lightly sketched character than Spina, and hence by no means as complete an embodiment of the representative hero; but he is even more clearly symbolic. His name is the Italian name for Lazarus; and we are intended, I am sure, to recall, at the mention of him, that biblical Lazarus who rose from the dead (in the story which played so central a role in Moravia's *Two Women*, as noted earlier). Lazzaro represents the possibility and the means of rebirth in the contemporary world. Returning to the village which had for long been in a condition of death, Lazzaro suggests that life may be renewed through the exertion of a radiant humanity; in this respect, also, he possesses one of the characteristic qualities of the second generation saint. And the metaphor by which Rocco identifies him ("a cart loaded with sacks of wheat in a starving village") emphasizes the special feature of Lazzaro: he is potentially the spiritual nourishment for the community he lives in; he is himself the *panis* shared with others in his moments of companionship. He is the living bread—not come down from heaven, like Christ in the church hymn —but come up from the soil of truest humanity.

The novel comes to its close on the same tone of explosive calm: as Rocco, who has safely made the journey from the pole indicated by Oscar, the Communist, to that indicated by Lazzaro, moves quietly with Stella amidst their small circle of friends, active in a a movement of farm laborers but animated by the belief that the most powerful weapon they possess is the fact of their friendship. Friendship, by making them human, has made them alive. "*Amo ergo sum*," says Rocco.

A Handful of Blackberries is a modest book and takes modesty of ambition as a part of its subject.[45] There is wisdom in it; unlike its predecessors, the novel seems itself to be wiser at every moment than the behavior it describes. It is the wisdom begotten of suffering, the wisdom that history and politics spent themselves to create: a vigorous but humble insight accessible peculiarly to the artist in action—the artist who acts in and against history, but who does so on the basis of an artistic apprehension of experience. But still more important is the fact that the experience recorded *in* the book and the experience of writing it have made it possible for Silone not only to continue writing but to enter a stage of creativity in which he is altogether and unqualifiedly a novelist—*The Secret of Luca* being, one trusts, only the first example of this new creativity. The career of Silone is thus representative of one of the finest achievements of the second generation of novelists—the achievement of fiction that makes is possible for fiction itself to endure, against many kinds of odds in a death-infected world.

One needs merely to sketch the plot of *The Secret of Luca* to indicate the immense change that has occurred. The story begins, like most of Silone's books, with a return to the valley of the Marse— that of Luca, a seventy-year-old *cafone* who has been away forty years, locked up in a penitentiary for a crime he did not commit, but against the accusation of which he refused to defend himself; and of Andrea Cipriani, a popular political figure, who comes back to his constituency to garner adherents in a forthcoming election. Encountering the rugged figure of Luca, and recalling a childhood involvement with his history, Andrea gives up his political mission in order to search out Luca's "secret"—the secret of his refusal to explain where he had been on the night of the crime, the choice of life imprisonment rather than of speaking out. *Luca* is a mystery story, but a most unusual one; for the mystery is not the identity of the real criminal—who has made a deathbed confession before the story begins—but the source and cause of a man's behavior. In solving the mystery, Andrea comes upon a strange, utterly hopeless, and completely chaste love affair. But that is not the solution, either. Luca's secret is a certain quality of character that makes the whole village—mayor, police, townsmen, and peasants—profoundly uneasy upon his reappearance. What frightens everyone is exactly what is terrible and dangerous about Lazzaro in *A Handful of Blackberries:* a stubborn integrity, a rocklike loyalty, beyond reason and beyond recompense, which, if ever it became infectious, would start a riot, possibly a revolution, all across the valley. Luca is in his very person bread and wine for those who, beneath their selfish ignorance, do still hunger and thirst after some mode of righteousness—an extraordinarily perilous fellow, and one best suppressed or even killed, like Christ in *The Brothers Karamazov*. This is what Andrea quickly, if dimly, perceives, and it is why he continues urgently on his spiritual detective work, against every demand of courtesy, tact, and former friendship.

The Secret of Luca is a brief and tightly woven novel, with the color of dark gold. There are fewer characters than usual, and there are no characters who do not participate significantly in the action. The latter is taut, direct, and irresistible; and for once, the action is inseparable from the plot. No novel of Silone has been so artfully designed, or executed with such sure control. Its quality is so evenly distributed through its entire texture that illustrative quotation, in this case, is not very useful; the whole little book is its own illustration. But the following fragment of dialogue, in which Andrea drags information from the hostile and fearful miller, Ludovico, may suggest how swiftly and economically Silone sketches the world of law and procedures and politics—and by implication, Luca's way of transcending and disconcerting that world, in a gesture of fantastic charity (as the man who became Pope Celestino once dreamed of the replacement of the age of law by the age of the spirit):

"Did you hear me?" Andrea asked him.

The old man finally raised his eyes and looked at him.

"What do you want to know?" he demanded. "That accursed trial? But no one could ever understand that."

"Did you know that Luca was innocent?" asked Andrea.

"There has only been one innocent, Jesus Christ," replied Ludovico.

"Don't be clever," insisted Andrea. "I mean, did you know that Luca was innocent of the crime for which he was condemned?"

"Oh, everyone knew he was innocent of that," said Ludovico. "More or less."

"What do you mean, everybody?" protested Andrea. "The jury too?"

"I think so."

"And the judges?"

"But of course. The judges weren't fools."

"And why, in your opinion, did they convict him?"

"They had to convict someone. A man had been killed, and Luca was implicated."

Flickering behind this passage is Silone's adolescent experience with the law court and its ritual placation of the invisible state. But the moral content of *The Secret of Luca*, the felt life in it, and the warm confidence of its artistry ("It is the most *written* of Silone's books," as one Italian critic correctly and admiringly observes): all of these derive, I suggest, from the long journey that Silone set out upon as the immediate result of that early experience and of his interpretation of it. It was a journey into history and beyond it: an inquiry into the abrasive reality of modern power, and the discovery of what power concealed or suppressed—the timeless reality of conscience. The journey and the discoveries it led to permitted Silone to find his own proper theme: which is the theme of charity in motion, the theme of the replacement of inhuman force by the human force of everything that friendship means to him. The journey provided Silone also with the vision to perceive and sustain that theme, and the art to record it. The journey was itself the subject of *Bread and Wine* (as, by way of rehearsal, of *A Handful of Blackberries*); *The Secret of Luca* tells instead of a spiritual arrival. There will always be those who prefer the journey to the journey's end, and *Bread and Wine* remains the book by which Silone deserves most to be honored. But in the figure of Luca—following hard upon that of Lazzaro and similarly, I imagine, containing biblical echoes in his name—Silone has reaffirmed the conviction announced in *Bread and Wine* that "a new type of man" must be born. Luca, too, is impressively and literally "a new type of martyr," or perhaps a new version of a very old type. As a martyr and as a man, he is the "new type of saint" that Silone has always been seeking to describe for us, and that is the best image of sacrificial human heroism that contemporary fiction can offer.

CHAPTER 5

William Faulkner:
The Hero in the New World

> "He saw the land already accursed even as Ik-
> kemotubbe and Ikkemotubbe's father old Issetib-
> beha and old Issetibbeha's fathers too held it,
> already tainted even before any white man owned
> it by what Grandfather and his kind, his fathers,
> had brought into the new land . . . as though in
> the sailfuls of the old world's tainted winds which
> drove the ships—"
>
> FAULKNER, "The Bear"

THE STEINBECK PERSPECTIVE

"As to SILONE, who speaks to the whole of Europe," Albert Camus
has remarked, "the reason I feel myself so close to him is that he is at
the same time so incredibly rooted in his national, and even provincial tradition." [1] It is a generous statement, which we emend by
saying that if Silone speaks not merely to the whole of Europe but
to the whole world, it is because he has always drawn primarily
from his provincial resources and has taken only very selectively
from his national tradition. The latter might have ruined him; but in
his own province, he could find traces of an ancient dream, and he
could witness the present reality of suffering neighbors. By relating

179

the dream to the suffering, he arrived at the universal questions to which his life and his art could be dedicated. William Faulkner, too, is "incredibly rooted" in local and provincial traditions. And his way of enlarging upon those traditions to possess himself of and to transcend his national culture—to evoke out of Mississippi and America a contemporary and a timeless human image—is the subject of this chapter: Faulkner's way, and the dangers that beset it.[2]

Faulkner appears in these pages as the representative *American* novelist—the writer who subjects the complex and painful sense of life, which for the most part he shares with his European contemporaries, to the special pressure of a home-grown American imagination; and who constructs thereby strangely new images of experience in an odd and baffling new world. This is the quality in Faulkner that is not unhappily forced into prominence by the predominantly European context of this book; in other contexts and associations, other not less significant qualities would no doubt be seen to emerge. But to speak of Faulkner as American is, first of all, merely to identify him, by giving a name to the tendencies and motifs he has brought to fulfillment, and which, in fact, it has been his business to move beyond. I want to praise Faulkner, but not necessarily that which he represents; and indeed, in calling him American, I am pointing to the elements upon which he has practiced his own art of conversion—as Moravia may be said to represent the erotic element, not only because he converts other human actions into the sexual act, but also because he has sought to transform sexual experience into the sense of being alive and human; as Greene can be called the representative religious novelist, not because priests turn up in his stories, but because of his unique talent for converting backward and forward (as it were) to and from the religious impulse. Faulkner's concern, for a long time, was his own country and the portion of it that was his own countryside; he looked upon the latter not only as a subject but as a kind of prison; all his vigor was directed toward breaking out of it. In "The Bear" he succeeded, I think, in breaking out by a robust and formidable act of artistic conversion. Whether his liberation was helpful or not to his career as a novelist is at least open to the question I shall raise about it later in the chapter.

Superficially at least, Faulkner is by no means the most unmistakably American writer of his time. John Steinbeck, for example, is in many obvious ways more persistently engaged with the daily lives and habits of American people, with the shifting American idiom, and with the facts of American history from the westward migrations of the nineteenth century to the dust-bowl tragedy of the twentieth. At the same time, in other and equally obvious ways, Steinbeck has addressed himself more plainly than has Faulkner to the subjects and themes that have occupied Ignazio Silone (and to a lesser extent Camus)—the novelistic concern with social injustice and the paradoxes of morality in an oppressive world; and in the figure of Tom Joad, in *The Grapes of Wrath*, Steinbeck offers an illuminating example of what I have been calling the picaresque saint. It might therefore be sensibly argued that an entire chapter should be devoted to Steinbeck. But there is a distinct uneven-ness in his work, and a certain failure of artistic promise. Steinbeck can more fittingly appear here as a link between writers as seemingly remote from one another as Silone and Faulkner, a link that helps us see more clearly the essential pattern of second generation fiction. If Steinbeck has not provided original and enduring treatments of major themes, he offers a very valuable perspective on those writers who have.

Between Steinbeck and Silone, one observes a lengthily unfold-ing analogy that changes at last into a marked difference. The two men were born in the same year (1900), and in their first fictional writings, about three decades later, both men chose to deal with primitive penniless persons—the cheerful California unregenerates of Tortilla Flat and the rugged Abruzzese analphabets of Fontamara. Steinbeck and Silone alike regarded these folk with affectionate humor; they chose them as their companions, as against the "civil-ized" and law-abiding people in the distant citified society. When hard times came—the depression in America, the congealing of the Fascist movement in Italy—both writers again chose the wretched and the victimized as companions and as the models for their fiction; both examined the situation local to them in terms of a poetry flavored with Marxism; and both articulated dramatically the im-mediate need to unite—to organize—to rally together and strike back. This was the point reached by Steinbeck in his severely naturalistic novel *In Dubious Battle* and by Silone at the conclusion of *Fonta-*

mara and the beginning of *Bread and Wine*. In Steinbeck's case, the problem was not new. He had always been interested in the nature of human unity, in the formation and decay of social units: even through the haze of legend that he wrapped around the episodes of *Tortilla Flat* (1935), we glimpse the rise and fall of a tiny social entity—its creation ("How Danny's Friends swore comradeship"), the challenge to it ("How the poison of possessions wrought with Pilon"), its disintegration ("How each friend departed alone"). But that was all good chivalric fun, in the mock-epic spirit. *In Dubious Battle* (1936) confronts the problem without laughter, and, with some reservations, commits itself to group activity as the only instrument of survival amidst the murderous forces of greed.

One character in the novel, to be sure, voices some of the doubts hinted at in the title. Doc Burton, a non-Communist sympathizer, tells the organizers and strikers to whom he ministers that they are "group-men," a new kind of being, something potent but also distinctly dubious. "A man in a group isn't himself at all, he's a cell in an organism that isn't like him any more than the cells in your body are like you," he says to the radical leader. The latter replies irritably that Doc Burton simply doesn't "believe in the cause"; and Doc agrees: "I don't believe in the cause, but I believe in men." But the questioning note is lost in the violent events that hurry the novel to its climax; and thereafter John Steinbeck, for all his ardent and admirable humanism, has not sufficiently pursued Doc Burton's anxious insights. Or perhaps he has pursued them in artistically unfruitful directions; for Steinbeck has tended to examine the sociology of the problem and its biology; even, we might say, its physics and its chemistry. He has talked about nodes and nuclei and organisms and cells, wasting his poetic vein on scientific and social-scientific abstractions.

It was during this period that the divergence between Steinbeck and Silone became enlightening; for while *The Grapes of Wrath* (1939) follows a mainly political and sociological course (however emotionally intensified), its counterpart in Silone's career—*Bread and Wine*—registers a defeat of political ambition that is at once a triumph over it, in the name simultaneously of humanity and of art. This is the event acknowledged by Pietro Spina when he tells

Luigi Murica that "politics have become something different for us," that the real questions are "What is man? What is this human life?" and the real revolution that of becoming a new human being. It was by thus transcending his political theme that Silone succeeded in truly engaging it, because he was no longer engaged *by* it.

So brief a treatment as this is bound to be unfair to a writer as voluminous, varied, and energetic as Steinbeck. But it seems to me that Steinbeck's writings, from *The Grapes of Wrath* onward, are marked chiefly by the moment and kind of their failure, and for reasons to be hazarded: though in the case at least of *The Grapes of Wrath* (as I have remarked elsewhere [3]) of a failure that is in the end almost indistinguishable from success. For *The Grapes of Wrath* is all compact of the themes and qualities we have been everywhere discovering in second-generation fiction. It confirms our sense of what that fiction has aspired to, in its typically creative moments; and even as it fails to fulfill its own aspiration, it reveals, by recompense, the nature of the aim and the requirements for arriving at it. *The Grapes of Wrath* is a picaresque novel in the modern manner, an episodic long tale of encounters along the way of a harried and difficult journey—the journey of dispossessed Oklahomans toward and into the deceptively promising land of California. Steinbeck is at his best as a contriver of episodes, and *The Grapes of Wrath* is crowded with memorable instances of his skill. The hero of the book, Tom Joad, moreover, shares with the heroes of Silone, Camus, and Greene, the contradictory elements that have gone into the contemporary heroic profile: he is something of a criminal, something of a saint, something of a poet. He has killed a man and served some years in jail for doing so; and, as the book concludes, he is an outlaw in that profounder and more saintly sense, a rebel against institutionalized and legalized cruelty, a refugee witness to truth and hence a man—like Pietro Spina and like Graham Greene's Mexican priest—to be hunted down and destroyed. *The Grapes of Wrath* moves to rhythms also sounded by Camus and Silone: it celebrates revolt in the name of human solidarity; the essence of its rebellion is the assertion that "we are." Its angry, personal, conversational tone anticipates with no less eloquence the more severe formulations of Camus in *The Rebel:*

One man, one family driven from the land [it is Steinbeck's voice, in chapter fourteen]. . . . I am alone and I am bewildered. And in the night one family camps in the ditch and another family pulls in and the tents come out. The two men squat on their hams and the women and children listen. Here is the node, you who hate change and fear revolution. Keep these two squatting men apart; make them hate, fear, suspect each other. Here is the anlage of the thing you fear. This is the zygote. For here "I lost my land" is changed; a cell is split and from its splitting grows the things you hate—"We lost *our* land." The danger is here, for two men are not as lonely and perplexed as one. And from this "we" there grows a still more dangerous thing: "I have a little food" plus "I have none." If from this problem the sum is "We have a little food," the thing is on its way. . . . This is the beginning—from "I" to "we."

There is no more compassionate paragraph in American fiction; and yet the seeds of artistic defeat are in it. One sign of them is the names given the human relation: node, anlage, zygote; for it is a sign of abstraction at the instant when the human demand is most intense. Steinbeck's quasi-scientific interests seem to have prevented him from focusing on the elements that make up the human relation: sharply outlined and inviolable single persons. He has somehow missed the truth lying behind Martin Buber's insistence that distance (or "distancing," as Buber more actively describes it) is a prerequisite of relationship; and in missing it, Steinbeck has reversed a failure noted earlier in Camus. The distance between persons in *The Plague* remained, psychologically and metaphorically, too large (though, as I have said, this is not so much Camus's failure as a failure in the world he accurately represents); but in Steinbeck, the distance is apt to be too slight for visibility. Steinbeck has always suffered from this: "You have never known a person," the hero of *To a God Unknown* (1933) is told by his sister-in-law; and we feel it is Steinbeck admonishing himself. "You aren't aware of persons . . . only people."

Steinbeck's characters, as a result, tend not to be related but to melt into one another. And they seem to want so to melt, rather than to commune: a recurring danger of individualism, as against another viewpoint that we may perhaps call personalism. *The Grapes of Wrath*, indeed, crowns the Steinbeckian evolution from uniting to melting by associating the latter with the metaphysical doctrine—borrowed from Emerson and introduced into the book by the ex-preacher Jim Casy—of the "oversoul," the doctrine of the one vast transcendent soul of humanity of which each individual has his small particular fragment. "Maybe all men got one big soul and evr'body's a part of it," says Casy; and Tom Joad, his disciple, echoes the notion later, in the much-quoted address to his mother: "A fella aint got a soul of his own, but on'y a piece of a big one." The big one was rent asunder, in Steinbeck's version of the fall of man and the loss of Eden, by the force of the individual acquisitive instinct; and the effort of men—the novel implies—is not merely to unite, but to restore the primal cosmic unity.

The doctrine of the oversoul, which is a doubtful contribution to political revolt, is also little short of disastrous for fiction; for fiction depends upon the idea that a fellow *does* have a soul of his own, and it often dramatizes historic conditions that seek to deny the fact. But mention of Emerson brings us closer to the nub of Steinbeck's difficulties; for Steinbeck has absorbed both too much and too little of Emerson. While saluting again, in colloquial language, the Emersonian oversoul, Steinbeck overlooked the constant insistence of Emerson upon the irreducible reality of the single person—the insistence in the essay "New England Reformers," for example, that human unity "is only perfect when all the uniters are isolated"; that "it is the union of friends who live in different streets and towns." But the ultimate cause of the honorable kind of failure I am attributing to Steinbeck is exactly an excess of the most characteristic Emersonian spirit: a zestful and insufficiently examined confidence in human nature; and thus an absence of the tragic and ironic spirit with which Steinbeck's contemporary, William Faulkner, is so richly endowed. The tragic spirit, let it be emphasized, is by no means necessary to all writers under all circumstances: for which we may be grateful. But it seems indispensable for a writer of the second generation directly confronting the complex challenges of his time. Steinbeck's work, for example, moves toward an image of what Malraux has called "virile fraternity"; but it does not arrive at the kind of image Malraux offered in his most recent novel—virile fraternity *with the enemy*. There is too indistinct an awareness in Steinbeck that the conventional terms of battle are no longer valid; that the guilt is everywhere and on all sides and in all of us, and the urge to expiate the guilt as well; that the very problem of the problematical novel is nothing less than the nature of man. To have reached that awareness and to have presented it in narrative would not have meant relapsing into the sad and the poignant; for tragedy has little to do with sadness, any more than it has to do with the otherwise healthy anger that, in Steinbeck, is a substitute for the tragic spirit. Nor would it have meant any loss of his appealing, compassionate earthy humor. It would have meant protecting that humor from the sentimentality to which it has often declined. It would have meant transforming it into something a good deal more compelling—what Hawthorne once described as "the tragic power of laughter."

Faulkner has much more of that special kind of laughter than Hawthorne; though Hawthorne is, of course, the American novelist to whom Faulkner has always been most deeply indebted.[4] The two men responded, a century apart, in a similar way to comparable challenges: to the (as it seemed to them) illusory image of man put forward in Hawthorne's time by Emerson, and in Faulkner's time by an entire culture and, as a part of it, by John Steinbeck. To take hold of this image was in neither case to destroy it. There is a tension amounting to an anguish in both Hawthorne and Faulkner, a tension between the yearned-after hopefulness and the tragic reality. In Faulkner's darkest passages and his earliest fiction, we sense a strong current of amazement, of pity, of (to use one of Faulkner's favorite words) outrage—the shock of unbelief and the outrage at the betrayal of human promise, the pity for betrayed humanity. Faulkner thus contains and exploits more of the fertile contradictions of his country than any writer since the great age of fiction in the nineteenth century; and this is what is meant by naming Faulkner, in the present company, as the representative American.

But to insist upon Faulkner's encompassing American quality is to remind ourselves that no American novelist in decades has been so highly esteemed abroad—has been, in fact, so often accommodated to and even naturalized in the different cultures of very different countries. This singularly native writer has spoken sharply and directly to the human condition in almost all the languages of the West, so to say, and he has seemed or has been made to seem peculiarly at home in each of them. The profile of Faulkner in the several mirrors of Europe is a part of his real profile, though only a part of it: the dark part, as we might say, the passionately negative side of him. In the developing Old World view, Faulkner was seen as providing images of a world a good deal older yet: a world with the very mark and feature of oldness upon it, a world like that of the Old Testament, seen in a certain exterior perspective. The radical novelty of the world Faulkner went on to imagine is measured by the radical antiquity, something deeper than time, of the world he inhabited or could persuasively be alleged to inhabit, during the first decade or so of his literary career.

FAULKNER IN THE OLD WORLD

What Europeans have been saying to each other about Faulkner is an important element in their more general conversation about art and experience. It is as though a sort of *pax Faulkneriana* permitted them to cross national frontiers and discuss those larger issues, a common concern with which has made the writers of the second generation a distinct group. Nevertheless, Faulkner's reputation in Europe is of course inseparable from the literary conditions and intellectual tensions of each country; and, in the absence of a detailed sketch of those conditions, any account of his reputation must be incomplete and misleading. If this is true everywhere, it is especially true in France, where the popularity of Faulkner, which began in the middle nineteen thirties (long before it did in America), reached phenomenal proportions both of sales and of admiration by the late forties. Faulkner's prestige, as the hostile Italian critic said about Silone, was formed abroad, and for not entirely dissimilar reasons. French readers saw in Faulkner's work ingredients that Americans were temperamentally slow to recognize or to honor. For there is a certain impressive arrogance about French criticism and French taste; they are profoundly functional and spring from a wise if sometimes exasperating ability to identify the internal dialogue of French culture at any moment with the fundamental problems of mankind. Faulkner became thus a figure in the central debate of the aging generation in France—the debate between the Catholic writers on the one hand (Mauriac, Claudel, Jammes, and Bernanos), and their "demoralizing" adversaries on the other (Gide, and then Sartre and Camus). The debate concerned the questions of existence and salvation, of the degree of rationality in the universe and the degree of man's dependence upon it. It is the debate traceable as an international affair between Camus and Graham Greene. This was the context in which Faulkner rose to eminence: a context indicated by the contentious title and paradoxical content of Sartre's play *Le Diable et le Bon Dieu* (1951), Sartre's own major effort in the picaresque vein with his own ironical version—in the person of *le diable*, a Renaissance adventurer—of the picaresque saint.[5] Faulkner over the years has managed to appeal to both sides. He was first embraced by the devil's advocates; for Faulkner's earlier fiction gave a picture of human experience so seemingly nihilistic that the nonreligious or even antireligious writers found it extraordinarily authentic. The Christ-imagery of his later work is more likely to attract the followers of *le bon dieu;* though Camus, who once extolled the splendid absurdity of Faulkner's novels, has recently (1957) and successfully adapted for the stage Faulkner's quasi-religious mystery drama, *Requiem for a Nun*—an enterprise that may itself offer a clue to Camus's personal evolution.

Trying to explain the current fashion of the American novel in Europe and above all in France, Henri Peyre has suggested that it was because American books had "assumed a prophetic character." [6] M. Peyre, one feels, has his tongue in his cheek as he makes the statement; there is an air of polite disbelief behind much of what he says on the subject; but his main point is well taken. The American novels of the thirties and forties, he remarks, were the books "best attuned to a tragic era of incomprehensible violence and of brutal inhumanity to man." So well attuned have they seemed that one of the best critics in Europe, Mme. Claude-Edmonde Magny, found it meaningful to name the era *L'Age du Roman Americain*,[7] an era symbolically represented in and by the American novel. By the "American novelist," Mme. Magny and most other French critics meant Hemingway, Steinbeck, and Dos Passos, along with Faulkner, with one or more writers added to make up *"les cinq"* or "this new *pléiade*" as the case might be. Faulkner seems now to occupy a place by himself (partly due to the brilliance of the translations and the comment); but for two decades, "the American novelist" was a usable composite—who seemed to Europeans to be describing actions sufficiently unmotivated and sudden and shocking to typify a time of undeliberative and suicidal violence. A colossal image of slaughter and self-slaughter traveled across the ocean from American fiction; it was the image seized upon and celebrated abroad.

Camus was to say, in *The Rebel*, that the secret of modern Europe was that it no longer loved life; and a Europe unable to do so found in the Americans and especially in Faulkner a dramatic rendering that was at once an explanation of its cosmic distaste. Like St-Exupéry, Faulkner seemed to be crying out that he hated his epoch; for not enough was being made, in those days, of Quentin Compson's tormented iterations at the close of *Absalom, Absalom!* (1936) —"I don't hate it! I don't hate it!" Missed too, were the implications of the character of Dilsey in *The Sound and the Fury* and the structural suggestions of *As I Lay Dying* and *Light in August*— all symptoms (to which I shall return) of a buried, furious, indestructible bias toward life. But meanwhile the role assigned to Faulkner in Europe was large and momentous: the very type of the modern artist, combining violence and metaphysics, according to André Malraux; a writer whose accomplishment, according to the periodical *Esprit*, was "the resurrection of myths and the renewal of tragedy"; a novelist who had found the means to convey in narrative, as Jean-Jacques Mayoux said in 1948, the unbearable pressure of time as a "quality of existence." These were the grand and terrible themes exposed in Faulkner by French observers, at a moment when he was still looked upon at home (with several distinguished exceptions) as an artless and unnerving primitive, a writer of preposterous melodrama who was devoid of a single recognizable idea.

Sartre, exercising classic French taste and relating all the themes at once in a comment on *The Sound and the Fury*, remarked in 1939 that he loved Faulkner's art but hated his metaphysics. Faulkner wrote, according to Sartre, as though man were completely without a future, possessed only of a past; but he should write *as though* man might have a future. The glance was all backward in Faulkner; and human life (Sartre added, in an excellent image that could be illustrated from almost any page of Faulkner) appeared as a road watched despairingly as it flowed away, from the rear window of a moving car. Mme. Magny made still more of the obsessive onslaughts on the baffling retreating past in *Absalom, Absalom!* and *The Sound and the Fury*. She pointed to a view of the human condition comparable to that of portions of the Old Testament— the condition of man prior to the Incarnation of truth that made history meaningful; the condition of man groping with awful pain through his own still undecipherable history. And Mme. Magny, writing at the close of the war, underlined the relevance of that sense of experience to a generation that was itself groping its way through the inexplicable horrors of the time. Faulkner ranked high among the prophets, Mme. Magny implied; for he had uncovered in his local South and its legends the outlines of a nearly worldwide myth of enormous tragic impact.

Perceptions of this kind and enlargements upon them have not been restricted to France, though nowhere else in Europe is the mind so engrossed in ultimate and universal considerations. But a fragment of the views of Sartre and Mme. Magny were, for example, presented and given a Danish twist by Tom Kristensen of Copenhagen, in a short article on *The Wild Palms*, in 1939. Kristensen was peculiarly alert to the combination in Faulkner of grimness and gaiety, of the suicidal and the jaunty: something less visible to the French, but which we can recognize as distinctively Danish. The Danes have an acute sense of the conditioning—the imprisoning —aspect of the human condition; and the concept of escape has for them an unusual and often an ironic significance. Cultural predispositions like those, anyhow, led Kristensen to see in "The Old Man" and "The Wild Palms" (which Faulkner sewed together not unartfully under the title of the second) a double drama of imprisonment: a dialectic of modes of jailing, each mode sardonically illuminating the other; and a startling and grotesque image of absolute defeat.

Another and less hectic appraisal of the defeat imputed to Faulkner's fiction was recorded as early as 1935 by the erudite Italian critic Emilio Cecchi, in a general essay on Faulkner called "The Crisis of Barbarism." Cecchi, rather anticipating Sartre, said in substance that he loved Faulkner's art but hated the culture and society and manner of living it so accurately reflected. Cecchi offered a version, too, of Mme. Magny's thesis. Almost alone among European critics at the time, Cecchi had a real grasp of American cultural history, an understanding reinforced by a visit to America that Cecchi described in a little threnody called *America Amara (Bitter America)*.[8] His verdict on Faulkner is one that gently indicts the American scene while praising Faulkner's picture of it: the picture of a world without an illuminated conscience—without, at least (according to Cecchi), a specifically Christian conscience, and hence prone to collapse into pagan excesses and, by consequence, self-destroying remorse. It is an appealingly Florentine verdict, benign and not impatient, deriving from a gracious and learned commitment to classical moderation in all things, including the exercise of 'he specifically Christian conscience.

In contrast to the Tuscan moderation of Emilio Cecchi, it may have been the Piedmontese restlessness and sense of frustration (combined with unique personal abilities) that led Cesare Pavese of Torino—the most promising talent in Italy until his suicide in 1950—to identify the special complex value of Faulkner's novels. Pavese had translated both *Moby-Dick* (a stupendous literary feat) and Faulkner's *The Hamlet;* and both books went into the metaphysical struggling of his last and probably his best novel, *The Moon and the Bonfire*. The literary principles at work there were made articulate by Pavese in a posthumous essay on "myth." Both the principles and Faulkner's importance to them may be summarized as a conviction that "returning" is the major contemporary subject for literature, and the major contemporary method for realizing that subject. Much—and the best—of Italian fiction during the Fascist period and after has been almost obsessively concerned with the need and process of returning. Each of Silone's novels, except *Fontamara*, begins with an actual and physical return, from exile or from hiding or from jail, to the hero's neighborhood or family home; and the novels go on to describe the effort to convert the physical into a significant psychological return. The same motif was given exquisite treatment in Vittorini's *Conversations in Italy*, and by a number of other writers (Mario Soldati, for example) in a number of other books. The shared image is the effort to return from a kind of death to a kind of life; to return from the imprisonment of the spirit to its freedom; to come back from various dark caves of withdrawal and paralysis to the sources of vitality. In

The Moon and the Bonfire, the image takes the form of a man returning to Italy from a plainly symbolic voyage to America: and then—in a manner for which Pavese had stressed his debt to Faulkner—of seeking to evoke reality by a different kind of return: by the mind and imagination turning back upon themselves, circling back again and again over the elusive events of private history. The imaginative adventure springs from the belief (argued explicitly in Pavese's essay on myth) that the real is virtually the product of memory, of the mind's return to its own past: a notion writ large in the fiction of Proust, but found by Pavese rather in Faulkner. But for Pavese, the impulse to return was invariably thwarted; so he wrote himself, and so he apparently interpreted the stories of Faulkner. Pavese's unhappy death, while certainly due to extremely personal reasons, none the less bespoke in a violent act (as we have seen Silone suggest) the sense of ultimate and irremediable defeat.

 We discover, in short, in different countries and in the views of different critics a developed impression of Faulkner—begotten in the thirties and elaborated in the forties—as the supreme contemporary artist of defeat, betrayal, and death: an impression greatly honored by a Western world that felt itself defeated and dead, that was yet fighting its own past in order to get out of it and beyond, and back to the shores of life. Faulkner appealed to all those whose picture of man was the one indicated in the title and contents of a book of poems by the Swedish lyricist Erik Lindergren: *Man Without a Way,*[9] a volume whose new Swedish idioms and rhythms owed much to the novel Lindegren was then translating: Faulkner's *Light in August.* Lindegren is perhaps the most gifted Swedish poet of his time, and *Man Without a Way* was the germinating work of an entire literary generation (known, because of the time of its flowering, as "the Fortyists"). His excitement over Faulkner's language is all the more suggestive since it was precisely Faulkner's *language* —his use of the English language, that is—that prevented Faulkner from winning much acceptance in England. The English regarded Faulkner's verbal eccentricities in somewhat the way Italians of a traditionalist temper regarded the unconventional irregularities of Silone's prose. The irregularities of James Joyce, for the English, remained conventional ones: recognizable deviations from the known center, the only center; but Faulkner's idiom, which came from no center known to them, seemed simply unforgivably bad writing. His hot Southern American Protestant rhetoric fell on deaf Anglican ears; his "ideas" seemed extravagant and intrusive; and his recurrent expression of outrage appeared dubious to a country which was to wait another decade or so before producing its own race of angry young men. But in Sweden, Erik Lindegren was unencumbered by the legacy of classical English prose; and he was driven by a native and personal demonic fury. Faulkner's prose, which Lindegren wrestled with over the months while trying to break free from his own earlier and more conventional poetic style, acted at last as an explosive liberating agent. For the prose exactly suited Lindegren's theme: the baffled wandering of the individual, spun loose from any orbit, burdened by an unsharable secret, a dreadful memory, seeking communion as a means of life but expecting only death. It is the very theme of *Light in August;* or rather, it is half of that theme. The other half went unrecognized, while the Old World was paying Faulkner its tribute as the contriver of his generation's truest myth: the myth of modern man who had lost his way.

"THE BEAR": AMERICA TRANSCENDED

If, then, as several European critics suggested, Faulkner's novels and stories through, say, *The Hamlet* (1940) possess an atmosphere not unlike the Old Testament in its most tragic and baffled moments, we can perhaps take *Go Down, Moses* (1942)—and especially its longest and richest component, "The Bear"—as Faulkner's first venture into a world of light like that following the Incarnation. Faulkner is himself our warrant for so heady an analogy; though, before pursuing it, we should also remember that "The Bear" is a story about the American South in the eighteen-eighties when the frontier was rapidly disappearing; and the vividly invoked setting is the ground of the story's being and of all that it becomes. "The Bear" is a work in the tradition of Cooper and Twain; another tale of a boy growing up and growing wiser along the border between the civilized and the still unspoiled; and it partakes, too, of that even more widespread drama of American literature, the effort of youth to mature in the face of all the obstacles our culture has erected. Historical and traditional elements provide a fertile base. None the less, it is in "The Bear" that we meet Faulkner's first full-fledged hero in the old heroic meaning of the word; and he is a young man who quite self-consciously takes up carpentering, once he has accepted his peculiar moral mission, because

> if the Nazarene had found carpentering good for the life and ends He had assumed and elected to serve, it would be all right too for Isaac McCaslin. . . .

"The Bear" is a canticle or chant relating the birth, the baptism, and the early trials of Isaac McCaslin of Yoknapatawpha County in Mississippi. It is ceremonious in style, and it is not lacking in dimly seen miraculous events. We get moreover *an* incarnation, if not *the* Incarnation. Or better, we get a re-incarnation; and we witness an act of atonement which may conceivably flower into a redemption.

"The Bear," consequently, is a pivotal work and the key to the whole of Faulkner's fiction: though perhaps only to the whole of it. The notion is reinforced when we encounter the same reanimated human will and the same illuminated human mind at work in the novels that followed, as against those that preceded "The Bear." Beginning with "The Bear," and there more emphatically than anywhere else, what is positive in human nature and the moral world envelops and surrounds what is evil. The corrupting and the destructive and the desperate have their ageless being in human experience, but here they become known to us exactly in their opposition, even their subordination, to the creative and the nourishing. That process of knowledge is one of the things "The Bear" is about: how evil is recognizable through and by good. "The Bear" thus presents us with just the sort of dramatic clarity that has seemed otherwise denied both to American and European writers for many a long decade. The highest reaches of modern literature, in fact, have often taken the form of an ultimate duplicity, the best account of the world that honest genius has been able to construct—the poetry of unresolved dualism, with every virtue and every value rendered instantly suspect by the ironic coexistence of its forceful contrary: Ahab and Starbuck and all their fellows, in a never-ending shift of the reader's, and the author's, allegiance. Those splendid discords and artful confusions are the determining marks of Faulkner's earlier fiction. And that is why "The Bear" appears as pivotal; though persons permanently at home with contradictions and who listen happily (as Emerson once said that he did) to the endless "clangor and jangle of contrary tendencies" are likely to regard it as merely old-fashioned; and to regret it, the way *Billy Budd* is sometimes regretted, as a regression to lucidity. Certainly *Requiem for a Nun* and much more so *A Fable*—where the moral dilemma is dissolved under the pressure of a dismayingly naked New Testament allegory—are grounds for wondering whether the pivotal achievement of "The Bear" was not artistically too costly.

Yet there were hints of the lucidity to come in the earlier novels as well. *As I Lay Dying* and *Light in August*, for example, have been compared to Jacobean drama, and rightly so. They project worlds wherein, as in the terrible world of John Webster, what is human or decent or pure flickers uncertainly in a darkness charged with a hideous violence; the violence and the darkness being the norm, the known and the knowable, and the measure of such pitiful virtue as stirs feebly to combat them. But even there, something more ancient and enduring than the central characters and their wicked propensities seems to flow through them and to reaffirm itself as it flows on into the future. It is what, with a wry face, we have to call life itself. The grimace is due to the guise in which life is reasserted: a new set of false teeth in *As I Lay Dying;* a new wife for the implacably selfish Anse Bundren: "a kind of duck-shaped woman all dressed up, with them kind of hard-looking pop eyes like she was daring ere a man to say nothing"; an illegitimate child that Dewey Dell has not found the medical means to get rid of. Life in *Light in August* is personified at the beginning and the end by Lena Grove, moving calmly and with animal obstinacy across a stage littered with death and depravity, with abominable cruelty; carrying in her womb her own bastard child, to be born on the other side of town. Still, it would be seriously misleading to describe either of these novels as a drama of the triumph of life: even to the extent that Moravia's *The Woman of Rome* may be said to be, with its violence culminating in illegitimate childbirth. The design of these two Faulkner novels is closer to that of Greene's *Brighton Rock:* a sustained tension, almost a war, between the creative and the destructive impulses.[10]

In "The Bear," however, the balance is tipped and the former situation reversed; change is the essence of this story. What we discover first, along with young Ike McCaslin, and what determines his and our subsequent judgments is not strident evil, but the qualities of an archetypal or ideal being. A cluster of virtues is unambiguously present from the start, as qualities to be striven for, prizes to be won: proving their efficacy in the mastery of self and the victorious confrontation of evil: pity and humility and courage and pride and the will to endure and the rest. Their names recur with musical regularity, like the burden of a song. And together they comprise what we may call the honorable: something Roman and a trifle stiff, to some degree traditionally Stoic and to a greater degree unmistakably Virgilian. It is the honorable that permeates the wilderness, scene of the main action and home of the main actors in the drama. Old Ben, the bear, patriarch of the wilderness, embodies the virtues in some undefined and magical way; and like Old Ben, the honorable exists as an ethical reality before the story opens, "before the boy was born"—as a glimpse of immortality. This reality is independent of shifting urban moral fashions; it is an ideal prior to civilization. But it is not an uncivilized ideal; its priority is logical rather than temporal; it is prior because it is ideal, not so much older as timeless. It has nothing to do with "primitivism," or with noble savagery, or even the American Adamic dream of unspoiled original innocence in the New World—nothing except this, that in Faulkner's handling of it the honorable emerges by a dialectical transformation, a "transvaluation" of that dream and that innocence: at the instant the falsehood is exposed and the existence of evil is acknowledged.

The humanly recognizable embodiment of the honorable in "The Bear" is an action, a repeated ritual pattern of conduct: "the yearly rendezvous . . . the yearly pageant-rite of the old bear's furious immortality," the annual duel between the skilled hunters and the shaggy, tremendous, indomitable Old Ben. The duel is enacted within a soiled set of conventions and rules, older than memory and faultlessly observed on both sides; the men *hunt* all other bears in the wilderness, but with Old Ben they engage rather in a kind of ritual dance. It is by participating in this ritual that the young hero, Isaac McCaslin, is reborn and receives, as it were, a sacramental blessing. That process is the substance of the first half of the story.

In a sense I will suggest, it is the whole of the story; the rest of "The Bear" tells us how a hero, if properly initiated, may behave in the presence of evil. But to explain these seemingly extravagant remarks, and to take hold of the experience more firmly, we need to examine the experience in its actual and living form: its artistically realized form, unabstracted. To do so is to look closely at the story's structure.

The difficulty of most of Faulkner's stories lies in the order of their telling. He has always provided us with lots of action; and if his unconventional arrangement of the incidents sometimes resembles a random shuffle through a fateful crazy-house, it at least avoids another extreme of modern fiction. It never evaporates into atmosphere or aesthetic self-indulgence. What *happens* in a Faulkner story is the most important thing in it, except perhaps the moral excitement that produces the happening. But we are let in on the event secretively, gradually, almost grudgingly, from different viewpoints and at different times. This is to say that Faulkner's structural experiments—like his verbal ones—are significant, but not significant in themselves; only in what they are intended to disclose. The structure of *A Portrait of the Artist as a Young Man* is crucial because it is what the book is really about; the creative imagination and its shaping power was Joyce's subject and his hero. But the structure of "The Bear" or *The Sound and the Fury* is, rather, a fascinating executive technique whose aim is to reveal the substance of the life within. Artistically as well as chronologically, Faulkner belongs among novelists of the second generation, but he has absorbed more from the first generation writers and made better use of it than any of his contemporaries (contrast the misguided use of Joycean monologue in Greene's *England Made Me*). Much insight can be gained into Faulkner and much drawn from him by placing him alongside Joyce and Proust and Virginia Woolf, as Leon Edel has done with striking results in *The Psychological Novel*. Yet Faulkner's peers are, I think, the present ones; and his literary ancestry, like theirs, jumps a generation back into the nineteenth century. He belongs with Silone and Greene and Camus; and in that company, he is the greatest master of narrative technique.[11]

"The Bear" has a plot relatively simpler than some in Faulkner's

earlier writings; but here again Faulkner has played weird tricks
with the temporal ordering. He has concluded his tale, for instance,
with an episode that occurs at a moment earlier in time than several
episodes that have preceded it in the telling. The story is divided
into five sections. But if we follow the direct temporal succession of
the events in the life of Isaac McCaslin—noting in parenthesis the
story's arrangement of them through the successive numbered sections—we come upon this personal history:

(Sections 1, 2, 3) A boy named Ike McCaslin grows up in Mississippi in the years after the Civil War. From the time he is ten, he
accompanies his cousin Cass Edmonds and several of his home-town's
leading citizens, every year, on bear-hunting expeditions in the un-
tamed wilderness north of the town. Ike begins to acquire some of
the skill of the older men, and with them the severe masculine
virtues that the solemn game of hunting can produce. In that game,
the greatest and most honored rival (not enemy or prey) is an
enormous and ancient bear known as Old Ben. During the boy's
sixteenth year, Old Ben is at last killed by one of the men, Boon
Hogganbeck, and a mongrel dog called Lion.

(Section 5) Two years later, the boy, now eighteen, comes back
once more to the wilderness to find it no longer a wilderness. The
old hunting lodge is gone, the group of hunters disbanded; and
lumber companies have begun to invade and transform the forest.
Ike encounters Boon Hogganbeck, who is lost and nearly hysterical
in the new "civilized" era.

(Section 4) Three years later, when Ike is twenty-one, he comes
into his inheritance of the land and the money that have been
handed down through his father (Uncle Buck) from his grandfather, Carrothers McCaslin. But Ike decides to renounce his legacy,
since he has previously discovered it tainted at the source by his
grandfather's misdeeds. The latter had seduced and had a child by a
Negro slave, Tomasina, who was probably his own daughter as well.
That combination of incest and miscegenation represents for Ike the
evil condition of the South, and its betrayal of moral possibility:
a version of the human legacy of evil generally, from the "original
sin" at the beginning of time; but deriving, in the New World, from
the corrupting effects upon both parties to it of the institution of
slavery. He determines to dissociate himself from his own particular

corrupt legacy; and he continues to live a simple huntsman's life in or near the forest, basing his conduct on an emulation of Jesus. He takes up carpentering and marries the daughter of his partner. He has no children.

Thus, the "real-life" career of Ike McCaslin, so far as we know it from the furtive disclosures of "The Bear." [12] But keep in mind that the incidents of his twenty-first year and of his later years are given us—as Faulkner actually wrote his narrative—*before* we learn about the return to the woods, at eighteen, in the fifth and final section. Our question is with the relation between the chronological order and artistic order of the events, and the value of Faulkner's rearrangement.

André Gide, when he was writing *The Counterfeiters*, confided to his journal a desire to render the events of his novel *légèrement déformés*, so that the reader's interest might be aroused in an effort to restore the original aspects; the reader becoming thereby the author's collaborator. Faulkner's motive may in part be the same. His alleged contempt for his reader has the effect, anyhow, of involving the reader nearly to the extent of devouring him. No other American writer engages his readers so mercilessly; and except for those who fear and resent him on quite other grounds, readers of Faulkner can and do get an immense satisfaction from that participation with him that verges on the creative. This is one of the first generation features of Faulkner—one that links him with Gide and Joyce. But the aim of Faulkner's deliberate deformations is not finally aesthetic; he wants the reader to participate not in a creative act but in a moral act. He wants to define a moral experience of mythological proportions and of ambiguous reality: an aim that of necessity makes heavy demands on the reader. Conrad, for example, asks no less of us when he makes his arduous way through the thickets to release his prophetic myth of modern history in *Nostromo;* nor, to name a writer even closer in feeling to Faulkner, does Virgil in his myth of Roman history. In the *Aeneid*, the last event of the poem—the duel between Aeneas and Turnus—occurs many centuries before some of the events already described: the long course of Roman history across the centuries and up to the battle of Actium, as given in the preview by Anchises in Book VI and in the pictures engraved on the shield of Aeneas in Book VIII. In the

Aeneid, of course, the chronologically later events appear explicitly as prophecies, almost as dreams. But that, I propose, is exactly the nature of the fourth section of "The Bear," with its narrative of Ike's twenty-first and later years.

Before I press the suggestion, some mechanical observations may be helpful. The fourth section has the same formal organization and is roughly the same length as the first three sections combined. This gives it, suitably, the appearance and function of a counter-weight. Both of these two large parts begin at certain moments in Ike's life (when he is sixteen and twenty-one, respectively), retreat to earlier moments, and then spiral back through their starting points. The recurring insistence of Faulkner upon his hero's age is too striking to be overlooked; it is almost a plea: "He was sixteen then . . . then he was sixteen." Ike's age is the chief structural element; and his sixteenth year was his *annus mirabilis*. The story flows through that year on three distinct occasions; as though only by this means could the contradictory richness of the year's experience be made manifest.

But while we are aware of strong currents carrying us forward and backward in "The Bear," we receive also the corollary impression that time is motionless and everything is occurring simultaneously; the high mobility of the story concludes in a sense of the fixed and the frozen. Faulkner achieves this effect by bringing in past events only as they are returned to in present memory, in the manner Cesare Pavese was to adopt: by parentheses, and by parentheses within parentheses, like one memory jogging another. He achieves it, too, in his narrative order, by the triple journey through the sixteenth year. We might even say that "The Bear" arrives at an image of the conjunction of time and eternity.

The story begins in Ike's sixteenth year, the year he is to complete his rite of initiation. Till this moment, he has grasped the importance but not the meaning of the experience.

> It seemed to him that there was a fatality in it. It seemed to him that something, he didn't know what, was beginning; had already begun. It was like the last act on a set stage. It was the beginning of the end of something, he didn't know what except that he would not grieve. He would be humble and proud that he had been found worthy to be a part of it too or even just to see it too.

"The beginning of the end of something"—an end *and* a beginning, in fact: which is why Ike has reason to be humble and proud. For the drama he is engaged in is a vast drama of death and birth: the death of Old Ben, of Sam Fathers (Ike's foster-parent and tutor), of the dog Lion, of the wilderness and the companionship Ike had known there, of an entire world; and the birth or rebirth of Isaac McCaslin as the solitary reincarnation of those dead and the lone witnesses (very much in the second generation "tradition") to that world and its truth. This is what Ike is disciplined to perceive, as the story returns to the great year in section three. When Old Ben dies in that section, he dies metaphorically in childbirth. He has, indeed, many features in common with the "terrible mother" of heroic mythology; and in this context, the name of Sam Fathers, Ike's spiritual guide, is intrusively significant. It requires only a twist of the tongue to convert the story's title into "The Birth."

In the fourth section we find that it was also during Ike's sixteenth year, on a December night after the last bear hunt, that he solved the riddle of his family's history. The section begins with the sentence, ominously uncapitalized: "then he was twenty-one." The defining occasion of most of it is a conversation between Ike and his cousin Cass Edmonds in the plantation commissary on the date of Ike's legal coming-of-age. But, while the entire span of Ike's very long life is touched upon, it is the discoveries of his sixteenth year that account for the intensity of his speech and the resoluteness of his decision to reject his inheritance. With the conversation as foreground, those discoveries pass through Ike's memory like shadows on the wall behind—shadows themselves in a ghostly conversation; for they appear as remembered entries in the commissary ledgers, written in a question-and-answer style. The entries had been made decades earlier by Ike's uncle and his father, and they had been pieced together with amazement and horror by Ike five years before the present moment. Their language has the sparse, foreshortened quality of memory:

[Uncle Buck:] *Eunice Bought by Father in New Orleans 1807 $650.
Marrid to Thucydus 1809 Drownd in Crick Cristmas Day 1832*
[Uncle Buddy:] *June 21th 1833 Drownd herself*
[Uncle Buck:] *23 Jun 1833 Who in hell ever heard of a niger
drownding himself*
[Uncle Buddy:] *Aug 13th 1833 Drownd herself*

The motivation for Eunice's suicide is revealed only in its impact upon Ike's oddly mythopoeic imagination. It is up to us, collaborators in the hunt, to discover that Eunice had been the mistress of the grandfather, Carrothers McCaslin (Uncle Buck's "Father"), bought by him and—when she was pregnant by him with the child Tomasina—married off to another slave, Thucydus; and that Eunice drowned herself twenty-three years later when she realized that her daughter, too, had become pregnant by Carrothers McCaslin: by her own father, by Eunice's lover. For Ike, the tragic event has the formality of legend:

> . . . he seemed to see her actually walking into the icy creek on that Christmas day six months before her daughter's and her lover's *(Her first lover's,* he thought. *Her first)* child was born, solitary, inflexible, griefless, ceremonial, in formal and succinct repudiation of grief and despair who had already had to repudiate belief and hope

Ike has a shocking revelation of the literal fact of human brotherhood: Turl, the child Tomasina bears, and Jim, the child Turl later begets, are actually Ike's cousins, and have their rights in the legacy he renounces.

The first essential link between the two large parts I have been discussing—the first three sections taken together, and the fourth as their counterweight—is the near simultaneity of the death of Old Ben and the discovery of mixed blood and incest in the McCaslin clan. The fourth section of "The Bear" is not merely the further adventures of Isaac McCaslin. The harmony of the parts may be summarized in ancient formulas: the birth into virtue, and the vision of evil. Only the person adequately initiated can have the vision at all; and only the potency of the initiation enables the reborn individual to withstand the evil when it is encountered. The action in section four (the discovery and the renunciation) is made possible by the experience that preceded it; the ritual in the wilderness *contains*, implicitly, the decision in the commissary.

This leads to a somewhat more complex view of the relationship. It is true that the fourth section is contained within the sections that have the wilderness as their setting: the containment achieved when Faulkner brings his story back to the wilderness in the fifth and final section, returning to the life of Ike before he has reached the age of decision, returning to the atmosphere and the rhythms of the hunting world. The fifth section reverts to the style—relatively straightforward, though highly orchestrated and charged with autumnal splendor—of the first, second, and third sections; picking up that style where it had been left almost sixty pages before, and so enveloping and containing the very different style in between. We may illustrate by quoting from the last lines of section four and the first of section five, breaking in anywhere on the endlessly flowing matter of section four:

> . . . and on their wedding night she had cried and he thought she was crying now at first, into the tossed and wadded pillow, the voice coming from somewhere between the pillow and the cachinnation: 'And that's all. That's all from me. If this dont get you that son you talk about, it wont be mine': lying on her side, her back to the empty rented room, laughing and laughing

> He went back to the camp one more time before the lumber company moved in and began to cut the timber. Major de Spain himself never saw it again.

Faulkner has even gone to the extreme, as we notice here, of employing a single quotation mark in the conversations of the fourth section: the conventional sign of the speech contained within the speech—as against the double quotation mark elsewhere. It is the sort of device peculiarly trying for those not already persuaded by Faulkner; but it is an instance of his anxiety that we should recognize the mode of existence of that phase of the whole experience.

Its *mode* of existence is as important as its content. For what we are given in the fourth section is not so much a narrative of events that have happened, as an intense, translucent vision of the future. Its appearance between the third and fifth sections—between the episodes of Ike's sixteenth and eighteenth years—allows us to suppose that it is a dream; perhaps a dream that occurred during the year between. It is a true dream, to be sure, a true prophecy, issuing securely from the gate of horn; but passing before our eyes incidents that at the moment of perception exist only in a state of possibility. The sense of something not yet realized is carried in the prose itself. We are struck by the decrease in visibility. Against an immeasurably vast setting, actions and dialogue have curiously hazy outline. Sentences spray out in all directions, almost never (within

our hearing) reaching their probable periods. Everything is potential, unfinished, pushing toward completion. But the experience
is not a *mere* possibility, in the sense that a quite different experience is equally possible. We have to reckon with Faulkner's notions
about time and reality: according to which events become real not
when they occur but only when they are looked back upon in
memory. The fourth section creates the real by dreaming how it
will eventually be remembered. *Forsan et haec olim meminisse
iuvabit.* Aeneas can say no more than that; and if Faulkner permits
Ike to dream in some detail how these things will later seem to be,
it is partly because Faulkner has dared assume (as Mme. Magny has
observed) something like the divine viewpoint. But not altogether.
The events are certain, but not yet. They are only partially visible
to the human perception. A spirit or a goddess might see them
whole, as ghostly Anchises and Venus can see the future of Rome;
but the most illuminated human perception is fully competent only
with the past; and the dream remains dreamlike. And beyond all
that, the *content* of the dream is such that the most illuminated
human art can—or should—present it only through a liquid mist of
prophecy.

To justify the latter contention, we must come back to actualities,
to the national and provincial traditions it is Faulkner's role in these
pages to represent. It is a long way from ancient Rome to nineteenth century Mississippi; and it is time to take account of the
boundaries within which Ike acts out his backwoods drama; the
force of the larger implications is derived from Faulkner's artistic
conversion of specifically American materials. Like *Moby-Dick*,
"The Bear" is most in tune with perennial rhythms of experience
when it is most solidly American; and if we close in on the particular portion of America that provides its scene, we recognize its
significant prototype in *Huckleberry Finn*. Both are narratives of
boys growing up in the nineteenth century South; both record a
sense of the troubled kinship between white and black, though
Twain does not carry that kinship literally into the blood streams.
Both suggest an ironic reversal of the conventional morality that
legitimizes social injustice—though, again, Twain's humor is in
charge of his outrage and prevents him from intruding lectures on
social legislation and warnings to the government up north, as it

protects Huck himself from a pretentious awareness of his own virtue. But the central insight Faulkner shares with Twain is one that both share with many another American writer: a sense of the fertile and highly ambiguous possibility of moral freedom in the new world. It is the possibility hymned by Emerson and Thoreau, and claimed again for the Far West by contemporary Californians like Steinbeck and Saroyan. In the Mississippi wilderness of the eighteen eighties, Faulkner has projected another image of the ethically undefined: undefined, like the river in *Huckleberry Finn*, because not yet fixed in the implicitly hypocritical conventions of civilized life. In so far as "The Bear" is a story about death, it is about the death of the frontier world and its possibility, of the new unspoiled area where a genuine and radical moral freedom—a kind of original innocence—could again be exercised.

But to say so without fundamental qualification would be to ascribe to Faulkner a view of innocence and the New World almost exactly opposite the one finally revealed in "The Bear." It would be to forget how often Faulkner has engaged in the ritual slaughter of the animal innocent—how he has penetrated the veil of innocence to arrive at the tragic fact, performing an operation on the hopeful world of his time similar to the one Hawthorne felt impelled to perform a century ago on Emerson. A part of the history Ike McCaslin rehearses for Cass Edmonds, on his twenty-first birthday, seems to echo the cheerful story Emerson and his colleagues used to tell each other:

> 'He [God] made the earth first and peopled it with dumb crea-
> tures, and then He created man to be His overseer on the earth and
> to hold suzerainty over the earth and the animals on it in His name,
> not to hold for himself and his descendants inviolable title for-
> ever . . . and all the fee He asked was pity and humility and suffer-
> ance and endurance. . . . He watched it. And let me say it.
> Dispossessed of Eden. Dispossessed of Canaan and those who . . .
> devoured their ravished substance ravished in turn again and then
> snarled in what you call the old world's worthless twilight over the
> old world's gnawed bones, blasphemous in His name until He used a
> simple egg to discover to them a new world where a nation of
> people could be founded in humility and pity and sufferance and
> pride of one another. . . .'

The identification of the New World as a divinely offered second chance for humanity after the first opportunity had been so thoroughly muffed in the Old World—the association of America with Eden—has never been more eloquently made. But Faulkner's hero is examining the myth precisely to see where it went wrong; and Faulkner himself, in writing "The Bear," was returning to the wilderness for the reason Graham Greene had gone to the Liberian jungle: driven, as Greene said in *Journey Without Maps*, by a "curiosity to discover . . . from what we have come, at what point we went astray." It is the familiar moment in the career of the second-generation novelist, when he returns to the sources to understand the bewildering fatalities of his age. Faulkner and Isaac Mc-Caslin conclude that the mistake was inherent in the myth; that the New World was not ever devoid of evil, from the moment of its settling—that it was 'already tainted even before any white man owned it by what Grandfather and his kind, his fathers, had brought into the new land . . . as though in the sailfuls of the old world's tainted wind which drove the ships.' It was the evil of slavery, rooted in the sin of spiritual pride and the lust of possession. What Grandfather and his kind brought with them into the New World was themselves; what they brought was the nature of man.

After probing to the falsity of the myth, "The Bear" goes on, by way of atonement, to construct a new and more durable image of innocence and moral freedom: a new image of a new kind of New World. Qualities undergo a profound dialectical transformation in "The Bear"—and of a nature indicated at once in the opening sentences:

> There was a man and a dog too this time. Two beasts, counting Old Ben, the bear, and two men, counting Boon Hogganbeck, in whom some of the same blood ran which ran in Sam Fathers, even though Boon's was a plebeian strain of it and only Sam and Old Ben and the mongrel Lion were taintless and incorruptible.

The change is already apparent in the paradoxical attribution to a mongrel dog of "taintless" and "incorruptible" qualities. It is there, too, though we do not immediately know it, in the same attribution to the man, Sam Fathers, who is also a mongrel, the half-breed offspring of a Negro slave and a Chicasaw Indian. The purity transcended is, in short, a physical purity, a matter of blood, something misleadingly suggested by the physical purity of the land—a very dangerous illusion. What takes its place is a tougher kind of purity, of innocence, of moral freedom; virtues not of a historical and accidental but of an ideal and permanent kind; qualities not given but achieved, by conduct and by art, through discipline and submission. The new innocence is not other than conscience.

"The Bear" thus moves toward a "transvaluation of values" at once large and homely—as large and as homely as the one symbolized in Silone's *A Handful of Blackberries* by the battered trumpet of the peasant Lazzaro. The two achievements have a good deal in common; for both manage to take hold of the mystery of power, in order to subdue it and transcend it: as Camus would do also in *The Plague*, and Greene (as his very title suggests) in *The Power and the Glory*. In assessing Faulkner's tale, we may permit ourselves still broader references; for it belongs to a still broader tradition, the tradition of heroic legend. In that tradition, where power is always a major factor, the special character of the hero's power is often represented by a "magic weapon," and by the use made of it.[13] We may contemplate a significant range from the great bow of Odysseus, with which he ruthlessly slays a houseful of political and domestic rivals, to, say, St. Martin of Tours telling the pagan Emperor that, "Armed only with the Cross, in the forefront of the enemy, I will fear no evil." Aeneas enters his supreme battle wearing on his shield the recorded destiny of Rome, a predestined power that makes him invulnerable to the mightiest of the Latins; and the secret source of Ahab's power is the giant harpoon baptized "not in the name of the father, but in the name of the devil." Isaac McCaslin's weapon is nothing so grandiose; but it is not much less meaningful. It is, of course, his hunter's rifle.

His first gun is too big for him, a man's weapon in a boy's hand. Then at eleven years old, the year he first encounters Old Ben, he receives his own gun, "a new breech-loader, a Christmas gift; he would own and shoot it for almost seventy years. . . ." The imagery of the gun is diffused through the story, one of its unifying motifs; an association is noted with the taintless mongrel dog, whose color is gunmetal gray. But what is important is the use Ike makes of his gun in his relation with Old Ben. The first time he meets the bear, Ike has abandoned his rifle, along with his watch and compass, to present himself in humility before the ancient patriarch: an act of communion, verging on the holy. The second time, he throws his gun aside and risks his life to rescue a little fyce who was barking helplessly in the bear's path: an act of charity. That, I think, is the main symbolic movement of the narrative. For what we comprehend in "The Bear" is a movement generically similar to that of *Bread and Wine*. It is the transmutation of power into charity.

That is what the conversion of innocence amounts to, and Faulkner's artistic conversion of the historical image of America. In it, power suffers no real loss, but undergoes a sea-change. It comes under the control of moral understanding; a kind of grace enters into it. More concretely: Ike does not give up his weapon of destruction; on the contrary, we have swift glimpses of him in his later years as the greatest hunter in Yoknapatawpha County. But he uses his power with restraint and fidelity; he uses it with conscience. Boon Hogganbeck is the vulnerably innocent man, in the inferior sense of the word, and he is last seen nearly out of his head and rabidly dismantling his own gun. Ike continues to live near and in the dwindling forest, as close as possible to the source of his moral energy: a Natty Bumppo who is also an imitator of Christ. But Ike is not intended to represent Christ in a second coming; it is only that he seems to move in a world of light—a meager light but definite enough, for instance, to read the past by (in a way Quentin Compson could not); a new world in which values are confirmed only by raising them to a higher power; not the historical and physical New World —this is precisely what is transcended—but a world so perpetually new that Ike appears to be its only living inhabitant.

And here we observe the significant difference between Isaac McCaslin and some of the other fictional heroes who make up the image of our picaresque saint. Ike is in part a saint, according to part of the loose definition I have drawn from second generation novels. He does stand for a lost hope and a future possibility; he does represent a vanished Eden and is prepared for the purgatory to come. He is an extraordinary individual, an energetic outsider— his natural home not the society and the town of Jefferson, but the big woods. Ike differs from Pietro Spina (and Greene's Mexican priest) and from some of Camus's heroes in that he is not an outsider in the other and more painful and perilous sense. There is no roguery in him; he has not fully shared in the adventure of being human. Hence he does not share in the suffering and roguery of others, and there is thus no impulse toward companionship, toward reducing the tragic distance between man and man. History has taught him much; but it seems also to have taught him that history itself enforces a condition of solitude. His lifelong mission of atonement and of bearing witness is of necessity solitary: as though only in solitude might purity remain undamaged.

The transcendence enacted in "The Bear," to put it differently, was if anything too successful and complete. It carried Ike out of the quicksands of history, but at the same time it nearly carried him out of the company of mortal men. He has moved dangerously close to the person of the savior-god, to the person of Jesus: dangerously close, at least, for the purposes of fiction. It is worth insisting that the life of Christ is not under any circumstances a fit subject for literature: not because such a subject would be irreverent, but because within the limits of literature it would be impossible; or, what is the same thing, it would be too easy. And this is exactly why the quality of the fourth section of "The Bear"— the mode of its existence—is so uncannily appropriate to its content. It was perhaps Faulkner's most extraordinary poetic intuition to present the affinities between a human being and a divine—a Mississippi hunter and the figure of Christ—not as an actuality, but as a foggily seen prophetic possibility: something longed for and even implicit in present circumstances and character, but something that has decidedly never yet happened. "The Bear," reaching to the edge of human limits, does the most that literature may with propriety attempt to do.

THE LOSS OF IMPURITY

Most of the conclusions I have expressed here about Faulkner were arrived at and put into print a number of years ago, at a time when rumors were heard that Faulkner was at work on a fictionalized life of Christ. In my essay,[14] I had at first included a reference to the rumors, and a pious hope that they were not true; but this I deleted. The appearance of A Fable (1954) may have confirmed both instincts as not unsound: both the apprehension, on principle, over the subject matter, and the deletion of any specific allusion as dangerous critical impudence, given Faulkner's unpredictable genius. *A Fable* does demonstrate, I think, the dramatic unfitness of the unmodulated Christ figure; and it demonstrates, too, the risk of so richly American a novelist abandoning his native materials—as he does here—to deal with European characters in a European scene. But ravaged though it is, the book (as someone said about Captain Ahab) has its humanities, and they are mighty ones. There is a kind of deadness at its center, but the amount of life that is thereby stricken remains enormous. *A Fable* carries a certain theme and style further than art may carry them; perhaps it fails; but so did Orpheus.

The action of the novel takes place in 1918, on the Western Front in France, during a simulated or analogical Holy Week: not the actual Holy Week of the Christian calendar that provided the setting for *The Sound and the Fury*, but a second Holy Week, with its own Maundy Thursday, Good Friday, Easter Even, and Easter morning; a succession of days and nights during which—as the action spirals its way through them, with many long digressions and reminiscences—a second Christ moves through the second inevitable Passion that climaxes his second coming. The motivating incident is the "mutiny" of a French regiment, which, at the instigation of a foreign-born corporal and his eleven faithful followers, simply refuses one May morning to make the attack upon the German trenches it has been ordered to make. In the ensuing excitement, it becomes clear that all the Allied forces and the German troops, too, had been ready for the French regiment's gesture; and that what was happening was a vast effort by the common soldiers to stop the war by refusing to fight any longer. But the book's emphasis is less upon that effort than upon the significance of its immediate failure. The story opens as the entire regiment is being hustled back to headquarters under arrest, with a special truck for the corporal and his followers, who have now mysteriously become twelve. A mob of civilians is dehumanized by rage and by fear for its relatives in the regiment, all of whom may now suffer a mass execution. The incident generates violent emotions on all sides, and it concludes in a carnage more wholesale than anything known even to the Elizabethans or Jacobean stage: an inordinate number of shootings, suicides, and immolations, framing the death of the corporal before a specially selected firing-squad. The military authorities, both Allied and German, manage by a tremendous concerted effort to get the war started again and hence get their world back to normal; though in fact the war would lose momentum and end by its own rules in November of the same year.

Throughout, the pace of the narrative is forced by the religious allegory: at first an echo, then a likeness that grows into a virtual identity between the figure and career of the martyred corporal and those of Jesus. The corporal is the illegitimate son of a married peasant woman and, if not definitely of a god, at least of a godlike person—a young French nobleman who later becomes supreme commander of troops on the Western Front and whose task it is to settle the mutiny and condemn the mutineers, his son among them. The corporal had been born in a stable, there being no room at the nearby inn; his half-sisters are named Martha and Mary, and later in life his betrothed, like Magdalene, is a prostitute. Little is known or told about his childhood and adolescence, but miraculous suggestions gather about his maturity. He joins the French Army and draws to himself a band of disciples: one named Paul, one named Peter—Pierre Bouc, who at first denies him and then begs to become a member of the doomed company, and does become its thirteenth man—and one named Polcheck, who betrays the mutiny in advance, and is last seen desperately trying to press thirty pieces of gold on the bereaved half-sisters and is obscurely associated with death by hanging. For his years-long effort to enforce the precepts of charity and to put an end to human hatred, the corporal is executed —along with two thieves named Lapin and Casse-Tête; his last words are a familiar translation: "It's all right," he says to one of the thieves, "we're going to wait. We won't go without you." His body is buried on the family farm; but whether because of a heavy shelling that plows up the ground, or for some other cause, by Sunday morning it has vanished.

There are many more such correspondences, but it becomes tedious to list them: and exactly because they are not, after all, correspondences but repetitions. Most of the serious critics were harsh on *A Fable*, but not always for the right reasons. Perhaps they were irritated by the ill-advised pretensions of the dust-jacket: "That many controversial interpretations will be read into *A Fable* is inevitable. Countless symbolic meanings will be attributed to the central characters and events," and so on. But the book's difficulty is just the opposite: it permits of no controversial interpretations and the main episode is pretty well devoid of symbolic meanings (which under no circumstances should ever be "read into" a novel, in any case). The trouble with *A Fable* is its lack of complexity in the undefiled purity of the hero, and the undefiled purity with which his person and career repeat those of Jesus. There are symbols in the book, but the corporal, the women, the disciples, the thieves, the judges are not among them. They do not *symbolize* anything; they *are* their originals, with French or Middle European —or rather, always with Faulknerian—accents.[15]

This difficulty was not the one commonly criticized. The chief objections were on the grounds of willful and intolerable obscurity. The book was condemned as fantastically extravagant in style and entangled in composition, and the whole of it declared lost in a thick darkness out of which a voice could be heard raving gibberish as in delirium tremens. A rereading confirms my initial impression that something like the opposite is the case. *A Fable* is not, in fact, hard to read; it is almost impossible not to read, for Faulkner's words are as clawlike as ever, and his most circuitous sentences (long sections average about a sentence a page) retain that unmatched prehensile quality that is the instant mark of a writer of genius. It is another aspect of Faulkner's style that, like his Jacobean ancestors, he pushes closer and closer to caricature, as a part of his theme; and here perhaps he slips over the edge once or twice. But the force behind the book is prodigious. And if that force has not found its way altogether into the book and distributed itself there evenly, it is not because the book is hard to understand, but because it is too easy to understand; not because the events and characters are hidden beneath a cloud of unknowing, but because they are seen all too plainly in the univocal glare of a deadening gray light.

A Fable is Faulkner's largest effort, within his largest context, to dramatize one of his generation's most striking impulses—the impulse, observed in "The Bear," to transmute power into charity. As such the novel has a massive grandeur that criticism is hard put even to describe. The corporal addresses his charitable energies not to a symbol of power, but to power's very being in the fullness of its form and movement; the totality of the armed forces of the world, locked in a battle that intensifies the power on both sides and that has lasted so long that the human warriors seem figures no longer in a world war but rather in a war world. The extreme discoloration of the human element in the novel, and especially of the mob (which, as Faulkner describes it, has been reduced by war to a mere brute fact of nature, an ugly throb of existence), is explained by the corrosive forces of the setting. The charity intended is not less total. It is the coming-to-be not of an armistice or a rest period, but of an entirely new condition of things, a new age for mankind—something like Silone's Abruzzese dream of the age of the Holy Spirit as replacing the age of law, "the ancient hope"—valid for both Silone and Faulkner—"of the Kingdom of God." The power is pure power: *mana*—what Melville symbolized in the whale, according to Newton Arvin: "the half-conscious, half-unconscious power of blind, restless, perhaps purposeless, but always overbearing and unconquerable force." And that force is to be transformed by the corporal and his followers into pure charity. It is perhaps the very purity of these elements that gives the book its essentially static quality.

At the book's center, the measure of its meaning, is a character who has the effect of divesting all other characters of their own actuality, as though draining them of blood. To apply the distinction made by W. B. Yeats, the corporal is a rhetorical figure, the product of Faulkner's quarrel with others; not a poetic figure, the product of Faulkner's quarrel with himself. It is a rhetoric that nearly drowns any protest against it in the warmth and beauty of its torrential flow. But through it all we feel a particular presence orating in endless fury against the majestic imbecilities of the modern world. The quarrel is outward, not inward; and the corporal is its instrument. *A Fable* is the best and biggest example in second generation fiction of what happens when the novelist's assault upon his age—the novelist's effort (as Camus and Malraux have described it, in remarks quoted earlier) to rectify the universe, to fabricate a better and more human universe—when that endeavor gets out of hand and gets away from the control of art. What happens is that the representative figures lose their vital complexity; and the representative hero loses the contradictions that animate him. In losing its impurity, the human image loses its life. The only sense in which *A Fable* is obscure is the sense in which it is lifeless.

We touch here upon the thorny old question of "belief" or even of "truth" in literature: and of the response of reader or critic to the substance of belief he comes upon. The question has again been made urgent by contemporary novelists, because they have somewhat departed from the traditional aim of presenting a picture or telling a tale, with pleasure as the sole end in view; and have directed fiction toward rebellion or conversion or inquiry—disguises of another and equally traditional aim, the aim of instruction. One talks as if there were rules in the matter, but writers as well as critics proceed empirically, obeying a new instinct or try to come to terms with a new kind of literature. One tends also, as in the present case, to take refuge in an impersonal tone, to subdue the intrusive personal factor with which belief is always enmeshed. But a general principle may be hazarded: and that is, that the substance of belief in a novel or a poem has force in so far as it has form; that it has radiance in so far as it has energy; and it has all this in so far as the shape of belief is dialectical—displaying the invigorating play of opposites. The best novel, Lionel Trilling has remarked elegantly, is the one that best contains and expresses the yes and the no of its culture; and the best novelist, Scott Fitzgerald once said, is the one who can hold two opposite ideas in his head at the same time and not crack under the strain.

No principle could be more important in a time when novelists are driven by a desire to deny and to affirm—engaged in a monumental effort to record a movement from death to life—but when, as a consequence, their compelling image is the one we have been watching: the image of the saint. The principle would be not less imporant in a time when the representative image was that of the devil; though the necessary artistic compensation would in that case be the reverse. The saintly image seeks of its own nature to gain altitude by getting rid of its human ballast; it moves toward the divine and evolves into the image of Christ; the tendency should be resisted. Gods may walk in the pages of fiction and poetry, as long as they are the gods of Homer or, shall we say, of Jean-Paul Sartre, with all their human imperfections written in their faces and accented in their speech. But the limits of literature are human limits, and contain the inescapable challenge to art of the contradictory nature of man. To create a fictional character is to effect an incarnation; when the character is himself God incarnate, the writer's job has been done for him in advance—which is what I meant by saying it would be too easy. And the writer must try to persuade us that the figure is a man, too: which is what I meant by saying it would be impossible. When, within the limits of literature, there appears the figure of Christ or even that of the truly sanctified, we have either the soft sentimentality of *The Passing of the Third Floor Back* or the stiff abstractions of *A Fable:* both—one at a vulgar and the other at a magnificent extreme—betrayals of art by their false transcendence of man.

That is why the contemporary profile of the fictional saint has, in most cases, retained the element of the picaresque: out of fidelity at once to art and to human nature. The purity of aspiration must be humanized and kept alive by a measure of impurity: moral impurity and artistic impurity; either within the character or in the perspective upon him. I am extending the sense of the word suggested by Robert Penn Warren in his healthy advocacy of what he calls "the impure novel"—the novel in which what is good or ideal is prevented from escaping into the merely misty by the pressure of an ironic or skeptical perspective upon it: as (in Mr. Warren's illustration [16]) the romantic idealism of Romeo is given proportion, and the play kept sane, by Mercutio's wise poetical realism; as in "The Bear" mistiness-is avoided by the brilliant strategy of representing it exactly as mist. Such dramatic impurity is the distinguishing mark, as I shall try to show, of Graham Greene's novel *The Power and the Glory:* a book built flawlessly out of two absolutely co-equal and co-extensive perspectives, that of the drunken but saintly priest and the upright agnostic lieutenant, as the two modify and characterize each other. A contrast more telling with *A Fable* is Dostoevski's *The Idiot*, wherein the protagonist, Prince Myshkin, is plainly a Christ figure in some degree, but where the beauty is in great part derived from the Prince's fragile physical and mental condition and from the disastrous results of his errands of redemption. The corporal's errand proves disastrous enough, but the fatalities do not derive from his own fatally equivocal character. Closer yet to *A Fable* is the story of Christ and the Grand Inquisitor in *The*

Brothers Karamazov. And the one scene in *A Fable* that does achieve
a well-nigh unbearable pressure, where the rhetoric is entirely controlled by the poetry, is a scene loud with echoes of Ivan's dream
legend.

It is the scene between the supreme commander and the young
corporal, between father and son (as the former knows but the
latter at the start does not); a scene that re-enacts also the moment
of Christ's temptation, when the devil took him to a high place and
showed him all the nations of the earth—his to possess and command,
if he would but bow down and worship his temptor. The old
general's fee is his son's consent not to be executed: he offers freedom, then the world, and finally the sheer sensation of existence;
and what he demands, in exhorting the other to give up his martyrdom, is a submission to the human condition, as though he were
pleading for art not less than for the human part of humanity. The
matching of the forces is a trifle marred, as elsewhere in Faulkner,
by an immense and verbose awareness of it; but the forces have
rarely been more impressively matched.

> 'We are not two Greek or Armenian or Jewish—or for that matter,
> Norman—peasants swapping a horse [says the general]; we are two
> articulations, self-elected possibly, anyway elected, anyway postu-
> lated, not so much to defend as to test two inimical conditions which,
> through no fault of ours but through the simple paucity and restric-
> tions of the arena where they meet, must contend and—one of
> them—perish: I champion of this mundane earth which whether I
> like it or not is, and to which I did not ask to come, yet since I am
> here not only must stop but intend to stop during my allotted while;
> you champion of an esoteric realm of man's baseless hopes and his
> infinite capacity—no: passion—for unfact. No, they are not inimical
> really, there is no contest actually; they can even exist side by side
> together in this one restricted area, and could and would, had yours
> not interfered with mine. So once more: take the earth. Now,
> answer as I know you will.'

And it should be stressed that Faulkner's most frequently quoted
salute to man (the one he adapted from Conrad's essay on James
and offered as his speech accepting the Nobel award in Stockholm,
in 1950) is given, in *A Fable*, to the old general to enunciate: demonstrating that here at least the old general bespeaks a part of Faulkner and that the debate between father and son projects Faulkner's

own inner debate, his internal quarrel. The result is poetry. To his father's last and most cunning offer—the offer of the feeling of life—the corporal has replied: "Don't be afraid. There's nothing to be afraid of." And the old general, after a long moment, continues:

'Afraid? No no, it's not I but you who are afraid of man; not I but you who believe that nothing but a death can save him. I know better. I know that he has that in him which enables him to outlast even his wars; that in him more durable than all his vices, even that last and most fearsome one; to outlast even this next avatar of his servitude which he now faces: his enslavement to the demonic progeny of his own mechanical curiosity. . . . Oh yes, he will survive it because he has that in him which will endure even beyond the ultimate worthless tideless rock freezing slowly in the last red and heatless sunset, because already the next star in the blue immensity of space will be already clamorous with the uproar of his debarkation, his puny and inexhaustible voice still talking, still planning; and there too after the last ding dong of doom has rung and died there will still be one sound more: his voice, planning still to build something higher and faster and louder; more efficient and louder and faster than ever before, yet it too inherent with the same old primordial fault since it too will fail to eradicate him from the earth. I don't fear man. I do better: I respect and admire him. And pride: I am ten times prouder of that immortality which he does possess than ever he of that heavenly one of his delusion. Because man and his folly—'

'Will endure,' the corporal said.

'They will do more,' the old general said proudly. 'They will prevail.'

A Fable rises to that high peak of impurity, and declines from it. The corporal and what he represents gradually dissolve the vigor of everything that resists them; the rhetoric defeats the poetry, the allegory destroys the symbol, and at the book's end the old general is sent dishonored to his grave: dishonored by the book, that is, and amidst the great French public honor of his funeral ceremonies. Taken as a whole, therefore, *A Fable* discloses a further loss of impurity, a continuation of the process first noticeable in "The Bear." The second installment of Faulkner's Snopes epic, *The Town* (1956), seems to indicate a regathering of imaginative strength: it is comic writing of a high order, if not of the highest Faulknerian order. But as final measure of the loss and of Faulkner's characteristic achievement, as well as of the human and artistic issues here at stake, we may cast a brief glance backward, in closing, at *Light in August*. For *Light in August* is not only Faulkner's most splendidly impure novel, with his most wonderfully imagined impure hero: the outlaw and murderer Joe Christmas, who carries the burden of his name through a ritual emulation of Christ's martyrdom. The book also gives a dramatic rendering of the most urgent of all our issues: the task Silone assigned both himself and Pietro Spina, the task of Greene and his Mexican priest, of Camus and Dr. Rieux: the task of creating and of becoming a human being.

In the story of Joe Christmas, Alfred Kazin has eloquently written, Faulkner managed "to pull off the tremendous feat of making us believe in a character who in many ways is not a human being at all—but struggling to become one. And this, after all," Mr. Kazin continues, "is the great problem of the novelist today. Joe Christmas is an incarnation not only of the 'race problem' in America, but of the condition of man. More and more, not merely the American novel, but all serious contemporary novels, are concerned with men who are not real enough to themselves to be seriously in conflict with other men." [17] The present book is, among other things, an attempt to document the truths reflected in those (as it seems to me) luminously accurate remarks. Mr. Kazin concludes about *Light in August* that it is representative exactly because in it "there is no engagement between man and man—only the search of the 'stranger,' *l'étranger*, to become man." And to that I have to add only the following: that in Faulkner, too, up to a certain point, as in the Camus implicitly referred to by Mr. Kazin, and as in Silone and Moravia and Malraux, "the search of the 'stranger' . . . to become man" has eventually taken the shape precisely and of necessity of an effort to reach an "engagement between man and man." Companionship is the matrix of humanity in the representative fiction of the second generation.

Faulkner knew this in *Light in August* and presented it in the contrast between Joe Christmas and the figure and especially the name of Lena Grove's protector and companion: the utterly human person whose name sings through the novel in a soft and often smothered counterpoint to that of Joe Christmas: Byron Bunch. Faulkner knew it, too, in *As I Lay Dying*. The possibilities hinted at in the name of Byron Bunch (the aristocratic *picaro*, and the crowd in which he mingles and renews his humanity) are properly subordinated, in *Light in August*, to the savage Marlovian farce of Joe's endeavor to become a man. But the process that might have crowned that endeavor is bespoken in the long cry of Addie Bundren that arises from the very heart of *As I Lay Dying:*

> And when I would have to look at them [the students she used to teach in the local school] day after day, each with his and her secret and selfish thought, and blood strange to each other blood and strange to mine, and think that this seemed the only way I could get ready to stay dead, I would hate my father for having ever planted me. I would look forward to the times when they faulted, so I could whip them. When the switch fell I could feel it upon my flesh; when it welted and ridged it was my blood that ran, and I would think with each blow of the switch: Now you are aware of me! Now I am something in your secret and selfish life, who have marked your blood with my own for ever and ever.

In that recorded passage by pain and blood from secret selfishness and death to "awareness" and life, Faulkner touched almost all the chords there are in second generation fiction. But from "The Bear" onward, a different suggestion began to predominate: the suggestion that humanity can be asserted only in a refusal to be contaminated by the humanity of others; that in order to become a man, one must leap beyond the condition and company of men, and take upon one's self the role of the solitary and purely saintly redeemer. There are flickerings of the older notion in *A Fable:* as when the British sentry, the personification of vicious selfishness, screams at the moment of his death by enemy fire, " 'No! no! not to us!'—not even realising that he had said 'we' and not 'I' for the first and last time in his life probably . . . not even realising that in the next moment he had said 'I' again." But in *A Fable*, with a kind of insurpassable finality, the stranger has become man by a transcendent assertion of his function exactly *as* a stranger, in an apotheosis of the image of *L'Etranger*.

CHAPTER 6

Graham Greene: The Religious Affair

What bore / tore;
the horror and the glory are the same.
Man's hope the wound / God's memory the scar!
R. P. BLACKMUR, "The Rape of Europa"

BETWEEN THE HORROR AND THE GLORY

To FAULKNER'S YOKNAPATAWPHA COUNTY, to the Rome of Moravia and the Abruzzo of Silone and the North Africa of Camus, we now add and enter into the world of Graham Greene—a baffling landscape, at once harrowing and seedy, which English critics call Greeneland. It is the first thing to mention, and not only because its creation is an accomplishment that marks Greene as a writer of stature, but also because the landscape of Greene's writings is never simply a background; indeed it is never a background at all—it is a setting, a situation. It is the human situation made scenic. At the same time, it bears a curious resemblance to fragments of the actual world and to the actual places it names. Greene has always tried to embed his anagogical nightmares in meticulously described settings: the journalist and the theologian in him have conspired to give physical surroundings their due, though with reservations to be noted. Sometimes those surroundings are the dingier sections of English cities, but more often they are those portions of the earth that, from the Western center, appear remote, primitive, fantastic; there is a close relation, for Greene, between the dingy and the primitive. His aim, moreover, is less to describe surfaces than to evoke the natural "genius" of the place, to summon up its ghosts. In *The Quiet American*, recently, it was Indochina; earlier it has been Stockholm, Tabasco and Liberia, Brighton and the English countryside; and one sometimes feels that the best of Greene's books are the two in which a disturbing energy of atmosphere is almost everything—*Journey Without Maps* (1936), a sketch of West Africa, and *The Lawless Roads (Another Mexico)* (1939), about Mexico. But Greeneland is primarily the scene of certain recurring dramas and characteristic personalities; and the nature of both comprises the substance of this chapter.

Greene is, of course, the representative *religious* novelist among the writers I have selected. But he is representative, in his genera- tion, exactly because of the unorthodox manner in which the reli- gious element appears in his pages. Greene understands and has artfully dramatized the contemporary feeling—made emphatic in the writings of Camus—that the religious sense is hostile to human aspiration. In so far as that is actually so, the religious sense would seem also to be hostile to the art of narrative, which normally takes as its subject the natural urgings of man. But out of both forms of hostility, Greene has drawn a peculiar human anguish and a peculiar tension which are the determining features of his work. Out of them, too, he has drawn—in the figure of the priest in *The Power and the Glory*—as clear an instance as we can find of the picaresque saint: a figure himself made up of internally hostile attributes.

Greene's fiction thus depends for its success upon a delicate balance of paradoxes, each one of which is in a state of imminent eruption. When the balance holds firm, the result, in my opinion, is literature of a high order: the highest, perhaps, of any English novelist in the second generation. When the paradoxes erupt or collapse, the result is cleverness without force, well-made plots with very little action; and then the author of so impressively strained a novel as *Brighton Rock* looks like nothing so much as a tired James Hilton, wearing a faint neo-Augustinian scowl. No one is more prone to the meretricious than is Greene; and no one is capable of a more resounding impact.

Greene writes best when he is truly *inside* the special world he has himself envisaged. It is helpful at the outset, therefore, to attempt to locate that world in relevant symbolic terms. In order to do so, we may make use of a series of phrases, Greenean in their surprising sequence, that were once employed by T. S. Eliot: the boredom, the horror and the glory.[1] The phrases define the limits of Greene's world, and even plot a way through it. For boredom guards the entrance to life, in Greene's view of it; it is the first condition he remembers in his own experience, and it is the first condition in which we encounter many of the characters in his earlier novels; it is the condition back into which, with ill fortune, Greene's stories occasionally slip. For vitality and the communicated sense of vitality lie further along the way: on the far edges of the horror, on the outskirts of the glory.

"It was the early autumn of 1922. I was seventeen and terribly bored." In one of the essays collected in *The Lost Childhood* (1951), Greene tells of the immense boredom that afflicted him during all the years spent at the school in Birkhamstead, of which his father was headmaster and where Greene had been born in 1905. Boredom was what had once prompted him to run away from home: a lack of feeling or interest no doubt related to the not uncommon sense of emptiness in the presence of his (in the context) illustrious father. Running away was a listless act of rebellion against the father—or so it would be described in Greene's first novel, *The Man Within* (1929), when Francis Andrews takes to the road and to crime to escape the oppressive memory of his late, revered parent. In Greene's own case, the parental reprisal was to send him to a London psychoanalyst. It was possibly a shrewd enough move, for the boredom was complex and went exceedingly deep, but, Greene remembers, "the psycho-analysis that followed my act of rebellion fixed the boredom as the hypo fixes the image on the negative." He felt wrung dry, and remained so for several years. His second effort to escape, in 1922, was more radical. He took to playing Russian roulette in secret, with a revolver he found one afternoon in the cupboard of his bedroom.

The technique of this terrible game is well known. Greene's technique, anyhow, and the motivation behind it, he explained in

the concluding poem of *Babbling April,* a volume of almost re-
freshingly immature verse published when he was twenty.[2]

> I slip a charge into one chamber,
> Out of six,
> Then move the chambers round.
> One cast of the dice for death,
> And five for life.
> Then, eyes blind and fingers trembling,
> Place the revolver to my head,
> And pull the trigger.
> Will it be mist and death
> At the bend of this sunset road,
> Or life reinforced
> By the propinquity of death?
> Either is gain.
> It is a gamble which I cannot lose.

The game brought the boy an immediate and delicious sense of
life; but after three or four tries, it grew dull, and Greene himself
grew more irresponsible in the playing of it. He then wrote what
he rightly calls "a very bad piece of free verse" intended to comfort his parents if the game was ever lost: verses falsely suggesting
that he believed the revolver not to be loaded, so that his death, if
it occurred, would be put down to a frightful mistake. It is the
opening poem of *Babbling April:*

> How timorously, like an old-fashioned collector of wild flowers,
>   do we gather our sensations. . . .
> How we make our timorous advances to death, by pulling the
>   trigger of a revolver, which we already know to be empty,
> Even as I do now.
> And how horrified I should be, I who love Death in my verse,
>   if I had forgotten
> To unload.

"I who love Death in my verse." Here, as later, Greene invites
us to consider to what extent his involvement with death is purely
theatrical. If the poem speaks true, then the game itself was pure
pose, a self-indulgence of a sort Greene is the warrant for our label-
ing as sexual. ("It was like a young man's first successful experience
of sex.") But if the poem, as Greene declares, is deliberately misleading, then the emotion expressed in it—a virile contempt for the

timidity of man's exposure to sensation—is manufactured, while the author imaginably hugs himself in secret for his personal courage in facing up to a supreme challenge. Some of Greene's most serious work raises a comparable question about the relative degree of the challenging and the stagy. But what is to be noticed, in any event, is the sureness of Greene's adolescent instinct in seeking to get beyond boredom by contriving the sense of terror. The boy's flirtation with suicide, as a device for acquiring a sense of vitality, provides a sort of précis of some of Greene's later plots; and it is a dubious but real-life parallel to Camus's *The Myth of Sisyphus*, wherein, as we have seen, Camus discovers the terms for living by examining the case for self-slaughter. The interplay of the suicidal and the life-affirming would be for Greene, no less than for Camus, a central and representative motif: between Camus and Greene we observe a number of parallels that change eventually into a sort of implicit debate.

Terror was one way to conquer boredom. Another intimately related way, which Greene had already hit upon, was submission to the shock of evil. It was in part a vicarious experience, and it began during his fourteenth year when he first read Marjorie Bowen's melodramatic historical novel, *The Viper of Milan*. Greene's favorite book theretofore had been that splendid adventure story, H. Rider Haggard's *King Solomon's Mines;* but with the characters of Haggard young Greene could not, as the saying goes, "identify." He felt them as too simply good; they seemed to him unreal. But he could easily recognize the treacherous della Scala in *The Viper of Milan*, and the handsome Visconti with "his genius for evil." He knew Visconti in his own English neighborhood:

> His name was Carter. He exercised terror from a distance like a snowcloud over the young fields. Goodness has only once found a perfect incarnation in a human body and never will again, but evil can always find a home there. *Human nature is not black and white but black and grey.* [Italics added.] I read all that in *The Viper of Milan* and I looked round and I saw that it was so.[3]

"Perfect evil walking the world where perfect good can never walk again": this was both the lesson of *The Viper of Milan* and the subject decided upon by the aspiring novelist. For Miss Bowen had also decided the boy's future career for him: he would write fiction.

But in trying to assess Greene's developing religious sensibility, we must take note of the crucial remark that concludes the essay I have quoted from. "Religion might later explain it to me in other terms, but the pattern was already there." Religion came later, to supply terms for explaining an impression of human nature and experience that had long before taken possession of Greene's imagination. Why Greene was seized so early by just such a sinister impression is beyond our speculations here. But Greene's fiction, in any event, is not applied Catholicism; it is absorbed Catholicism, and the process and amount of absorption are fascinating to watch. Greene does not write from within the familiar, the always known interior of Catholic Christian doctrine; he writes from a peculiar vision of life which—when given intellectual content by the vocabulary of Catholicism—always appears as something more agitated, almost, as it were, more important than Catholicism is for those who are Catholics by inheritance. This is not merely to say that Greene is a religious convert; it is to say that the religion to which he was converted was deeply modified by the personal experiences that flanked the conversion: direct and personal responses that came before and after, responses to life that were in fact responses to death and to evil—acknowledgments of the invigorating horror.

Perhaps the best adjective to describe Greene's primary and pre-religious impulse is "Conradian." There is, indeed, a striking "Conrad aspect" to Graham Greene, though it is not easy to define it with precision; it is a parallel or a tangent, and only occasionally a specific influence. Conrad's swelling Latinisms and his large translucent comments on human destiny find little echo in Greene's swift and nerve-racked paragraphs; but subjects and themes from the best of Conrad find their way into Greene's work. *It's a Battle-field* (1934) is indebted to Conrad's *The Secret Agent* for its portrayal of the London police official just back from the colonies, and for its ironic account of violence and confusion in the great metropolis. Both writers share a taste for the exotic, for wandering amid the uncharted sections of the earth; Greene quotes Conrad appropriately, at the outset of *Journey Without Maps*, to formulate his sense of the Liberian adventure by allusions to the heart of darkness; and in dealing with the English scene, Greene, like Conrad, sometimes looks upon it with the curious glance of the traveler returned from afar. In Greene, too, we find that alternation of skepticism and faith that animated Conrad's stories; and characters —especially wicked characters—whose energy is created by a sort of purity in their evil intention: the boy, Pinkie, in *Brighton Rock* reveals an intense austerity in his satanism that is a recognizable inheritance from Mr. Jones in *Victory*. Greene has written about Mr. Jones, and about Conrad in general; it was perhaps in Conrad (again, in *Victory*, and the reflections of Axel Hyst) that Greene found the most usable dramatic version of the idea that Greene has often emphasized—the idea that pity is a disguised form of contempt and a dangerous human weakness. Perhaps the main parallel between the two novelists, however, is in their image of persons who feel themselves psychically nonexistent, who flirt with death and horror in order to come alive. Conrad has bequeathed this theme, of course, to an entire generation. "How to be! *Ach!* How to be!" Stein exclaims to Marlow in *Lord Jim*. "The way is to the destructive element submit yourself, and with the exertions of your hands and feet in the deep deep sea keep you up." That is, the way Francis Andrews and Oliver Chant arrive at "being" in *The Man Within* and *The Name of Action;* and it seems to be the notion behind Greene's trips to Liberia, to the awful discomforts of Tabasco, to the battlefields of Indochina.

But if Conrad helped to supply a dramatic structure, it was in Henry James that the apprentice writer found the most compelling portrait of evil. The James aspect of Greene is so pronounced that it extends to the slightest verbal trifles. The narrator of *The Quiet American*, for example, awaits probable death by gunfire in a paraphrase of James's much-quoted dying remark: "Now it comes. . . . I awaited, with a sense of exhilaration, the permanent thing." [4] And even while charging James's play *The Other House* with the capital offense of incompetence, as he has done in one of his five essays on James, Greene is seduced into some Jamesian syntax: "It was just the sense of the abyss that he failed on those flat boards ever to convey." Greene has evidently studied to excellent effect James's "dramatic" or "scenic" theory of narration— his scrupulous concentration on the action, his technique of foreshortening and compressing, his method of alternating the scene and the "interval." But what Greene has found overwhelming in James—whom he has called "as solitary in the history of the novel as Shakespeare in the history of poetry"—is this: "a sense of evil religious in its intensity"; and "a passionate distrust in human nature."

Behind so selective a view of James, there lurks not only Greene's extraordinary hospitality to the evil element, but also his assumption about American literature—that the best of it was the product of a nerve-end Calvinism, wherein the sense of goodness is swallowed up altogether in the consciousness of evil. That is just what we often feel about Greene's own fiction, and the question of accuracy arises when Greene goes on to say that in James's novels "the rage of personality is all the devil's," and that Milly Theale's "courage has not the supernatural support which holds Kate Croy and Charlotte Stant in a strong coil." It is the Kate Croys who interest Greene more, in any case, and he regards them as James's great creations—demon-driven egotists who include Gilbert Osmond and Mme. Merle and (to me astonishingly) Mme. de Vionnet. But the essential form of evil in James has been detected by Greene with exactness: James's "main fantasy," he has written, was "the idea of treachery." It is because Greene holds so passionately to the same ancient conviction—that treachery is the most awful of human sins—that he could see the theme at once in James. And it was Greene's obsession with the act of betrayal that led him to the archetypal story that he has been rewriting, with endless variations, since *The Man Within:* the story of Holy Week, the story of betrayal and sacrifice that, for Greene, is primarily the outrageously puzzling story of Judas Iscariot. That story, too, like the terms of Christian religion, came later and served to explain—by virtue of being the supreme instance of its kind—the pattern of human conduct already discovered.

As Greene came to the religious account, propelled by his personal intensities, so he came to the sense of good only under the impetus of his sense of evil. Heaven was a scanty inference from hell.

One began to believe in heaven because one believed in hell, but for a long while it was only hell one could picture with a certain intimacy. . . . One began [later] to have a dim conception of the appalling mysteries of love moving through a ravaged world. . . .[5]

"Of course there's Hell," the Boy says with scornful assurance in *Brighton Rock*. "And Heaven too," the girl adds anxiously; "Oh maybe," the Boy replies, "maybe." Lines like these show that it was the consciousness of evil and hell and death that brought Greene to life, that aroused him from his congenital boredom. The alternative consciousness, for Greene, is occasional and dim; it is of a grayness through which white may be faintly guessed at. But the stimulation of the darker sensibility did carry Greene over the threshold, into his own area of vitality—that dangerous ground beyond boredom, between the actual horror and the possible glory.

THE DESTRUCTIVE ELEMENT

Greene's adolescent experiences and his reading provided him with the basic materials and patterns for most of his fiction. One later experience seems, in retrospect, to have settled things once and for all—the Liberian journey in 1935. But by that time Greene had graduated from Oxford, had flirted briefly with communism, had worked as a newspaper reporter, and had joined the Roman Catholic Church—"convinced," as he wrote later, "by specific arguments in the probability of its creed." He had also published six works of fiction, along with the little volume of verses.[6] The importance for Greene of the Liberian journey, as we shall see, was due to the critical point at which he had by then arrived as a narrative artist.

In the most provocative and memorable of Greene's apprentice work—in *The Man Within*, *The Name of Action*, and (especially) *England Made Me*—the problem of the action, as against the dilemmas contrived by the plots, is the problem of sheer existence. It is the question posed to Conrad's Marlow by Stein—"How to be?" This was exactly the question confronted unsuccessfully, as we recall, by so many of Moravia's characters from *The Time of Indifference* onward; and it is one of the key mysteries faced up to by second-generation fiction in general. It is by no means a sudden or a novel mystery; Continental European literature in the nineteenth century reflected repeatedly the wearing struggle against ennui and the sense of nothingness; and, to pick a single major novel, the alternation of vitality and collapse, of the nourishing and the withering, was the mainspring of *The Charterhouse of Parma* more than a century ago. But Moravia, Camus, Malraux, and others testify, along with Graham Greene, that the effort to come into felt life is somehow more necessary, urgent and radical in our time—a time when the opposite inclination, the radical bias toward death, has become almost equally vehement.

In *The Man Within*, Francis Andrews—a young man who falls among smugglers and then betrays them—is bitterly conscious that "there was nothing in him but negatives. . . . How could any one believe in him if he did not even exist?" Andrews' particular trouble is a self-draining reverence for his dead father—a note generalized at the outset when Andrews, frightened and hurt, stumbles into a lonely cottage dominated by the candlelit coffin containing the corpse of the girl Elizabeth's late guardian. In *England Made Me*, Anthony Farrant's slenderness of spirit is also related to his lost boyhood and parental power, but here the symptom is rather a "deep nihilism," a shabbily elegant hopelessness. Anthony is indifferent: in the large and complex French and Italian meaning of that word—in the meaning carried by Moravia's title *Gli Indifferenti*. Like Moravia's Michele, Anthony is quite unable—though unlike Michele he is bereft even of the desire—to "galvanize his dead spirit into life." "I haven't a future, Kate," he tells his twin sister with a kind of flourish. "You know that as well as I do. . . . I haven't a future." If Anthony resembles Michele, the hero of *The Name of Action* is first cousin to Claude Vannec in Malraux's *The Royal Way*. For Oliver Chant also enters deliberately onto the field of danger, motivated by a profound distaste for the empty surfaces of civilized society and stirred into being by the thought that he may get himself killed.

All three of these heroes confront varieties of the destructive element. The element submitted to by Chant is the totalitarian authority of Demassener, the dictator of a small European buffer state. Chant comes there bringing his wealth, his idealism, and his boredom, on an ill-conceived mission to overthrow Demassener by force. The effort is nominally successful; but Chant is awakened to the complexities of power, to the blackness and grayness discoverable on both sides of the conflict. By thinking too precisely on the event, Chant loses for his mission "the name of action"; and all his efforts, at the end, are to rescue Demassener and get him safely out of the country. Francis Andrews likewise achieves a modest portion of identity and is reconciled to the angry man within him—when he exposes himself to destruction by his former colleagues. It is the girl, Elizabeth, who is in fact destroyed; and Andrews' crowning gesture is to give himself up to the police for a crime he has not committed, but for which he is, in a deeper sense, responsible; he thus finds humanity through the gratuitous assumption of guilt, like Spina in Silone's *The Seed Beneath the Snow*. Of Greene's three protagonists in these early novels, only Anthony Farrant fails completely to keep himself up in the deep, deep sea by the exertion of his hands (to reorganize Stein's Teutonic syntax); and it is singularly appropriate that Anthony should sink to his death, an assassin's victim, in the icy waters off a Stockholm pier.

If the sense of terror is what may bring a man to life, it is love— of a rather special order—that can fulfill him. The element of human love was to have a strange career indeed in Greene's mature fiction; and even in these earliest works, there is a curious extrahuman aura about it. The energy that might have warmed Anthony Farrant into durable being was his sister's obscurely incestuous—almost, one feels, demonic—love and need for him. The energy that does redeem Francis Andrews is the love of Elizabeth, which combines with the stimulus of danger to give him a glimpse of the ultimate *sources* of existence. His awakening is thus vaguely religious and takes the form of a charitable love transcending (or, in what would be a typical Greene pattern, replacing) the purely erotic—a suggestive contrast to the failure of Carla, in Moravia's *The Time of Indifference*, who reaches for existence precisely through sheerly sexual experience, and so reaches in vain. When Andrews turns on Elizabeth for not yielding to him before marriage, she replies:

> "You can't understand. It's not what you call respectability. It's a belief in God. I can't alter that for you. I'd leave you first."
> "What has He done for you?"
> Her candor was evident to him in the manner in which she met his challenge. She did not sweep it aside in a rush of words as some pious women might have done. She was silent, seeking an an-

swer . . . and at last with a faint note of apology she brought out the brief reply, "I am alive."

As early as *The Man Within*, the religious sense is dissociated from, is set over against, the moralistic and the pious: everything that a young rebel in the nineteen twenties would scorn as Victorian. And the Jamesian hesitancy of dialogue there is not coincidental; it is in a passage on James that Greene made his most unequivocal statement about the dependence of the feeling of existence upon the authentically religious consciousness. As the quotation will show, Elizabeth's remark—"I am alive"—does not mean only that God created her; it means that her awareness of being alive is rooted in her belief in God. Here is the passage, from a review by Greene of Mauriac's *La Pharisienne:*

> . . . With the death of James the religious sense was lost to the English novel, and with the religious sense went the sense of the importance of the human act. It was as if the world of fiction had lost a dimension: the characters of such distinguished writers as Mrs. Virginia Woolf and Mr. E. M. Forster wandered like cardboard symbols through a world that was paper-thin. Even in one of the most materialistic of our great novelists—in Trollope—we are aware of another world against which the actions of the characters are thrown into relief. The ungainly clergyman picking his blackbooted way through the mud, handling so awkwardly his umbrella, speaking of his miserable income and stumbling through a proposal of marriage, *exists* [italics added] in a way that Mrs. Woolf's Mr. Ramsay never does, because we are aware that he exists not only to the woman he is addressing but also in a God's eye. His unimportance in the world of the senses is only matched by his enormous importance in another world.[7]

Several kinds of quarrels could be started over those sentences: over the particular literary judgments handed down, and over the logic from which the judgments derive. But the general contention, it seems to me, makes a good deal of sense; and the implicit attribution to Henry James is valid. Not enough has been made of James's allusion in *Notes of a Son and Brother* to an order of goodness and beauty that is other than—and hence, James hints, a measure of—any order the visible world can show. We note, too, that not only persons but places as well—not only characters but the world through which they wander—gain existence and importance (for Greene) by means of the religious perspective. The passage is highly relevant also to any appraisal of the typical Greene "hero"— or antihero, or, as some would say, nonhero. It is as though Greene, by a religious twist which sometimes becomes simply a religious trick, can detect and expose even in (say) the seamier sections of Brighton and in a vicious adolescent some of the stature we associate with the classical heroic figure: "his unimportance in the world of the senses . . . matched by his enormous importance in another world." Greene, as always, carries things to extremes; but his is a major contribution to the whole difficult question of the heroic image in our tattered and democratic times, a question that is by no means simply literary.

The danger and the love that animate Andrews in *The Man Within* culminate thus in a religious insight which liberates him at last from the restrictive memory of his father. He has to absorb the force of Elizabeth's reply when—after he has blamed all his inadequacies on his parents: "It's not a man's fault. . . . It's all in the way he was born. My father and mother made me"—she gently answers: "You always seem to leave out God." But to leave out God, it is now time to admit very bluntly, is just what so many modern novelists and critics are above all things anxious to do— and not without good reason. The religious sense, one has heard it well argued, has the opposite effect of the one Greene claims for it; it tends in our day to reduce existence rather than to enhance it. The complaint (made by persons as religiously sensitive as Allen Tate) about religious literature in the twentieth century is in great part legitimate: namely, that its concern with grace has quite blotted out its vision of nature; that, in the theological perspective, the common inclinations of men appear dim or ugly, and their suffering insignificant. This is the whole meaning of the implausible figure of the priest, Paneloux, in Camus's *The Plague*, preaching to the afflicted congregation of Oran that human health and happiness are not items to be valued.

Greene is far too canny a novelist to link together by fiat religion and the sense of life. How little he does so may be seen from his comment on Conrad—a comment that compares Conrad with James under this head, and reverses the proposition in the passage about James quoted from above.

James spent his life working towards and round the Catholic Church, fascinated and repelled and absorbent; Conrad was born a Catholic and ended—formally—in consecrated ground, but all he retained of Catholicism was the ironic sense of an omniscience and of *the final unimportance of human life under the watching eyes*. [Italics added.] [8]

Greene's fiction illustrates betimes this underhalf of the religious paradox: for it is a paradox, and a perfectly sound and traditional one, that human life is both infinitely important and infinitely unimportant from the divine standpoint. Greene can find value and meaning in the worst or slightest of places, by hinting at God's mysterious concern for human beings; but he also takes a disturbing pleasure in so arranging matters in his plots that religious belief cannot help but oppose and diminish every normal and natural impulse; religion in Greene is frequently an insidious, a perverse, an exhausting and life-denying emotion. We recall the elderly Catholic ladies in *The Living Room*, whose psychic deathiness—rooted in a miserable fear of dying and disguised as religious piety—gives the play's title its hideous irony. More memorable still (to return to Greene's earlier work) is the figure of Minty, the soiled but oddly touching remittance man in *England Made Me*.

Minty is the counterpoise to the unimpassioned Anthony Farrant in that novel's enervating pattern of exiles, failures and wreckage. He is charged with an intense secret passion, but it consists in a loathing of things human and a hidden lust for things sacred. "Yes, it was ugly the human figure," Minty broods; and all its sweaty ugliness beats in his brain like a bird's heart. In a representative moment, Minty is seen sneaking toward the sacred as another man might furtively approach the pornographic: "A church claimed him. . . . It was Lutheran, of course, but it had the genuine air of plaster images, of ever-burning light, of sins forgiven. He looked this way and that, he bent his head and dived for the open door, with the caution and dry-mouthed excitement of a secret debauchee." Even inside the church, the human dimension of Christianity literally nauseates Minty. "To think that God himself had become man. Minty could not enter a church without the thought, which sickened him, which was more to him than the agony in the garden, the despair upon the cross." To find the full elaboration of the other side of the paradox, and the other side of Greene's deceptive coin, we must look—as, in the next section, we shall—at *The Power and the Glory*, and the celebration of the meanest of men as the image of God.

Anthony Farrant and Minty show an equal resistance to incarnation, to becoming a full-fledged human being; but the one fails to arrive at it from below, while the other detests it drearily from above. The one person in *England Made Me* who is piercingly alive is Anthony's tough-spirited sister Kate: whose first name, I suspect, is a reminiscence of Henry James's Miss Croy in *The Wings of the Dove*. Her hard vitality, in any case, is drawn from the same ominous source that Greene detects behind Kate Croy and behind all of James's truly vigorous characters. It is a source opposite to the one to which Elizabeth, in *The Man Within*, more faintly attributes her own existence: opposite yet oddly similar and nearly equal; a demonic power that manifests itself humanly in a driving egotism, all the more driving since exercised in the apparent interest of someone else. For what Greene was gradually, if confusedly, establishing in these early novels—and what, I trust, has been gradually established in these pages—is that the source of existence is two-fold: supernatural evil and supernatural good. Only persons who fall prey to one or the other really come alive; but those who do so are and have remained the privileged people in Greene's universe, the high society of the best and the worst. Greene, like the James he has described, has had difficulty galvanizing goodness into being, and when he has done so it is in the most improbable form. But the principle that has been at work from the beginning is confirmed explicitly in *The End of the Affair*, when Bendrix tells himself that it is the saints "who come alive. . . . They stand outside the plot, unconditioned by it. But we have to be pushed around. We have the obstinacy of non-existence." The same book takes as its motto a remark of Léon Bloy: "Man has places in his heart which do not exist, and into them enters suffering, in order that they may have existence." In the modern or ontological work of literature, it is *existence* rather than—as in classical literature—*wisdom* that is the reward of experience, the product of suffering, the fortune acquired either by the fortunate fall or the reluctant ascent.

I have been trying to make explicit certain ideas that were at most only fuzzily implicit in Greene's early novels; they are visible mainly in retrospect. It was the trip across Liberia in the year following the completion of *England Made Me*, a personal journey into the heart of darkness, that seems to have given Greene the full and final shape of the vision from which he would henceforth offer up his narrative impression of life. The Liberian adventure was the turning point in Greene's development, and the book he wrote about it—*Journey Without Maps* (1936)—is the pivotal item on the list of his writings. What Greene discovered in West Africa and his formulation of it serve to explain, in so far as such matters are ever explicable, the remarkable improvement in momentum and texture and dramatic focus from *England Made Me* to *Brighton Rock*, the first novel after the journey; and *Brighton Rock* in turn made artistically possible (as I shall suggest) its two excellent successors.

Greene went to Liberia as Henry James went to Europe and as Hawthorne, in his imagination, went back to the seventeenth century: in a moment of creative crisis, and in order to experience a richer reality, for artistic purposes, than the local or contemporary world seemed able to provide. He found in Liberia what James found in Europe: an atmosphere where (as Greene put it), "the sense of taste was finer, the sense of pleasure keener"; he found, too, what Hawthorne described in the second chapter of *The Scarlet Letter*—a place where (again, as Greene put it) "the sense of terror was deeper and purer." But the pleasure and the terror, profoundly interrelated for Greene, were not the product of civilized manners or an implacably moral culture. They were the gifts of the altogether primitive and childlike, seen through a haze of the highest romanticism; they were the immediate and childlike responses to the assaults of supernature.

The doomed responsive children of *Brighton Rock* were the first fruits of Greene's discovery; and, in fact, the trip across Liberia was consciously conceived by Greene as a return to a forgotten childhood. For Greene, as for many other writers, the process of self-renewal involves such a return, but in his case it took (and continues to take) the form of an invigorating journey back to hell. Greene's first remembered sensations, as he would later articulate them, were of the devilish impurity in the schoolboy world that surrounded him; and it should be said of Greene that he has never proved unfaithful to the initial hellish vision. Those who avert their eyes from it end up (he evidently believes) like Philip in the best of Greene's few effective short stories, "The Basement Room," written in the same year as *Journey Without Maps*. They end up in the "deep dilettante selfishness of age," the sterile nonexistence that Philip's betrayal of the butler in that story had ensured for him. Greene's fictional children, like Wordsworth's, are in a secret and usually declining communion with supernature; but in Greene the secret has become a frightful one. "Hell lay around him in his infancy," Greene remarks about Pinkie in *Brighton Rock*, and about his childhood fellows and himself in *The Lawless Roads*. As the vision of evil becomes crusted over with characteristically deadening maturity, the need becomes urgent to seek it out again by returning to the youthful terror. That is why Greene went to Liberia; but with the larger mission of rediscovering not only his own lost boyhood, but the lost childhood of the modern human race. He went to Africa driven by a "curiosity to discover . . . from what we have come, to recall at which point we went astray."

It is a commonplace that a man receives from any experience what his imagination and sensibility prepare him to receive. Another traveler might have found stray anthropological amusements in the jungle; still another might have found the whole business simply uncomfortable. Greene found it uncomfortable enough, appallingly and endlessly so; the destructive element was literally and physically present at every turn in the path and change in the weather. But he was prepared for an experience of considerably deeper psychological force; and it began for him at Mosambolahun, just across the Liberian border from Sierra Leone. Here his quest was first rewarded. He witnessed a devil dance, wherein the devil, played by the village blacksmith, was ceremoniously introduced by the tribal elders to a group of terrified children, the initiates of the day. It was not much of a dance, but Greene reacted at once to the potent ritualistic impulse behind it. It brought back an English village dance he had watched as a boy; and it made him feel strangely at home. "Here one was finding associations with a personal and a racial childhood, one was being scared by the same old witches." A boy screamed when the devil mouthed him; a girl danced "with the sad erotic infinite appeal of projecting buttocks and moving belly . . . like Europa before the bull." Neither of them knew that the devil was only the Mosambolahun blacksmith—a lazy and useless fellow—in disguise. The elders, who did of course know, could acknowledge the blacksmith without losing their faith in the dreadfulness he had practiced to represent.

What Greene realized then, and by means of several similar occasions later, was the real nature of the destructive element—the power to be submitted to, immersed in, along the way to being. It was the devil himself; and by recognizing him, Greene could also, at last, give expression to his own devil-infested childhood. What had been lost in the maturity of the West, he decided, was equally the children's right instinctive terror and the elders' unspoiled symbolic imagination. The devil dance, along with other terrors and fierce cruelties, both natural and human, led to a singularly acute sensation of pleasure; and both as a man and a writer, Greene came back alive from Liberia. In a coastal town, toward the end of the journey, he summarized his conclusions in a long postscript.

> This journey, if it had done nothing else, had reinforced a sense of disappointment with what man had made out of the primitive, what he had made out of childhood. Oh, one wanted to protest, one doesn't believe, of course, in "the visionary gleam," in the trailing glory, but there was something in that early terror and the bareness of one's needs, a harp strumming behind a hut, a witch on the nursery landing, a handful of kola nuts, a masked dancer, the poisoned flowers. The sense of taste was finer, the sense of pleasure keener, the sense of terror deeper and purer. It isn't a gain to have turned the witch or the masked dancer, the sense of supernatural evil, into the small human viciousness of the thin distinguished military grey head in Kensington Gardens with the soft lips and the eyes which dwelt on girls and boys of a certain age. . . . There was cruelty enough in the interior, but had we done wisely exchanging the supernatural cruelty for our own?

To return thus to hell was to return to life. And the climactic event of the entire journey was precisely that: the discovery of a wholly unexpected concern with being alive. It was the immediate result of a dangerous bout of malaria; but it was in fact the ultimate consequence of the experienced terror and pleasure, and of their supernatural sources. Seven days away from Grand Bassa on the coast, Greene came down with fever.

> [It] would not let me sleep at all, but by the early morning it was sweated out of me. My temperature was a long way below normal, but the worst boredom of the trek for the time being was over. I had made a discovery during the night which interested me. I had discovered in myslf a passionate interest in living. I had always assumed before, as a matter of course, that death was desirable.
>
> It seemed that night an important discovery. It was like a conversion, and I had never experienced a conversion before. (I had not been converted to a religious faith. I had been convinced by specific arguments in the probability of its creed.)

"The worst boredom of the trek was over"—dispersed by the horror; and Greene emerged converted, in as literal and actual a version as we may find of the underlying motion from death to life that typifies the progress of second generation figures. Greene himself, on his own evidence, would lapse frequently back into boredom, and the dose of danger and terror had to be repeated at regular intervals, but his conversion to an interest in life was sufficient to launch him on his most impressive creative phase. After *Journey Without Maps*, none of Greene's major characters (with the rule-proving exception of James Callifer in *The Potting Shed*) would suffer from the sense of nonexistence, even though several of them would feel, strongly, that death is desirable.

Christian doctrine, as it had done in the past, would come later and explain the pattern; but the pattern itself—so predoctrinal or sub-doctrinal as to be not only not Catholic but not even Christian—was provided by the personal experience. Returned to England, Greene could make out what he must go on to do as a novelist. He had to discover—or create—something equivalent to the Liberian interior: a universe of simplicity and passion where young boys might still scream and stiffen under the devil's muzzle, and young girls dance before evil with erotic innocence. If so pure a world were not visible upon the European scene, there was the next best thing. There was the seedy; for Liberia had also explained to Greene his congenital affection for the seedy, in both persons and places; "seediness represented a stage further back," closer to the primitive, something that had begun to go wrong but had only just begun and had not yet "reached so far away as the smart, the new, the chic, the cerebral." Greene set himself to explore the seediest setting he could find, uncovering within it aspects of the primitive and the horrifying not wholly lost. Greene, in short, began to write *Brighton Rock*.

THE "TRILOGY"

In Greene's early fiction, along with a definite but notably uneven development of style and vigor, there was an apparent failure to distinguish between various fictional genres. Even *Brighton Rock* betrays an initial confusion between what Greene calls an "entertainment" and what he finally offered as a tragedy; but here the confusion is unexpectedly exploited (as shall be seen) in the composition of an immensely impressive novel. The distinction of genres, in a somewhat Gallic manner, would become important for Greene, and in a sense the making of him; but prior to *Brighton Rock*, we observe an uncertainty of artistic purpose that led to an unstable treatment of the basic elements of fiction: setting, character and action. Part of the success of *Brighton Rock*, *The Power and the Glory*, and *The Heart of the Matter* is due to the preliminary sketching of elements in each of them—a process that, as it turned out, managed to release the special energy and "vision" that would characterize Greene as a writer of stature.

The settings of *The Power and the Glory* and *The Heart of the Matter*, for example, had already been explored by Greene personally and in two excellent travel books: *The Lawless Roads*, from which the whole passages are transcribed in the former; and *Journey Without Maps*, which concludes on the Gold Coast of poor Major Scobie. In the travel books, Greene's journalistic and photographic abilities exhausted themselves; and in the novels, consequently, physical settings could be managed so as to exude a meaning that transformed them into spiritual situations, into elaborated images of fate. Mexico, however discolored, is still Mexico in *The Lawless Roads;* in *The Power and the Glory*, the country has been reduced and reshaped to fit a particular action, of which indeed it contains the particular secret. Similarly, each one of these three novels has its correlative entertainment; a mystery story, in the popular sense, that functions ably as trial run for a mystery drama in a more ancient and theological sense. Here we touch the crucial distinction underlying the other distinctions, for the unsolvable mystery of the human condition, beyond or beneath any sociological or historical or psychological explanation thereof, has become Greene's obsessive subject. Raven, the killer in *A Gun for Sale* (1936), with his dumb conviction of injustice and his bleak yearning for a soul he can trust, is a purely human cartoon for the metaphysical monster, Pinkie, the killer of *Brighton Rock* (1938). In *The Confidential Agent* (1939), the weary and frightened fidelity to his mission of the Spanish agent, D., is a sketchy and political version of the behavior of the nameless Mexican priest, the agent of God, on his exclusively religious mission in *The Power and the Glory*, a year later. And *The Ministry of Fear* (1943), the most skillful of the entertainments and a very good story indeed, dramatizes what Greene regards as the most dangerous of human emotions—pity—the fatal flaw which would destroy Major Scobie in *The Heart of the Matter* (1948), but which is significantly contrasted in that novel with its real opposite, the primary attribute of God: mercy.

It can be said about the earlier novels, then, that the confusion of purpose and the blurry handling of the elements are rooted in a failure to disentangle the *mystery* of the mystery, to separate it out from the contingencies of melodrama and the staged surprises of the brain-twister. The disentanglement followed, as it seems, upon the Liberian experience examined above; for after that, the plot and the action of Greene's novels are increasingly given their meaning by the religious motif—a motif which, since it cannot always be called Christian, can scarcely be always called Catholic; a sort of shocked intuition of supernature. It is when the religious motif takes charge that Greene's resources—including his nervous, highly pressured style, and his uncommon talent for narrative—become ordered and controlled, and his artistic power fulfills itself.[9] *The Man Within* has an appealing youthfulness of viewpoint; but the religious element remains shadowy and generalized, and the whole story wobbles uneasily to (in context) a rather pointless climax. The real source of complexity in human events, as Greene would eventually see it, is not detected in *The Name of Action*, though that is what the novel is about; as a result, we are introduced here only to shapeless movements in a nightmare world. And in *England Made Me*, which is otherwise a genuine achievement, Greene so far misunderstood himself as to insert stream-of-consciousness meditations ill-advisedly but patently borrowed from James Joyce. Nothing could be further from Greene's intentions than those of Joyce—which achieve the careful rendering of the behavior of the mind, with the ultimate aim of celebrating the shaping power of art, the "stasis" that imposes value and meaning upon the chaos of mental experience. Greene has never reverted to the Joycean technique.[10] What Greene has envisaged and what he has become especially concerned with are better implied in the title of still another early book, *It's a Battlefield:* the human scene now described as a battlefield between transcendent warring forces. And in *Brighton Rock*, the metaphor of the battlefield is dominant: "It lay there always, the ravaged and disputed territory between the two eternities."

The three novels published between 1938 and 1948 are sometimes taken together as a trilogy; but the word should be enclosed in quotation marks, for the trilogic pattern, if it existed in Greene's awareness, took hold only belatedly. But it is worth juxtaposing the three books, to observe several striking aspects of Greene. All three show his affection for the primitive; like Silone, Greene often turns away from the relatively civilized to inspect human life in its cruder and more exposed conditions: in a dark corner of Brighton, the jungles and prisons of Tabasco, the coast of West Africa—all places where, as Scobie tells himself in *The Heart of the Matter*, "human nature hasn't had time to disguise itself"; places where there openly flourished "the injustices, the cruelties, the meanness that elsewhere people so cleverly hushed up." In these primitive scenes, we encounter the dramatis personae of Greene's recurring drama and of his troubled universe: the murderer, the priest, and the policeman, who are the heroes respectively of the three books. All three figures, in different embodiments, appear in all three novels; and they tend more and more to resemble each other. The murderer, Pinkie, is knowingly a hideously inverted priest; the policeman, Scobie, becomes involved with crime and criminals; the officer in *The Power and the Glory* has "something of a priest in his intent observant walk," while the priest in turn has queer points of resemblance with the Yankee killer whose photograph faces his in the police station. The three figures represent, of course, the shifting and interwoven attributes of the Greenean man: a being capable of imitating both Christ and Judas; a person who is at once the pursuer and the man pursued; a creature with the splendid potentiality either of damnation or salvation. The actualities of their fate exhaust, apparently, the major possibilities. If one can be sure of anything in the real world or in Greene's world, Pinkie Brown is damned—it is his special mode of triumph; the Mexican priest is saved—sainthood gleams at last through his bloodshot eyes; and the final end of Major Scobie is what is precisely in doubt, as difficult to determine as his own ambiguous last words, "Dear God, I love. . . ." Pinkie is a proud citizen of hell; Scobie's suffering is that of a man in purgatory; and the laughter in *The Power and the Glory* celebrates, perhaps, the entrance of a soul into paradise. The three careers are presented to us in three very different kinds of fiction: *Brighton Rock* just manages to escape melodrama and becomes a work *sui generis; The Power and the Glory* is, in its way, a divine comedy; and *The Heart of the Matter* is a tragedy in the classical tradition. These novels are, respectively, Greene's most strenuous, his most satisfying, and, artistically, his most assured.

Brighton Rock in particular is the most harrowing of Greene's stories about children; and Pinkie, the seventeen-year-old gangster (he is usually referred to simply as "the Boy") is "the most driven and 'damned' " of all Greene's characters, to quote his own words about the evil forces in that other fearful tale about children, James's *The Turn of the Screw*. There is, to be sure, a superficial movement in the novel from death to life: the narrative begins with the revenge-murder by Brighton race-track hoodlums of Hale, the man who is working a publicity stunt for a newspaper among the holiday crowds; and it closes with the pregnancy of Rose, the wan underage wife whom Hale's killer, Pinkie, has been forced for protection to marry. So far, there is a momentary likeness to Moravia's *Woman of Rome*, which similarly concludes with the heroine's pregnancy by a now dead murderer. Moravia's novel quite definitely suggests the painful victory of life over death. But Greene's artistic and intellectual purposes are almost always dialectically opposite to those of Moravia; and in *Brighton Rock*, not only is the death legally avenged, the birth itself will be altogether darkened by Rose's discovery of Pinkie's true feeling about her—via the "loving message" he has recorded by phonograph, and which, "the worst horror of all," she is on her way to hear as the story ends: "God damn you, you little bitch, why can't you go back home for ever and let me be?" [11] The implied denouement in *Brighton Rock* is as disagreeable as anything in modern fiction. But *Brighton Rock* is deliberately pitiless, and partly because it aims, by moving beyond human pity, to evoke the far faint light of an incomprehensible divine mercy.

Part of the disaster that threatens in this pitiless book is artistic: a threat to the shape and character of the book itself. Greene evidently began it as an "entertainment," and the first American edition announced itself as such. He began it, that is, as a melodrama of murder and detection in which contingency and coincidence would be allowed free play, the chase be exciting for its own sake, and with a larger and more kindly emphasis than the novel eventually allowed on Ida Arnold, the London lady of easy virtue who had known Hale in his last frightened hours and who sets herself to discover the criminal, an aim she formidably succeeds in. But evil has always stimulated Greene a good deal more than the righting of wrongs; and in this case, the figure and story of Pinkie Brown (unlike those of Raven in *A Gun for Sale*, of which *Brighton Rock* would otherwise have been a repetition) expanded in Greene's imagination until a recognizable tragedy took its place in the book alongside the well-made entertainment. The entertainment is Ida's; it begins with the first sentence ("Hale knew, before he had been in Brighton three hours, that they meant to murder him"), and ends with the police closing in on the culprit. The tragedy is Pinkie's; *it* begins more subtly in the atmosphere of the place (implied by the adjectives used for the jostling crowds: "bewildered," "determined," "cramped," "closed," "weary"); and its action is defined in advance by the book's motto, from *The Witch of Edmonton*, with overtones of *Macbeth:* "This were a fine reign:/To do ill and not hear of it again." In the open world of the entertainment, happenstances accumulate; but in the tragedy there is no space for contingency, no time for the accidental. Evil is fertile and is always heard from again; every move Pinkie makes—from the killing of Hale, through the further necessitated murders and the detested courtship and marriage, to the climax in which, like Oedipus, he blinds himself (with vitriol)—has a convulsive inevitability, the more dreadful since it seems rooted neither in private temperament nor in social background. It derives from the inexplicable power of evil, one of the two things that Pinkie believes in: *"Credo in unum Satanum."* *Brighton Rock* confirms Greene's statement in the preface to a book about him by the French critic, Paul Rostenne, that he has no a priori edifying purpose in writing his novels, but is carried along rather by the unpredictable energies of his characters. As Pinkie's perils increase and his ambitions enlarge, the very design of the book shifts and re-forms.

Brighton Rock could have been a kind of disaster, two different books, between the same covers only by mistake. But it emerges as an original and striking work: for the relation between the detective story and the tragedy expresses exactly what *Brighton Rock* is finally all about. It is a relation between modes of narrative discourse that reflects a relation between two kinds or levels of reality: a relation between incommensurable and hostile forces; between incompatible worlds; between the moral world of right and wrong, to which Ida constantly and confidently appeals, and the theological world of good and evil inhabited by Pinkie and Rose. It is, in short, the relation Greene had formulated for himself in Liberia, between the "sinless empty graceless chromium world" of modern Western urban civilization and the supernaturally infested jungle with its purer terrors and its keener pleasures. The abrupt superiority of *Brighton Rock* to anything Greene had yet written comes from the fact that for the first time he had separated the mystery from the mystery and confronted the one with the other.

Here, of course, the confrontation takes the form of deadly warfare: "She [Ida] stared out over the red and green lights, the heavy traffic of her battlefield, laying her plans, marshalling her cannon fodder." That sense of the universal drama is both ancient and modern; for *Brighton Rock*, to put the case in perhaps exaggerated and misleading theological terms, belongs with the early and late medieval tradition, the tradition now again in fashion: the tradition of Tertullian and the dark, negative, and incorrigibly paradoxical theology wherein everything supernatural stands in implacable hostility over against everything natural and human; and for the most part, vice versa. This is the view Albert Camus has identified and attacked as *the* Christian tradition.[12] But in another tradition, in so-called theocentric humanism, there are intermediate ends, intermediate goods, and intermediate explanations: because there is an intermediate figure, the God-man, Christ, who reconciles the realms and makes sense out of human history. But about Pinkie and his small explosive world, there is nothing intermediate—here everything is sudden and ultimate.[13] Pinkie has no great involvement with the things of this world, with money or with sexual love or even with Brighton. His Brighton is not a town or a "background" but a Fury-driven situation; and he is involved immediately with evil and catastrophe.

He is deeply implicated, too, of course, with good—with the forlorn waitress Rose, who has just enough information about Hale's murder to make Pinkie decide savagely to marry her in order to keep her quiet; and who is as doomed to salvation (that is how Greene prefers to describe it) as Pinkie is to damnation. He sees her as his necessary counterpart. "What was most evil in him needed her; it couldn't get along without her goodness. . . . Again he got the sense that she completed him." Their world, too, is a battlefield, but with a difference:

> Good and evil lived together in the same country, spoke the same language, came together like old friends, feeling the same completion, touching hands beside the iron bedstead. . . . [Their] world lay there always, the ravaged and disputed territory between two eternities. They faced each other as it were from opposing territories, but like troops at Christmas time they fraternised.[14]

In *Brighton Rock*, the theme of companionship, which takes so many forms in the fiction of the second generation, appears as the reluctant fellowship between good and evil and is symbolized in the illegal marriage of Pinkie and Rose and the uncertain sexual union of the two virgins on their wedding night. There, touching hands beside the iron bedstead, they peer out together at the "glare and open world," the utterly alien world of Ida Arnold. "She was as far from either of them as she was from Hell—or Heaven."

In Ida's world, the religious impulse is softened into a comfortable moralism; but in Pinkie's world, the human impulse shrivels and looks ugly. Pinkie sees only extreme alternatives—not even sacred and profane love, for example, but the supernatural and the obscene. Normal love is reduced to the pornographic, and is opposed only by fidelity to supernature; here, as in *England Made Me*, religion becomes a substitute for or even a heightened form of pornography. Pinkie quotes venomously from the cheap literature, "the kind you buy under the counter. Spicer used to get them. About girls being beaten." But in choosing the alternative, in submitting to the super-natural, Pinkie attaches himself primarily to supernatural evil. *"Credo in unum Satanum"* is the violent admission elicited on the same page by the outburst against pornography; and though he tells Rose scornfully, "Of course there's Hell," about heaven he can only say "Maybe."

As Pinkie pursues his dream of damnation, the tragic dimension of *Brighton Rock* turns into a sort of saint's life in reverse. The seven sections of the book dramatize one by one an inversion of all or most of the seven sacraments, dramatize what we might call the seven deadly sacraments: [15] as Pinkie is confirmed in the habit of murder ("Hell lay about him in his infancy. He was ready for more deaths"), is ordained as a priest of his satanic church ("When I was a kid, I swore I'd be a priest. . . . What's wrong with being a priest? They know what's what"), performs the act of matrimony (which here is a mortal sin), and receives the vitriolic unction in the moment of his death. The entire reversal accomplished in *Brighton Rock*, haphazard though it is, manages to dignify the repellent protagonist on the principle indicated to Rose, at the very end, by the sniffling old priest: *Corruptio optimi est pessima.* The worst is the corruption of the best; only the potentially very good can become so very evil, and only the sacraments that save can so effectively become the sacraments that blast.

Despite its singularly uninviting character, accordingly, the nar-row and oppressive world of Pinkie Brown is clearly to be honored —in the terms of the novel—over the spiritual bourgeoisie of Ida Arnold. Her world, for all its robust good humor, is increasingly represented as sterile, and she as a hollow, heartless menace. Ida, with her big breasts and her warm enveloping body, remains child-less; it is the angular, nearly sexless Rose who conceives at once, after a single sexual venture. And the final worldly victory of Ida, her destruction of Pinkie, coincides with a hidden defeat of her own world: a repudiation of it, accomplished relentlessly by the rhetoric of the book. That rhetoric aims at separating out and then destroy-ing the moral domain, in the name of the theological; the conven-tional values of right and wrong are lured into prominence and then annihilated. This is done by a series of seeming contradictions that sometimes appear strained and perverse, but often make arrest-ing similes. A remark about Pinkie—"his virginity straightened in him like sex"—aptly suggests the colliding opposites that animate his experience. Oxymorons are employed in the account of Ida and her behavior, and with the intention of transforming or "transvaluat-ing" our judgment of her. When allusion is made to Ida's "remorse-less optimism" or her "merciless compassion," the aim is to negate the familiar human attributes—in this case, cheerfulness and pity—by stressing their remoteness from the religious virtues: in this case, penitent humility and mercy. The adjective, from its higher plane, denies all value to the nouns on their lower human level. And the whole process culminates in the epilogue when the priest, coughing and whistling through the grille in that unattractive and seedy way Greene's priests almost always have, says to Rose about Pinkie—destroyed now by the ferocious pity of Ida Arnold—that no human being can conceive "the appalling strangeness of the mercy of God."

About this verbal technique, which may best be defined as a technique of befuddlement and concerning which one has the un-easy suspicion of mere cleverness, there will be more to say. Mean-while, it is to be noted that as the detective story and the tragedy intertwine in *Brighton Rock*, we find ourselves in a universe wherein seeming opposites—good and evil—become closely allied, and seem-ing likenesses—the good and the right—are totally opposed. These paradoxes, too, are incarnate in the central figure. Pinkie, Greene's first memorable image of the character he had so cherished as a boy in *The Viper of Milan*—"perfect evil walking the world where per-fect good can never walk again"—is a replica of Judas who none the less has faint confusing echoes about him of the perfectly good, of

Christ. He is the worst *only* by virtue of being the corruption of the best. And so, when his unstable associate Cubitt is talking about him to Ida and when Cubitt denies being a friend of his—" 'You a friend of Pinkie's?' Ida Arnold asked. 'Christ, no,' Cubitt said and took some more whiskey"—there is the fleeting whisper of a memory: "A court-yard, a sewing wench beside the fire, the cock crowing." And Cubitt goes on to deny him thrice.

On numerous occasions Greene has quoted the lines from AE's poem, "Germinal":

> In ancient shadows and twilights
>   Where childhood had strayed,
> The world's great sorrows were born
>   And its heroes were made.
> In the lost boyhood of Judas
>   Christ was betrayed.

It is not only the realm of supernatural good and its unlikely representative Rose which are betrayed by the lost boyhood of this demonic Judas; it is also the flickers of the Christ in himself. It is within such a context and by such insinuations that Greene earns Pinkie the right to be regarded, as though reflected in a crazy-mirror on Brighton pier, as an image of the tragic hero. There can be no doubt, finally, about the damnation of Pinkie Brown: except the enormous doubt that, according to Greene, must attend our every human judgment and prediction.

The motto of *The Power and the Glory* is from Dryden: "Th' inclosure narrow'd; the sagacious power/Of hounds and death drew nearer every hour." The lines could apply to *Brighton Rock* and with a little stretching to *The Man Within*, as well as to most of Greene's entertainments; they summarize Greene's settled view of human experience. But they are peculiarly appropriate to *The Power and the Glory*, which is, one could say, Greene's most peculiarly appropriate novel and which comprises the adventures of a hunted man—the last Catholic priest in a totalitarian Mexican state—whom the hounds of power catch up with and to whom death does come by a firing squad. There is no complication of genres here: the novel has a single hero and a single action—and both are strik-

ingly representative of the special kind of hero and heroic adventure that characterize the fiction of the second generation.

According to the laws of the godless Mexican state, the priest is
an outlaw simply because he carries on his priestly duties; but he
has also broken the laws of his Church. He is a rogue, a *pícaro*, in
several kinds of ways; his contradictory character includes much of
the comical unpredictability of the traditional *pícaro;* and the narrative Greene has written about him is perhaps the most patently
picaresque of any we are considering—the lively story of the rogue
on his travels, or better, on his undignified flights from and toward
the forces of destruction. In no other novel of our time, moreover,
are the paradoxes of sainthood more expertly handled. The priest—
who is a slovenly drunkard and the father of a devilish little child
who giggles a good deal and is often helplessly weak at the knees—
is also a potential, perhaps finally an actual saint. He feels at the end
that he has failed: "It seemed to him, at that moment, that it would
have been quite easy to have been a saint. . . . He felt like someone
who has missed happiness at an appointed place." But other evidence throughout the book suggests that all unwittingly he had kept
his appointment with beatitude. *The Power and the Glory* stands
beside Silone's *Bread and Wine*. And the so-called "whiskey-priest,"
disguised as a layman and fumbling his way toward disaster, is, if
not the twin, at least a brother of Pietro Spina, a layman (a revolutionist) disguised as a priest, and similarly the last lonely witness to
truth in his own neighborhood, who is equally pursued by the forces
of oppression and who is likewise the attractive, incompetent, and
saintly source of damage and of death to almost everyone involved
with him. These two novels give the most revealing account in
second generation fiction of the hero as outlaw, fleeing and transcending the various forms that power currently assumes.

In terms of Greene's artistic and intellectual development, however, another motto, in place of Dryden's, might be drawn from the
book itself: when the priest, heading bumpily into the hills of
Tabasco on mule-back, daydreams in the imagery of a "simplified
mythology"—"Michael dressed in armour slew the dragon, and the
angels fell through space like comets with beautiful streaming hair
because they were jealous, so one of the Fathers had said, of what
God intended for men—the enormous privilege of life—this life."

This life. In this novel, by a refreshing contrast with *England Made Me* and *Brighton Rock*, the religious impulse no longer denigrates and undermines the human but serves rather to find in it or to introduce into it a kind of beauty and a kind of goodness. "I tell you that heaven is here," the priest cries out to the vacant-faced peasants gathered dumbly in a hut on the mountainside at dawn. It is, of course, characteristic of Greene that, in *The Power and the Glory*, where the divine image for once irradiates and redeems the human, it is seen doing so only to the most squalid, repellent and pain-racked of human conditions—just as omens of sanctity are seen only in an unshaven brandy-bibber. Natural beauty is not enhanced, but natural ugliness is touched by grace.

> At the centre of his own faith there always stood the convincing mystery—that we were made in God's image—God was the parent, but He was also the policeman, the criminal, the priest, the maniac and the judge. Something resembling God dangled from the gibbet or went into odd attitudes before the bullets in a prison yard or contorted itself like a camel in the attitude of sex. He would sit in the confessional and hear the complicated dirty ingenuities which God's image had thought out: and God's image shook now, up and down on the mule's back, with the yellow teeth sticking out over the lower lip, and God's image did its despairing act of rebellion with Maria in the hut among the rats.

Characteristically, too, it is less the splendor than the almost ridiculous *mystery* of the thing that Greene wants to dramatize. But let him do so in his own manner: in *The Power and the Glory* a compassionate and ultimately a very charitable manner. For it is by seeking God and by finding Him in the darkness and stench of prisons, among the sinners and the rats and the rascals, that the whiskey-priest arrives at the richest emotion second generation fiction has to offer: the feeling of companionship, and especially the companionship of the commonly guilty and wretched. Arrested for carrying brandy, crowded into a pitch-black cell, crushed between unseen odorous bodies, with a woman on one side hysterically demanding to make her trivial confession and an unseen couple copulating somewhere on the floor, announcing their orgasms with whimpering cries of pleasure, the priest is touched suddenly "by an extraordinary affection. He was just one criminal among a herd of criminals. . . . He had a sense of companionship which he had never experienced in the old days when pious people came kissing his black cotton glove."

To appreciate this scene—it is the whole of chapter three of part two, and in my opinion the most effective scene Greene has yet written—we should locate it in the structure of the novel. It begins a few pages beyond the mathematical center of the book; but it constitutes the center as well of an action that has its clear beginning and its firmly established end. The basic unit in the structure of *The Power and the Glory* is the encounter: as it is in so many other novels of the second generation with their picaresque tendency and their vision of man as an outlaw wandering or hastening through an anarchic and hostile world. In *The Power and the Glory*, as in *Bread and Wine*, the plot is episodic and consists of a succession of encounters between the harried protagonist and a number of un-related persons—while within that succession, we observe a pattern of three dominant and crucially meaningful encounters.

We first see the priest when, in disguise, he sips brandy in the office of Mr. Tench, the morose expatriate dentist. We follow him, episode by episode, as he is hidden and given food by Coral, the precocious daughter of an agent for a banana company, Captain Fellowes, and his miserable death-haunted wife; as he arrives in the village which is the home of the woman, Maria, by whom he has had the child Brigitta; as he travels onward in the company of a mestizo, the yellow-toothed ignoble Judas who will betray him to the police; as he is arrested and released and fights his way over the mountains to freedom in a neighboring state and the comfortable home of Mr. Lehr and his sister, German-Americans from Pitts-burgh, in charge of a mining operation; as he is enticed back across the border of Tabasco to attend the death of James Calver, an American murderer who has been fatally wounded by the police; is arrested again by the police lieutenant, taken back to the capital city, and executed. Tench, Coral, Maria, the Lehrs, Calver: these are all strangers to each other. The episodes with each of them thicken and expand the novelistic design (Coral, for instance, is the priest's good spiritual daughter, while Brigitta is his evil actual daughter). But the design itself is created by the three encounters between the priest and the lieutenant.

These occur at carefully spaced intervals, about one third and two thirds through the book, and then at length in the climax. The first time, the lieutenant—whose whole energy and authority are directed exclusively to capturing this last remaining agent of the Church—sees the priest and interrogates him; but he neither recognizes nor arrests him. The second time, the priest is arrested, but he is not recognized: the charge is carrying liquor. The third time, recognition is complete and the arrest final. But these encounters are mere indicators of a carefully constructed plot; the action is something different and more telling, and we are made conscious of it from the outset when—in separate, successive views of them—paradoxical resemblances are registered about the two men. The priest disappears wearily into the interior, giving up a chance to escape in order to minister to a sick peasant woman and feeling "like the King of a West African tribe, the slave of his people, who may not even lie down in case the winds should fail." On the next page, the lieutenant marches by with a ragged squad of police, looking as though "he might have been chained to them unwillingly: perhaps the scar on his jaw was the relic of an escape." Later, as he walks home alone, dreaming of a new world of justice and well-being for the children of Tabasco, "there was something of a priest in his intent observant walk—a theologian going back over the errors of the past to destroy them again." The exhausted and sometimes drunken soldier of God, the chaste and fiercely dedicated priest of the godless society: each one enslaved to his mission, doomed to his role and its outcome: these are the beings, the systole and diastole, between whom the force of the novel is generated.

Readers of Dostoevski or of the Book of Revelation will easily identify them. They are the "hot" and the "cold" bespoken by the angel in lines quoted twice in *The Possessed:* "These things saith the Amen . . . I know thy works, that thou art neither cold nor hot: I would thou wert cold or hot. So then, because thou art lukewarm, and neither cold nor hot, I will spue thee out of my mouth" (Revelation III, 14-16). The lieutenant has had the chilling vision of absurdity: "He was a mystic, too, and what he had experienced was a vacancy—a complete certainty in the existence of a dying, cooling world, of human beings who had evolved from animals for no purpose at all. . . . He believed against the evidence of his senses in the cold empty ether spaces." With a devotion only to the reality of the here and now, he is a rebel against all the misery and injustice and unhappiness he associates with the rule of a greedy Church and its insistence on the unimportance of the human lot in this world. He watches the children in the street, his love for them hidden beneath his hatred of the Church and its priests: "He would eliminate from their childhood everything which had made him miserable, all that was poor, superstitious and corrupt."

The lieutenant, in a word, is *l'homme révolté* of Albert Camus, seen—with respect—in the unorthodox religious perspective of Graham Greene. François Mauriac was right, in his preface to the French edition of *The Power and the Glory*, to call the novel an answer in narrative terms to the widespread European sense of absurdity—to that sense as somehow the one necessary prerequisite to the struggle for social justice. *The Power and the Glory* is not perhaps *the* answer; but it does contain, among other things, a potent allegory of one of the major intellectual debates of our time. Greene, too, it should be said, gives fairer and more substantial play to what he regards as the opposition—embodied in the lieutenant— than Camus gives to *his* opponent, the crudely drawn cleric Paneloux in *The Plague*. Camus contrasts Paneloux, and his helpless appeal to divine irrationality, with the rational and dignified Rieux and Tarrou; while Greene joins the upright police officer in a contest with the wavering and incompetent whiskey-priest. Yet the nameless priest, consecrating moistly amidst the unspeakable heat and the detonating beetles of Tabasco, sweating his way toward a sort of befuddled glory, is of course the representative of the "hot," and the lieutenant's proper adversary.

These two are the persons of stature in the universe of the novel, and eventually they acknowledge each other. "You're a good man," the priest says in astonishment when, at the moment of his release from prison, the lieutenant gives him five pesos. And: "You aren't a bad fellow," the lieutenant concedes grudgingly, during the long conversations after the final arrest. Most of the other characters, those whom Greene calls "the bystanders," are the lukewarm, and their artistic purpose is, by a variety of contrasts, to illuminate the nature of the hunt. A good many of the more "regular" members of the Church, in fact, both in the past and now in the pleasant safety of another state, appear as lukewarm; *The Power and the*

Glory may be a religious novel, but it is decidedly not an ecclesiastical one. The priest himself had been lukewarm in the old days, going smugly on his parochial rounds and attending the meetings of the guilds. It is only in his moment of degradation, arrested not even for being the last priest with the courage to remain in Tabasco but only as a common citizen carrying contraband, that the priest reveals the "hot," the heroic side. He does so unconsciously, out of humility and a conviction of his own unworthiness and an irrepressible sense of humor. We return to the prison scene mentioned above: it occurs just before the second of the three major encounters.

The whole of it should be studied, from the entrance into the cell to the departure next morning and the sudden sense of companionship even with the lieutenant. But perhaps the following fragments can suggest the remarkable interplay—not, in this case, the remote opposition—of sacred and obscene love, of beauty and extreme ugliness, of comedy and deadly peril: all of which gives the scene a rich multiplicity of action beyond anything Greene had previously achieved. Just as the key moment in *Bread and Wine* occurs in the darkness of a squalid hut, so here the "epiphany" takes place in the blackness and stench of a prison.

> Among the furtive movements came again the muffled painless cries. He realised with horror that pleasure was going on even in this crowded darkness. Again he put out his foot and began to edge his way inch by inch from the grill.
>
> *   *   *
>
> "They'll shoot you, father," the woman's voice said.
> "Yes."
> "Are you afraid?"
> "Yes. Of course."
> A new voice spoke, in the corner from which the sounds of pleasure had come. It said roughly and obstinately, "A man isn't afraid of a thing like that."
> "No?" the priest asked.
> "A bit of pain. What do you expect? It has to come."
> "All the same," the priest said, "I *am* afraid."
> "Toothache is worse."
> "We can't all be brave men." [16]

The voice said with contempt, "You believers are all the same. Christianity makes you cowards."

"Yes. Perhaps you are right. You see I am a bad priest and a bad man. To die in a state of mortal sin"—he gave an uneasy chuckle—"it makes you think."

*   *   *

A long train of thought began, which led him to announce after a while, "They are offering a reward for me. Five hundred, six hundred pesos, I'm not sure." Then he was silent again. He couldn't urge any man to inform against him—that would be tempting him to sin—but at the same time, if there was an informer here, there was no reason why the wretched creature should be bilked of his reward. To commit so ugly a sin—it must count as murder—and to have no compensation in this world. . . . He thought: it wouldn't be fair.

"Nobody here," a voice said, "wants their blood money."

Again he was touched by an extraordinary affection. He was just one criminal among a herd of criminals. . . . He had a sense of companionship which he had never experienced in the old days, when pious people came kissing his black cotton glove.

The pious woman's voice leapt hysterically out at him. "It's so stupid to tell them that. You don't know the sort of wretches who are here, father. Thieves, murderers. . . ."

"Well," an angry voice said, "why are you here?"

"I had good books in my house," she announced, with unbearable pride. He had done nothing to shake her complacency. He said, "They are everywhere. It's no different here."

"Good books?"

He giggled. "No, no. Thieves, murderers. . . . Oh, well, my child, if you had more experience, you would know there are worse things to be."

*   *   *

Somewhere against the far wall pleasure began again: it was unmistakeable: the movements, the breathlessness, and then the cry. The pious woman said aloud with fury, "Why won't they stop it? The brutes, the animals!"

"What's the good of your saying an Act of Contrition now in this state of mind?"

"But the ugliness. . . ."

"Don't believe that. It's dangerous. Because suddenly we discover that our sins have so much beauty."

"Beauty," she said with disgust. "Here. In this cell. With strangers all around."

"Such a lot of beauty. Saints talk about the beauty of suffering.

Well, we are not saints, you and I. Suffering to us is just ugly. Stench and crowding and pain. *That* is beautiful in that corner—to them. It needs a lot of learning to see things with a saint's eye: a saint gets a subtle taste for beauty and can look down on poor ignorant palates like theirs. But we can't afford to."

"It's a mortal sin."

"We don't know. It may be. But I'm a bad priest, you see. I know—from experience—how much beauty Satan carried down with him when he fell. Nobody ever said the fallen angels were the ugly ones. Oh no, they were just as quick and light and . . ."

Again the cry came, an expression of intolerable pleasure. The woman said, "Stop them. It's a scandal." He felt fingers on his knees, grasping, digging. He said, "We're all fellow prisoners. I want drink at this moment more than anything, more than God. That's a sin too."

"Now," the woman said, "I can see you're a bad priest. I wouldn't believe it before. I do now. You sympathise with these animals. If your Bishop heard you . . ."

"Ah, he's a very long way off." He thought of the old man now— in the capital: living in one of those ugly comfortable pious houses, full of images and holy pictures, saying Mass on Sundays at one of the Cathedral altars.

"When I get out of here, I shall write . . ."

He couldn't help laughing: she had no sense of change at all. He said, "If he gets the letter he'll be interested—to hear I'm alive."

Pinkie Brown and Major Scobie, the protagonists of *Brighton Rock* and *The Heart of the Matter*, are never seen to smile, much less to laugh; the former is in a constant state of fury, the latter of apprehension. It is the laughter, almost more than anything else, that distinguishes *The Power and the Glory:* laughter based on the recognition of God's image in man, evoked by the preposterous incongruity of it and yet leading naturally to a warmth of fellow-feeling. Here again, a similarity may be noted with the comedy and the companionship of *Bread and Wine;* and perhaps Silone was not wrong, after all, to turn the ridiculous Sciatàp of that novel into the treacherous figure of *The Seed Beneath the Snow.* In this particular comic vision, even the traitors—even the Judases—have a clownish aspect. Contemplating the mestizo (in another passage) and recognizing him as a Judas, Greene's priest remembers a Holy Week carnival where a stuffed Judas was hanged from the belfry and pelted with bits of tin: "it seemed to him a good thing that the world's traitor should be made a figure of fun. It was too easy otherwise to idealise him as a man who fought with God—a Prometheus, a noble victim in a hopeless war" (the very archetype, in short, of Camus's rebel). But the force of the comic consciousness in *The Power and the Glory* is indicated, properly enough, at the end, when the lieutenant, having completed his mission and arranged for the priest's execution, sits down at his desk and falls asleep. "He couldn't remember afterwards anything of his dream except laughter, laughter all the time, and a long passage in which he could find no door." It is the lieutenant, Greene suggests, who is the trapped man, the prisoner; and the laughter he hears is like that laughter recorded by Dante on the upper slopes of purgatory, the chorus celebrating the release of a captive human soul from punishment and its entrance into paradise.

The priest himself hears none of that laughter and goes to his death persuaded of practical and spiritual failure: "I don't know a thing about the mercy of God," he tells the lieutenant, in the phrase that also rounds out *Brighton Rock* and *The Heart of the Matter;* ". . . But I do know this—that if there's ever been a single man in this state damned, then I'll be damned too. . . . I wouldn't want it any different." It never occurs to the priest that if he should so far honor the mestizo as to call him a Judas, he might himself appear as a version of the man Judas betrayed. The book has been hinting as much all along, in the pattern and style of the priest's adventures. The relationship is far more pressing and elaborate here than in *Brighton Rock* or *The Heart of the Matter,* where the vigor of supernature is hardly sweetened by the figure of intermediary and reconciler. The priest, accordingly, preaches to the poor and the meek and downtrodden across the hilly countryside; is tempted in the wilderness; is betrayed, tried, and executed. Toward the end, he, too, is juxtaposed with a common criminal—the Yankee killer, whose name, James Calver, echoes two syllables of the mount on which Christ was crucified, and opposite whose picture in the prison office there is a picture of the priest, grinning within the halo someone had inked around the face for identification. There is even a kind of resurrection in the little epilogue—about which one has mixed feelings—when a new, frightened priest arrives in town and is greeted with reverence by the boy Juan, who, prior to the martyrdom, had been a disciple of the lieutenant. That epilogue, offering presumably the first of the priest's miracles after death, insists perhaps too much. But if the priest is associated not only with Christ but with non-Christian divinities—the god-king of an African tribe, and the surrogate for the god, the bull that was slaughtered in the early Greek ritual of sacrifice and rebirth ("Then there was a single shot . . . the bull was dead")—the entire pattern is nevertheless artistically redeemed by a full awareness of the grotesque disproportion between the model and its re-enactment. "The priest giggled: he couldn't stop himself. He said, 'I don't think martyrs are like this.'" It is the giggle that saves both the priest and the novel Greene has written about him. For it is when he laughs that we know this slovenly rogue, this unshaven *pícaro*, to be also a saint; and we know that here for once—as in only one or two other novels —the paradoxes have held firm and the immense delicate balance has been maintained.

The Heart of the Matter is the most traditional of Greene's novels, in both content and construction. As such, it is obviously less representative than *The Power and the Glory;* and as such, it has a special appeal for those who mean by the word *novel* the kind of work that was typical in the nineteenth century. We note a major paradox about second generation writers: they are developing a rather new sort of fiction—the novel as an act of inquiry or of rebellion or of expiation, rather than as a direct and unprejudiced impression of life; but at the same time, most of them turn for support not to the experimental achievements of the first generation but to the literary forms of the nineteenth century.

The paradox is further strained in the case of *The Heart of the Matter.* Here, for example, is the careful delineation, not altogether unworthy of Trollope, of various discordant elements in a multicolored society, the society of the coastal city in West Africa that Greene had known on his journey in 1935 and again as a government official during the war in 1942-43, the date of the novel's action.[17] In *The Heart of the Matter*, there is no savage eruption out of animal holes into the glare and open world that characterized *Brighton Rock*, and none of the rhythmic peregrinations through anarchy of *The Power and the Glory*. The incidents take place very much *within* the society of the book and involve—not proscribed outlaws but—persons of significance and authority whose intimate knowledge of each other provides much of the hero's tragic dilemma. Here, too, there is a narrative pace, leisurely but never slack, reminiscent of Greene's distant relation, Robert Louis Stevenson. Greene may not be a master of all the elements of fiction, but that he is a master of narrative can be doubted only by those too little interested in storytelling to be capable of discrimination; *The Heart of the Matter* is very handsomely told. And here, too, is an array of characters in the old tradition—and including one especially, the merchant Yusef, whose fat and candid dishonesty would have pleased Dickens and even more, Wilkie Collins. Here, in short, is a traditional, almost a conventional *novel* that is yet a novel by Graham Greene, and something the nineteenth century could scarcely have imagined. For what the action serves to expose is not the habits of a society or the nature of the human heart (no one, says Father Rank in the epilogue, knows "what goes on in a single human heart"); but, going beyond all that, the absolute mystery of the individual destiny.

"Why, why did he have to make such a mess of things?" This is the hopeless and embittered question raised on the last page by Major Scobie's wife, Louise: not "Why did he?" but "Why did he *have to?*" That Scobie, the late Assistant Commissioner of Police, had made an appalling mess of things cannot be denied. *The Heart of the Matter* is the progressive account of it, from the first moment when he is passed over for promotion, through the disappointment of his restless, vaguely artistic wife—a disappointment so great that Scobie makes a dubious if not illegal transaction with the diamond-smuggler, Yusef, to get enough money to send her on a trip to South Africa; through the adulterous affair with the schoolgirlish widow, Helen Rolt, on which he embarks during his wife's absence; through the now rapid deterioration of his public and private life; through the agony—for a Catholic of his temperament—of receiving the sacrament in a condition of mortal sin; to the still graver sin of despair and suicide by which Scobie ends his career. The mess is so great and Scobie's talent, at every turn, for making bad matters worse is so remarkable that the novel has occasionally been dismissed as implausible. George Orwell once wrote to the effect that no one who could get into such deep trouble so quickly could ever have had the honorable career Scobie is alleged to have had in the first place. In the sane and skeptical humanism of Orwell, the contention is reasonable; but it is a point made outside the world of the book; within that world, the issue of plausibility does not arise.

As a matter of fact, the novel offers a definite though still typically mysterious answer to Louise Scobie's question. It would not have satisfied Orwell, for it is not drawn, finally, from psychology: that, Greene thinks, is not where the real mystery lies. But, before approaching the real mystery, it should be said that *The Heart of the Matter* does also offer clues for a purely psychological explanation of Scobie and his conduct. He has the ingredients of a genuine tragic hero. He is presented as a good man, rather better than most, with an inviolable sense of justice irritating to some of his colleagues. "You're a terrible fellow, Scobie," the commissioner tells him affectionately. "Scobie the Just." He is an able man and within limits a forceful one; and he is a strong Catholic with that special religious intensity that only Greene's Catholics (not, that is, the Catholics one thought one knew) betray. And he has a fatal flaw: but it is not arrogance or any normal form of pride; Scobie calls down ruin on himself, plainly and articulately, but not through *hubris*. His flaw is an excess of the quality Greene calls pity—an inability to watch disappointment or suffering in others—with this portion perhaps of pride (in Greene's view), that he feels it peculiarly incumbent upon himself to relieve the pain. In *The Ministry of Fear*, the entertaining trial run for *The Heart of the Matter*, Arthur Row's troubles begin when he commits a mercy killing—or, to stick to Greene's verbal distinctions, a "pity-killing"—to end the intolerable physical suffering of his wife. Scobie kills no one, though he feels himself implicated in several deaths; like some other heroes of second generation fiction, it is his misfortune to harm most of those he longs to help or even to save.

Scobie's troubles begin with his attempt to alleviate the painful disappointment of his wife. His feeling of guilt about her is due partly to his failure to be promoted; but it is rooted more deeply in another failure, an inability any longer to love his wife; and it goes back, too, to the moment when Scobie was unable to be present at the death of his child. He is a man clearly given to self-accusation, and the pattern of it thickens as the story moves forward. It might well be that the suicide, a third of the way through, of Dick Pemberton—an assistant district commissioner at Bamba who hangs himself and whose mode of death affects Scobie enormously—may have released in Scobie a congenital self-destructive impulse.[18] Pemberton's name, Dicky, with which he signed the suicide note, and the nickname Louise has coyly pinned on her husband—Ticki (his real name is Henry)—blur in Scobie's mind while he lies ill with fever after the Pemberton affair; and from then on, the pace of his decline grows more rapid. Scobie, in summary, is an affecting human being, whose sorry career is all too understandable. He is burdened by his own habit of pity for others. But we can ally ourselves with him in that other kind of pity that Aristotle called one of the two emotions properly evoked by tragedy. Still, it is the second of the emotions named by Aristotle—the emotion of tragic terror—that is the more deeply aroused in us by this novel, according to Greene's intention. Tragic pity (to borrow Joyce's definitions of these ancient terms) associates us with the human sufferer, during his grave and terrible experience. Tragic terror springs rather from our stimulated awareness of the secret cause of the suffering; and in *The Heart of the Matter*, as traditionally, that secret cause is the action of God.

The "heart of the matter," as a phrase, occurs after the opening of the novel's second part, when Scobie, momentarily alone and looking up at the stars, wonders whether "If one knew . . . would one have to feel pity even for the planets? if one reached what they called the heart of the matter?" Less than ten minutes later, un-knowingly—though he does suddenly feel cold and strange—Scobie reaches the heart of the matter and gives up the peace of his own soul. Coming in from his reverie, into the resthouse where they have brought the stretcher-cases from a torpedoed ship, Scobie is asked to stand watch over two victims who lie unconscious on two beds divided by a screen. One is a six-year-old girl. Looking at her, Scobie thinks again of his own dead daughter; and he begins to pray. "Father . . . give her peace. Take away my peace for ever, but give her peace." We are to understand, I believe, that God does exactly that. He gives the child the peace of death and a release from suffering, and Scobie's peace is taken away for the remainder of his earthly career. This is the book's major turning point, when pity deepens into terror. And the human agent through whom God acts is the patient on the other side of the screen, "the young woman lying unconscious on her back, still grasping the stamp-album." It is Helen Rolt, whom pity and loneliness will drive Scobie to make love to, in an affair that so torments Scobie's Catholic conscience that only an overdose of tablets can rescue him.

Here, as in *The End of the Affair* and *The Potting Shed*, God moves in a singularly Mephistophelean manner, His wonders to perform—a deity with whom one bargains away one's peace or love or beliefs, for the life of someone else. In a letter to the French Christian existentialist Marcel Moré, Greene put Scobie's case plainly enough: "Obviously one did have in mind that when he offered up his peace for the child it was genuine prayer and had the results that followed. I always believe that such prayers, though obviously a God would not fulfill them to the limit of robbing him of a peace for ever, are answered up to the point as a kind of test of a man's sincerity and to see whether in fact the offer was merely based on emotion." [19] Literary criticism does not invite us to scruple over Greene's religious orthodoxy or lack of it; our concern is simply the dramatic effectiveness of any religious opinion he happens to show. On this ground, *The Heart of the Matter* should be reckoned as successful precisely by implying a terrible tension between the divine and the human—a somber and disturbing modern version of the Greek tragic tension between fate and freedom. As in almost everything Greene has written except *The Power and the Glory*, the supernatural power and the human religious impulse work against the purely human inclination: even when the result is an awe-inspiring fulfillment, the granting of a wish. We may be dismayed that things are seen to be happening so, but that they are seen dramatically cannot be doubted.

Greek classical tragedy customarily ended by a choral acknowledgment of the unsolvable mystery and the purgatorial terror. Father Rank performs a similar function in *The Heart of the Matter*, in the epilogue Greene has characteristically added to ensure our befuddlement over the exact meaning of the events. "For goodness' sake, Mrs. Scobie, don't imagine you—or I—know a thing about God's mercy. . . . The Church knows all the rules. But it doesn't know what goes on in a single human heart." Again, the institutionalized Church is opposed in the name of the religious mystery; and again, the sheer incomprehensibility of God's mercy and grace is the aspect insisted upon. Again, too, the hero, moving doggedly toward disaster, is oddly associated with the figure of Christ: in the manner of *Brighton Rock* rather than *The Power and the Glory*, for we are once more in a universe without intermediaries. The role of Judas is played out by the English government spy, Wilson, who covets Scobie's wife as well as his reputation for integrity; and Scobie tries desperately to condone his act of despair by seeing in it an imitation of Christ: "Christ had not been murdered: Christ had killed himself: he had hung himself on the Cross as surely as Pemberton from the picture rail"—a notion that turns up again after the suicide in *The Living Room*. All these items provide the reader, as planned, with a full measure of uncertainty about Scobie's conduct in this world and his chances in the next. It is suggested in the last lines that Scobie may really have loved God; and it is suggested that God may be the only being he did love. The night before he encounters the dying child and Helen Rolt, we hear Scobie murmuring the incomplete phrase as he falls asleep, "O God, bless—," and later, another incomplete phrase as he falls senseless and dying: "Dear God, I love . . ." Not even the reader, who knows more about Scobie than anyone else, can be sure of the objects of those verbs.

Psychology thus yields to a dark theology, the pity to the terror, the human sufferer to the secret cause. All we are meant to know is that we know nothing; that is the answer to Louise's question. Pinkie Brown *almost* certainly is damned, and he was without any doubt a vicious and wicked young man. The Mexican priest is almost certainly saved, and he was one of the most curiously sympathetic figures in modern fiction. We conclude, about Henry Scobie, in a purging sense of the unguessable nature of human conduct and divine intervention. In so far as they do constitute a trilogy, Greene's three novels reverse the direction of the greatest religious trilogy, *The Divine Comedy*. Dante's poem moves from ignorance to knowledge, from discord to harmony, from unspeakable darkness to overwhelming light. Greene's "trilogy" moves stealthily deeper into the darkness, moves through the annihilation

of our confidence in human knowledge to an awareness of impenetrable mystery, moves from the deceptive light to the queerly nourishing obscurity. All the truth of things, for Greene, lies hidden
in the darkness: whether of slum-ridden Brighton, of a squalid prison
cell, or of a West African night of wonder and despair. Scarcely
less mysterious is Greene's achievement of making visible in that
darkness, and exactly by means of it, the unforgettable dramas of
extraordinarily living human beings.

The Divine Intrigue

Since about 1945, Greene has enjoyed an astonishing popular and
financial success—much the greatest of any of the novelists we have
been considering, and of such proportions that it has inevitably in-
vited skepticism in high literary places about his real artistic merit.
His successive works of fiction [20] have sold enormously, both in
England, where he is admired especially for his mastery of narrative and his evocation of despondent, grubby, middle-class atmosphere, and in America, where readers take a more strained and
intellectualized attitude toward the serious fiction they decide to
buy. Not less than ten of his writings have been made into films,
including all three members of the "trilogy." Greene's success has
corresponded, as is often the case, with a partial and no doubt
temporary decline of persuasive artistic force. At the same time,
inevitably, some of the more searching critics have begun to question his achievement. Morton Zabel, for example, who wrote in
1943 that Greene was very close to becoming one of the masters
of modern fiction, is now inclined to express a certain disapproval
of the whole design of his work. And Mary McCarthy has advanced the ingenious theory that Greene's appeal lies in his presentation of religion as a fashionable form of the titillatingly illicit.
Miss McCarthy, who opines in the same article (a review of *The
Potting Shed* [21]) that practically everyone these days is a nonbeliever, suggests that Greene's aim is to make religion exciting for
the nonreligious; though she evinces a kind of hostile respect for
Greene's craftiness in doing so.

Such judgments come to us with a good deal of strength; and yet,
since they are at bottom indictments of the reading public and of

modern culture, they do not perhaps sufficiently cover the case. It is true that there is an exasperating slickness about some of Greene's compositions, especially of late; and it is true that he often seems anxious to impart a secret thrill to the religious impulse—notably, by confounding it expertly with the impulse to adultery, in a manner that we are about to examine. It is true also that Greene's God is a hidden god, never seen face to face but only, so to speak, through an unwashed glass, under shabby shop-counters, darkly. Minty diving like a secret debauchee into a Lutheran church in Stockholm; the love and fear of God crouching like an animal in Nelson Place, Brighton; the broken rosary hidden (as Miss McCarthy noted) like a French post card in Scobie's desk—these are Greene's characteristic images for the hidden relation between the individual and God. But they are equally images that reflect the conviction Greene shares with the best of his contemporaries: namely, that God must in the very nature of things remain hidden in our time—or, at most, be obscurely felt in odd and unlikely guises. Camus hides him by turning his back and betting He does not exist—except, perhaps, on the other side of a maddening contradiction. Moravia doubts the existence, too, but he prowls forward bravely in his own peculiar darkness, prepared at least for the possibility of a revelation. Greene, like Silone, does believe in a reality other and higher than the human and the visible; and like Silone also, he has tried to find terms to describe the nature both of the concealment and the occasional teasing manifestations. As we have already seen, the Silone of *Bread and Wine*, responding to the political aspects of modern experience, put the case in a political metaphor: "In times of conspiratorial secret struggle," Don Benedetto tells Pietro Spina, "the Lord is obliged to hide Himself and assume pseudonyms. . . . Might not the ideal of social justice that animates the masses today be one of the pseudonyms the Lord is using to free Himself from the control of churches and banks?" The quality of Greene's imagery indicates the very different aspects—the familial and erotic aspects—of experience to which he happens to be responding.

As to Greene's popularity, once we have granted his swift readability, his melodramatics, and his queer theological spiciness, something solid and puzzling yet remains. His appeal, I venture again, lies in the concern he shares with other second generation writers for the apprehensions and the hopes they have all found in their historic world and have represented in their fiction. Much profit has been stolen elsewhere from these aspirations by presenting them in spurious, cheap, and even satirical form—the work of box-office revivalists, writers for women's magazines, and various other sorts of popularizers. But this debasing invariably happens to the most deeply felt beliefs of any time; each culture, it seems, spontaneously throws up its own satyr play to accompany the tragic vision that has ennobled it. The fact should not tarnish our reaction to the vision itself, when it is handled with artistry and conviction—delicate as the problem is of determining just when it has been so handled. But Greene, I think, has brought to the surface, and in very attractive prose, several of the major preoccupations of our day; and he has gone on to treat them with an unsettling literalness and immediacy. *The End of the Affair* really is the story of a saint, complete with spiritual diary and recorded miracles; *The Potting Shed* really is about a resurrection—about a human being actually and physically rising from the dead. Greene is, after all, the opposite of the stage magician: he makes some of his observers so conscious, or so suspicious, of his devices that they sometimes miss the event he primarily wants them to attend to—the deep movement from death to life, for example. But Greene's saints, like his suicides, are only more literal than those of the other writers we have been studying because they are presented in the vocabulary of a religion that takes them literally; they are less hedged around with the suggestion of metaphor and analogy than the saints of Silone and Faulkner. And in pursuing the aim of investing contemporary experience with dignity and stature, Greene has exploited a basically simple device; that is, he has reported the many varying experiences as unexpected versions of the Passion of Christ. *The Third Man* was built on this pattern: the highly imaginative photography of the film included a shot of the criminal, Harry Lime, extended horribly on a sewer rail, in Vienna, his hands contorted as in some fifteenth century northern European Crucifixion. Behind the somewhat dispirited melodrama of *The Quiet American* we faintly glimpse, once more, the ancient Passion Play; here too, as in *The Third Man*, it is the supposedly decent and sensible fellow who acts out the treacherous role of Judas, and the dishonest or the dangerous man who is betrayed, and the unhappy story of the harmfully innocent Alden Pyle gains some pitiful portions of significance by its reflection of the story of Holy Week.

What is importantly lacking in Greene's novels, except for *The Power and the Glory*, is the emotion that has become everything for Ignazio Silone: the emotion of human love, or, as the case may be, of human companionship. This is far too bald a statement, but I make it in order to point toward a truth. Human love is distinctly present, in persuasive and even moving form, in Greene's entertainments; it is what they are mostly about, and exactly because they have their being all, as it were, on the exclusively human level. But in the novels proper, with the exception noted, we are too often confronted by a *choice* between the love of man and the love of God. The choice makes for engrossing drama but it does so at the expense of any feeling of continuity and involvement between the two orders of experience and the two kinds of love; the one never leads to the other or grows out of it, as both psychologically and doctrinally one might suppose that it would. Greene's representative character is Henry Scobie, about whom it could be said that "he really loved God," but about whom his wife can not unjustifiably complain that "he certainly loved no one else." Equally but inversely representative is the forlorn priest in *The Potting Shed*, whose love for his nephew is fulfilled at the cost of his belief in God. In persons like these, Greene matches the forces in the manner Camus has consistently accused modern Christians of matching them: the love of and the whole-souled involvement with God *or* the love of and the whole-souled involvement with man. The only difference is the choice made by the two writers. Greene chooses the first, Camus the second.

Greene further and no less characteristically pits not merely human love but illicit, inadmissible, adulterous love—against the love of God. The love relations of Scobie, of Sarah Miles, of Rose Pemberton cannot, by nature, flow directly into a loving relation with God; the latter can be achieved only through the annihilation of the former; so that the latter is not a consummation but a replacement of the former. The relation between man (or woman) and God in Greene's fiction is thus, more often than not, an *affair:* a religious affair, but with all the doubts, resentments, misunderstandings, jealousies, and secret assignations that are the normal attributes of an extramarital sexual relation. This is as much the case with Scobie as it had been with Minty; and it is precisely true of Sarah Miles in the cunningly entitled novel *The End of the Affair*. About their religion, there is something almost shameful and furtive; it has all the air of an intrigue, a theological version of the intrigue we traced in Moravia. And yet, in the world of Graham Greene, it is out of just such an oddly culpable religious affair that sainthood is achieved.

The End of the Affair is a thorough documentation of these various relationships, alternatives, and paradoxes. The novel suffers a little from Greene's incorrigible competence; it is too well-made for its own good. Its own good is not merely to tell the story of a sensual and unfaithful young woman reluctantly dragged toward sainthood, but also to dramatize the assertion (made in a soliloquy by the narrator, the novelist Maurice Bendrix) that "The saints . . . create themselves. They come alive. They are capable of the surprising act or word. They stand outside the plot, unconditioned by it. But we have to be pushed around. We have the obstinacy of non-existence. We are inextricably bound to the plot." The fictional allusions here are, of course, metaphorical, as befits a novel about a novelist. But they tempt us to say that Sarah Miles, for all her eventual sainthood, can scarcely be said to stand outside of Greene's skillfully contrived plot. She is as bound to it as her impotent husband, Henry, or the Dickensian private detective, Parkis, or Bendrix himself. No one of them leaps out of the pages, with a surprising act or word, and runs away with the story, as characters frequently do in Faulkner (where they tend literally to take off at a sprint, pursuing or being pursued, in some sudden outburst of grotesque excitement). All are pushed around relentlessly by their artistic creator. Yet, conditioned as they are, the figures in *The End of the Affair* are vivid and memorable; their adventure is a compelling one; and the book's limitations, one feels, are faults on the right and necessary side.

Sarah's story is told from without, by a belligerent nonbeliever. She is the wife of a government official in wartime London, a woman of many human imperfections who—partly because of her husband's sexual incapacity—enters into a prolonged adulterous affair with a successful novelist. Then, at a certain moment, she abruptly breaks off the relation; and after a time, both the hitherto unsuspecting Henry Miles and the lover, Bendrix, suspect her of secret meetings with another person. The plot turns on the inquiry, initiated by the husband and delegated by the lover to a private detective, into the identity of the new lover. He is, of course, God: as Bendrix finally learns from a stolen diary; God, who has again answered a human prayer in frighteningly meticulous terms. It was Sarah's prayer for Bendrix, who had apparently been killed during an air raid, while he and Sarah were sleeping together. She touches his hand: "I could have sworn it was a dead hand"; and, like Scobie praying for the dying child, she prays for her lover's deliverance. "Let him live, and I *will* believe. Give him a chance. Let him have his happiness. Do this and I'll believe. . . . I'll give him up forever, only let him be alive with a chance." Bendrix returns to life; Sarah instantly—but without explanation—gives him up forever; she begins to believe and goes on to fall resentfully in love with God. Through all the anguish of her new affair, her unswerving conviction (like the Mexican priest's) of her own abysmal unworthiness wins for her an exceedingly bitter beatitude. After her death, three separate miracles confirm her achievement of sanctity, as they regularly do in the traditional lives of the saints: Bendrix is prevented from seducing a young admirer, the detective's child is rescued from seemingly fatal illness, and a hideous disfigurement suddenly vanishes from the face of a stanch atheist named Smythe. The final anticipated miracle is presumably "the chance" Bendrix was saved for—he feels at the end that he, too, is being prodded into belief, that God is closing in on him; that God, who turned out to be the criminal pursued by the hired detective, is now the implacable pursuer. The closing note is a paradoxical echo of Job, from the midst of his divinely ordained miseries: "Are not my days few? Cease then and let me alone, that I may take comfort a little." Bendrix's words are: "O God, you've done enough. . . . Leave me alone forever."

The expansion and contraction of Bendrix's religious sensibility are, in fact, an imporant part of the action in *The End of the Affair*. The same would be true of Greene's next novel, *The Quiet American*, which is rather inaudibly narrated by the nonbeliever Fowler, an English newspaperman in Indochina, estranged from his Roman Catholic wife in England. The dust jacket of the American edition maintains that in the new novel Greene "has entered a new vein where religion plays little or no part." This is hardly accurate, for Greene is simply continuing here in the vein begun with *The Man Within* and renewed in *The End of the Affair*, a vein in which the absence of religious understanding and the hovering possibility of acquiring it play a vital part. If *The End of the Affair* is a piece of unwillingly and skeptically reported hagiography, *The Quiet American* is cast in the form of a frustrated confession—frustrated because Fowler is unable to make out the Being to whom his sins should be confessed. It opens with his question, "Am I the only one who really cared for Pyle?" (the American whom Fowler has betrayed to native assassins), and it closes with his weary lament, "I wished there existed someone to whom I could say I was sorry" —two reflections, the answer to both of which is the answer to the puzzle earlier explored by Henry Miles and Maurice Bendrix. The answer is God. The difficulty of Bendrix in the one book and Fowler in the other of arriving at that answer is a central ingredient in their experience.

The position of Bendrix in *The End of the Affair* also provides a sort of built-in skepticism, a large and lingering doubt as to the allegedly supernatural nature of the events recorded: the reader's skepticism, written into the book, is first made active and then (or such is the intent) dissipated. It is a device indispensable to most of the fiction we have been studying, with its concern with saint-hood and rebirth and redemption—items that cannot be presented "purely" or unambiguously in a time when agnosticism vies for dominance with sentimental religiosity. In *The End of the Affair* the device is less surely handled than it had been in *The Power and the Glory*, where the range of suggestion and insight was so greatly extended by the counterperspectives of the lieutenant and the priest upon each other. But the device is necessary to the later novel as well; and it is not without skill that Greene has Bendrix' grudging narrative discolor, by juxtaposition, the pure account of her conversion in the secret journal of Sarah Miles. And it is Bendrix' angry but waning skepticism through which we observe the movement of Sarah's relation to God—the leap of faith which, according to the evidence, has made her eligible for sainthood, or maybe is evidence *of* sainthood. Bendrix' words given here remind us of the hostility to the spiritual leap that Camus expressed in *The Myth of Sisyphus.*

> For if this God exists, I thought, and if even you—with your lusts and your adulteries and the timid lies you used to tell—can change like this, we could all be saints by leaping as you leapt, by shutting the eyes and leaping once for all; if you are a saint, it's not so difficult to be a saint. It's something He can demand of any of us—leap! But I won't leap.

The narrator's voice, unlike the customary voice of Camus or of his characters, is thick with premonitions of leaping. But Camus would be (no doubt, is) even more strenuously opposed to the leap as described in the work that followed *The End of the Affair—The Living Room,* the first of Greene's plays. Here, in a play about physical suicide, the leap is enjoined in the very terms Camus dismisses almost with violence as "philosophical suicide." *The Living Room,* despite its punning title, is as much a play about death as its successor, *The Potting Shed,* is a play about life; and the sense of the reasonableness of things suffers as great a death as the luckless heroine. Rose Pemberton, the young niece of two pious and feeble-hearted maiden aunts and of their brother, Father James Browne, kills herself over a hopeless love affair with a married man. Her lover arrives furiously in the Brownes' living room to demand an explanation: of the seemingly cruel treatment of Rose by her family, of her terrible act, and even of the entire pattern of human experience generally. Father Browne, a crippled and rather helpless and useless priest squarely in the Greene tradition, has only this to offer:

> There's one thing I remember from the seminar. . . . It comes from some book of devotion. "The more our senses are revolted, uncertain and in despair, the more surely Faith says: 'This is God: all goes well.' "

There, exactly, is the "ferocious hopefulness" Camus attributed to Kierkegaard, Jaspers, and Franz Kafka: the hopefulness of persons who (Camus argued) do not say, "Absurd!" when confronted with absurdity, but say, "God!"

The Living Room is quintessential Greene, with its atmosphere of the steady insinuation of death (the aunts abandon, room by room, any part of the house where death has occurred, and now cower in the small section still uninfected), its opposition of adultery and religion, its desperation, its suicide, its appeal—partly demoralized and partly a painful hope—to the unknowable mercy of God, and its highly polished technique of befuddlement. Doubt is gradually shed over the whole *human* order of discourse and experience, until it is annihilated as a meaningful and valuable order: inducing in us a desperation of the senses until we, too, can, if so inclined, make the leap and desperately infer the divine perspective from the ruins of the human. In *The Living Room*, Greene intensified the dramatic stress and strain, the pulverization of feeling (his characters' or his audience's) that he has so often drawn from an insistence upon the total discontinuity between the human and the divine. And yet, we feel, there is another side of Greene beyond that; and we encounter the rest of him, perhaps, in his second play, *The Potting Shed*. The two plays combine to give us Greene whole.

The spiritual leap in *The Potting Shed*, no less sudden than the one indicated in its predecessor, is all in the other direction. It is a leap into unbelief: and it is bound up with a movement that reverses the movement associated with the leap in *The Living Room*. The movement in *The Potting Shed* is from suicide to life. [22]

The play has to do with the inquiry of James Callifer, a man now approaching middle age and long since separated from his wife, into the mystery of his own being, into his sense of a lack of being. He begins his search after he returns home to attend the funeral of his father, a well-known scientific rationalist; and again, as in *The Man Within*, the clue to the feeling of nonexistence is related to parental suppression (as it turns out), with the supernatural element coming at last to the rescue. The action of the play is a motion from ignorance to knowledge, paralleling the motion from death to life. What has to be discovered is the secret of an event that occurred when James was an adolescent. At the age of sixteen, young James had hanged himself in the potting shed of the family estate; his uncle, a priest, had prayed over the corpse for the boy's return to life, offering in exchange whatever he (the priest) most cherished; the boy was revived, and God took from the priest his most treasured possession—his faith. The priest leaped into un-belief and thereafter spent many miserable and increasingly alcoholic years (he is probably the most wretched and the seediest of Greene's long line of unsavory clerics) practicing a faith he no longer be-lieves in. At the same time, his brother—the boy's rationalistic father —suffered a corresponding loss. It would have ruined his public position to admit belief in a miracle, and yet he could not disbelieve it either; and he, too, lived on hopelessly through a now fraudulent career, voicing the catechism of a faith (in a wholly materialistic universe) he did not believe. In the play's precariously happy end-ing, the priest is restored to faith; James is liberated by his acquired understanding of his late father's fearful, resentful attitude toward him; and James and his wife, now reconciled, agree in a gingerly fashion to live together on the edges of that formidable divine ges-ture.

The Potting Shed suggests that, while Greene's fictional talent may be in abeyance, his theatrical talent is on the rise. The style in *The Quiet American* seems worn out, the familiar similes seem limp, like rubber bands that have lost their snap. But *The Potting Shed* has much of the stripped, honed urgency, the dazzling but still sub-stantial play of paradox that characterized the best of Greene's prose.

The movement from death to life has always been one of Greene's dominant themes, side by side with its opposite. Andrews' thrust beyond the sense of nonexistence in *The Man Within;* the develop-ment from murder to childbirth in *Brighton Rock;* the renewed life of the priesthood in *The Power and the Glory*, as though a conse-quence of the martyrdom of the saintly *pícaro*—all these testify to the possibility that is finally given startlingly literal form in *The Potting Shed*. In Moravia's most recent novel, *La Ciociara* (trans-lated as *Two Women*), the resurrection hoped for by Cesira and her violated daughter is entirely spiritual and moral, though it is defined by reference to the New Testament miracle of Lazarus raised by Jesus from the dead. Greene, too, means to suggest these further ranges of meaning, but, good English dramatist that he is, he pins them down to concrete particular events. One has learned not to predict about the future work of any accomplished living writer, but the guess may be hazarded here that Greene may have ex-hausted the few rich entangled themes he has so long been using, and that perhaps he will turn his attention more hospitably to the open world he has hirtherto mistrusted. But with his sense of death and his sense of life, his highly original and tautly dramatic religious consciousness, and his fertile vision of the almost comical paradoxes of potential sainthood in our bedraggled time, Greene's has been a determining literary voice. He has participated with nervously sustained eloquence in the novelistic effort by which the writers of the second generation have shown their time its death-tormented form, its life-directed pressure.

The Shared Reality:
The Shadow of André Malraux

> Pity? he thought confusedly, as he had when he
> saw the troops coming back. It was a profound
> impulse of a very different sort, an impulse in
> which anguish and fraternity mingled inextri-
> cably, an impulse that came from very far back.
>
> MALRAUX, *Les Noyers de l'Altenburg* [1]

IN ANDRÉ MALRAUX'S most recent novel, a colloquy of intellectuals
is held in an Alsatian abbey. At the last moment, the topic for discussion is changed by the host and master of ceremonies, Walter
Berger. "The colloquy was to have had as its title: the eternal elements of art," one member confides to the book's hero. "And now
it has become: permanence and metamorphosis of man." Eternity,
the speaker adds in a sly whisper, isn't doing so well; but the irony
does not conceal a transition of great significance for the novel and
for the entire career of André Malraux—indeed, for the career of
the generation of writers that Malraux, more fully than any of his
contemporaries, almost allegorically represents.

The transition is from the primacy of art to the primacy of man,
as the central preoccupation of art itself and of human thought in

general. That development was traced in the first chapter of this book, in the movement from the aesthetic vision of Joyce and his fellows to the more doggedly human vision of their successors. In his own life, Malraux recapitulated the whole development of his time; and in *Les Noyers de l'Altenburg* he provides a dramatic symbol to explain it. The reason for Berger's change of topic is explicit: the unexpected suicide of his brother Dietrich—the shattering intrusion of death and, more, of self-annihilation. "Perhaps it seemed [to Walter] a menace"; and of a kind no longer to be met by a confident appeal to the eternal and to the eternalizing principles of art. Here, as elsewhere in the second generation, the almost overpowering sense of death forced attention elsewhere: to the very nature of man, and to the question of whether man had a nature.

To define, as well as we may, the reality shared by the five novelists we have been considering, we can hardly do better than to survey, as archetypal, the career of André Malraux at certain of its key moments. We should look especially at *Les Noyers*, a novel that (to some extent like Silone's *A Handful of Blackberries*) rehearses the spiritual pilgrimage it simultaneously concludes. Malraux is nearly two years younger than Silone (the Frenchman was born in November, 1901), and younger yet than Faulkner. But he became entangled with the cultural conflicts of his time more rapidly than the others; the earliest significant work of Malraux dates as far back as 1921. And, perhaps because of a natural impatience, he seems also to have arrived more rapidly at those same successive phases of the human image that his contemporaries—working at least partly in his nourishing shadow—were more slowly to work through.

Except in the case of Camus, however, where it is emphatic, we cannot speak precisely of an influence. In Malraux, we observe not so much the influential as the exemplary. We confront a familiar Gallic phenomenon, the French talent for moving directly to the point and from one point to the next, displaying each of them in what is offered as its universal aspect. If, in the generation-wide struggle to come alive, Moravia represents the erotic motif; if Camus represents human reason in its compassionate workings; if Silone represents the conversion of the political ambition into the charitable urge, and Faulkner the conversion of darkness into light and the old into the new; if Greene represents the interplay of the more than human with the less than human—then Malraux may be said to represent all of these things or versions of them. Thus, he may be said to typify the strongly marked evolution of the whole second generation.

And beneath all of those motifs, we sense Malraux's persistent dedication of himself and his novelistic art to the tragic condition of modern man. That dedication led Malraux to construct, in his last novel, as striking an image as we can find anywhere of the contradictory hero of the time: the picaresque saint. The image is the climax, and it may even be the end, of Malraux's career as a novelist.

In stressing his representative function and in slighting what is unique in him, we no doubt do Malraux some damage, though the damage will not be great in the case of a writer whose evolution, like that of Camus and Silone, has been away from the abnormal and toward the affinities between men, toward fraternity and companionship. The danger, anyhow, is not one of oversimplification; the complexities of Malraux are less interesting and persuasive than the sublime simplicities his tortuous and often muddled way eventually led him to. Like Camus again, whose youthful hero Malraux was, Malraux invites his admiring critics to engage in complex discourse about human destiny and about the paradoxes that prevail when man attempts to bring his destiny into question. Still, whatever we can do about the inhuman and the antihuman forces that hem us in and shake our hold upon our common humanity, we shall not talk our way around them—as Malraux himself potentially demonstrates in *Les Noyers*. We are wiser if, like blinded Gloucester in *King Lear*, we can learn to see feelingly—groping along the path that Malraux, now standing for his time, has painfully charted for us.

The path begins, as in most of the important writing of the twentieth century, upon the note of death, where Malraux lingered long and obsessively. *Lunes en Papier* (1921), his first memorable work, sends forth seven Protean figures, in an extravagantly written fantasy, upon the mission of finding and of killing Death. As it turns out, Death is already seriously ill and has been contemplating suicide; before the dream-work is over, Death is near extinction from a bath of acid. This slender piece suggests high and youthful spirits, and it is projected in the happy chaos of deliriously unstable imagery then *à la mode* in France. But amid its nonsense, we recognize in *Lunes en Papier* what was to be the first and deepest motivation of contemporary fiction, one treated in as grave and lucid a work as *The Plague*—the assault upon the force of death: "Death, thou shalt die." What happened during the years immediately following *Lune en Papier* was that Malraux gradually detached the motivation from the style that burlesqued it. In doing so, he also rejected "the private world of the imagination," [2] with its glossy aesthetics; he turned outword to confront the formidable fact of deadliness—physical, psychological, metaphorical—in the immediate historic world; and in an essay called *"D'une jeunesse européenne"* (1927), he made clear both the nature of his rejection and its grounds. He no longer sought to extend the frontiers of what Leon Edel rightly names "the psychological novel"; he would use a few of its techniques to develop the more troubled form of the human novel, the novel of inquiry and revolt and conversion: the novel that some critics—in dealing with Malraux, as with Silone and Faulkner and Camus and even occasionally with Greene—would call the non-novel. Surrealistic comedy gave way to humanistic tragedy.

The first characteristic of the reality that Malraux shared with the most distinguished of his true contemporaries—shared with them and imparted to them—was its absurdity. In *La Tentation de l'occident* (1926), the work for which the essay mentioned above was a sort of apologia, Malraux introduced into the language of Europe the notion later to be erected, particularly by Camus, into a necessary premise for all future thought and action. *"At the center of European man,"* declares a young Chinese in that book, with the help of Malraux's italics, *"dominating the great moments of his life, there lies an essential absurdity."* Malraux was writing in the wake of the First World War and its tangible devastations; and he was writing, more importantly, in the known wake of the century-long disintegration of Europe's cultural foundations—virtually, of the entire classical-Christian tradition. The war had only hastened and dramatized that disintegration. In both a long and a short view, the very *source* of meaning in human experience seemed simply to have evaporated. The Christian source was gone: Malraux, like the Nietzsche he always admired and later studied, felt that God was dead. The classical source had vanished at the same time: human nature, on its own, could no longer reveal the element that might give it coherence. In *La Tentation de l'occident*, via letters exchanged between Europe and Asia, Malraux conveys the feeling of absurdity with dreadful effect.

In an absurd universe, peopled by unrelated fragments behaving absurdly as the grand image of man declined in the West, Malraux found for the moment only a single resource: courage and action; metaphysical and physical courage, of a boldly hopeless kind, taking the form of adventure, the calculated precipitation of the self into perilous circumstances—the fevers and cruelties of the Cambodian jungle, the revolutionary fighting of China—in order to derive an irrational sense of living from a defiance of the irrational onslaught of death. Out of the Chinese experience came *The Conquerers* (1928); and out of Malraux's effort, a few years earlier, to penetrate the Cambodian jungle in search of medieval Khmerian statuary, came *The Royal Way* (1930). The latter is worth considering in some detail, in order to balance its intense preliminary urgings against the testamentary quality of *Les Noyers de l'Altenburg*, a decade and in some sense a lifetime later.

On almost every page of *The Royal Way*, we experience, if not the shock, at least the recurring nudge of recognition. It is as though Malraux, writing in 1930, had miraculously surveyed in advance the major motifs of a generation of fiction yet unwritten and had jumbled them together inconsequently in a short and hence somewhat overcrowded novel. Not all of this, to be sure, was of necessity prophetic. The year before its publication, Alberto Moravia had already offered in *The Time of Indifference* an image of radical ennui challenged only by that sexuality which is but one of the modes of would-be redemptive action in *The Royal Way*. And in the same year as the latter, Graham Greene published *The Name of Action*, a comparable but decidedly inferior work, dramatizing another mode of response to death, and one still more central to *The Royal Way*, in the story of a young man leaving the sterile circles of European city life to seek out deadly danger as the means of bestirring in himself a sensation of existence.[3] Because of both its echoes and prophecies, in any case, *The Royal Way* tends to be more impressive in context—the present context—than when taken separately. It has the quality often found in literature of the second order of providing pleasure by constantly reminding us of something else. On absolute terms, Malraux may have been right to omit it from the one-volume Pléiade collection of his novels, though it seems to me superior on most counts to the earlier work he did include—*The Conquerors*—which introduced in the figure of Garine the first of Malraux's "adventurers." But *The Royal Way*, with its own vivid adventurer, gathers together, as it were, an assortment of replies to the death-consciousness of the day, and moves forward in a many-pronged assault upon its determining element.

The Royal Way is the story of Claude Vannec, a gifted twenty-six-year-old French student of Asian art and anthropology; of his self-appointed mission to ransack the deserted temples in "unpacified" Indochina; and of the person he encounters and is profoundly drawn to on his outward journey, the aging Perken, who has gained considerable authority among the Siamese tribes and who is on a private mission of his own. The missions are joined, for the two men recognize a kinship:

> All that held the two of them together, the source of their fraternity, was what lies deepest in the heart of man. . . . Suddenly Claude realized what the link between them was, between him and this man who had accepted his companionship . . . : Their common obsession with death.

This obsession—the theme on one level or another of almost everything Malraux has ever written—is everywhere evident in *The Royal Way*. The book launches its assault amid the Dead Cities of Cambodia, "of all dead lands most dead," beyond Bab-el-Mandeb, the Gate of Death, and in the hideously decaying world of the jungle. It is the assault of wilfully solitary men, made solitary—and hence, in this case, oddly companionable—by the deep sense of meaninglessness in modern life. Claude's "plan had cut him off from the world, and penned him in a private universe"; and Perken is yet more cosmically homeless. Since his native land, Schleswig-Holstein, had been annexed by Denmark, Perken is both practically and psychologically *heimatlos*. His mission is to find another adventurer, Grabot, who challenges Perken just because he is "a man who's *absolutely* alone," and has "decide[d] to cut himself off completely—

completely, mind you—from his fellow men." The lesson of absurdity is handed down from the older to the younger man. "You know as well as I do that life is meaningless," Perken remarks flatly. And the student is faithful to the master: "To be a living man," Claude reflects, "was even more absurd than dying."

The multiple attack upon that power ends, in *The Royal Way*, with multiple failure: not merely the defeat that was inevitable in the nature of things, but defeat in the very terms of the modes of attack. The book, its characters, and indeed its author have only a fleeting and indistinct glimpse of the one mode of attack that might have rendered the failure so meaningful as to have turned it into victory—what Vincent Berger, in *Les Noyers*, recognizes as "the assault of pity," and of something deeper than pity. In *The Royal Way*, other possibilities are probed and abandoned or are proved worthless. Claude had come to Cambodia prepared to attack death through the medium of art. "Every artist has to ward off death by a sort of intermittent immortality," he muses, during his vexatious interview with the French authorities at Saigon; his aim is to wrest from dead Cambodia fragments of forgotten sculpture, and, by taking them back to France, to release within them their secret, continuing life. The mission is in part successful; in one of the book's most brilliant scenes, Claude does manage, in a fury of effort, to hack off some stone figures from a temple wall. But later—in a decision whose suggestiveness transcends the limits of the novel—the artistic mission is abandoned for a more immediately human purpose. The treasures are left behind, their secret life still hidden, and Claude chooses to accompany Perken on the latter's physical race against his own death (he has been wounded by a poisoned spike): Perken's effort to return to the Siamese tribes before he dies, to make one last stroke of resistance against the forces that are invading his personal Siamese kingdom. Those forces, in the form of an advancing railroad, represent civilization; and civilization of that modern and mechanical sort, for Malraux as for Greene and Faulkner, is also one of the disguises of death.

For Perken, along with his adventurous plunges and his defense of "the wild life of the jungle" against the dehumanizing power of the "civilized," there has been another way of resisting death. That is the way of eroticism—the way, one recalls, of so many of Moravia's characters. Sexual achievement as the potential key to life is a recurring note in Moravia, and it almost always turns out to be dismally unsuccessful. But Malraux's Perken knows an even larger failure, for his sexuality, in its soaring metaphysical intensity, has not even the "remote" and "ridiculous" but very human motivation of Carla's in *The Time of Indifference*—the desire to have a new life. Perken's sexual acts are acts of aggression, of appropriation; they are efforts to wrest from the female body its secret vitality, as Claude attempted to wrest the concealed life from the body of the temple. One of the last acts of dying Perken is to rally his waning sexual powers (impotence is still another mask of death in the book), in a ferocious venture of copulation with a native woman. The venture is physically impressive but humanly disastrous. The woman stirs into violent life, but it is a distant, unpossessable life, its secret still unyielded.

Perken sees dimly toward the end that the clue he had needed and missed was, very simply, love. But he had preferred the loveless response to death of adventuring in power—sexual power and, more importantly, the power of authority among the men and women of the tribes of Siam. Adventure itself becomes the chief form of resistance to the inevitable: "What was his quest of the unknown," Claude reflects, echoing Perken's ideas, ". . . that men who do not understand call adventure—what was it but his counter-attack on death?" This particular adventure concludes in dying, as Perken succumbs at last to his wound. But Claude, presumably, returns to France with a new perception of what it means to be alive and with a hint, at least, of the element that really can sustain life. That hint enters the book in its last and highly effective lines. Perken lies wounded, his consciousness full of the sense of solitude and the absurd:

> But then a look from Claude brought him back to his body, to himself. It was a look of deep understanding, of perfect fellowship, in which the fervent confraternity of courage and compassion intensified the vital unity of all living flesh in the presence of death's victim.

Death, having created that "vital unity," then instantly dissolves it:

> With a rush of hatred Claude recalled a prayer of his childhood. "O Lord, be with us in our last agony. . . ." Ah, could he but ex-

press by look or gesture, if not by words, the desperate fraternity that was wrenching him out of himself! He passed his arm round Perken's shoulders.

Perken gazed at him as if he were a stranger, an intruder from another world.

A great deal of the work of Albert Camus is implicit in those few lines—from the fraternity of flesh announced in *Noces*, through the last outburst of hatred and understanding of Meursault in *The Stranger*, to the episode in *The Plague* wherein Dr. Rieux exerts all the vigor of his compassion to keep alive the dying child. But to note these affinities and to catalogue the representative themes in *The Royal Way* is to give a misleading impression of the book. The themes do not, finally, come together in an internal order; they bump into one another and vie for primacy. One result is a sort of energetic incoherence, with wordy abstractions hammering at us as confusedly and angrily as Claude hammered at the temple wall. Yet, apart from or beneath those diverse and somewhat ill-assorted themes, we come upon a persuasive image that does give the book a quality of wholeness and of harmony—that may even justify the incoherence and that we may also take as representative of much more than this single novel.

It is the image of the blind man's quest. "Like a blind man wildly lashing out, [Claude] strove to fight death down." Throughout the story, a heavy stress is laid upon the fatally hampered effort of men to perceive—to make out, in the half-light, the features and form of the reality that surrounds them. In the first sentence, we find Claude "gaz[ing] fixedly at the man's shadowed face, straining to get at least some inkling of its expression"; and in the last, "Perken gazed at him as if he were a stranger. . . ." Elsewhere we encounter innumerable allusions to peering, to lamps and fires, to shadows and reflections, to two-eyed men and one-eyed men and eyeless men. The reference to the blind man playing his flute in a Djibouti brothel is followed by the appearance of another blind man twanging a guitar and chanting the Ramayana at Pnom-Penh. Both serve to prepare us for the figure of Grabot, who had long before put out one of his own eyes (to escape military service) and who has now lost the other through the savagery of his Moi captors. But the blind musicians, in addition to their contextual function, seem to me to symbolize—and to be intended to symbolize—the harried artist in the contemporary world.

For this is a world, so Malraux implies, in which the instruments of vision have been denied at the moment when the need of human perception has become urgent. We have lost those cultural means which for many centuries Western man has been accustomed to use in order to see: that is, to see his own human nature, and his society, and his history, and his destiny. The artist continues to peer at the shape of things, but his eyesight is badly damaged, or even gone. Such, at any rate, is the fundamental suggestion of *The Royal Way*. But Malraux, in 1930, was already on the verge of detecting the nature of the reality which lay waiting for perception: what Silone would call "the intimate reality of others." Malraux, in his own highly original manner, would take that reality as the object of supreme importance in every novel he wrote in the years that followed.

In 1943, Malraux published, via Skira in Switzerland, the fragment of a novel that in its entirety was to be titled *La Lutte avec l'ange*. It had been written in a German prisoner-of-war camp in 1941, and the Gestapo had seized and destroyed a good part of it; the remainder Malraux printed "for those who are interested in 'what might have been,'" under the title of *Les Noyers de l'Altenburg*. But if *Les Noyers* is a fragment, it is a singularly whole and organic fragment. Most critics agree that it is not only a substantially complete book, but a remarkable work of the narrative art as well, one of Malraux's great achievements, confirming his high and exemplary position among the novelists of his generation. In *Les Noyers*, Malraux's sense of life is articulated in a tone of ultimacy only hinted at in the preceding novels *(Man's Fate, Days of Wrath, Man's Hope)*. Central to this articulation is the image of companionship, or "fraternity" as Malraux more often calls it, as the one valid response to death and the one indestructible source and container of meaning. *Les Noyers* rehearses and meditates, recapitulates and makes explicit. And as it does so, it not only offers a dramatic demonstration, as brilliant and expressive as anything in second generation fiction, of the theme of human charity. It also provides a memorable new image of the representative and contradictory hero we have been studying. *"Les Noyers,"* Professor Frohock argues, "is a necessary key to the full meaning of the novels [of Malraux] that precede it." It may also serve as a key to the meaning of all the novels that have been discussed in this book.

The bulk of *Les Noyers* consists of a three-part account of the career of Vincent Berger, an Alsatian scholar-adventurer, up to the crucial event of his life in June, 1915. The account is written twenty-five years later by his son in a prison camp near Chartres, as the son's way of explaining to himself the meaning of his own experience. Echoes and parallels between the two men, the two sets of experiences, and the two wars abound; they thicken and empha-size the defining qualities of the novel's world, like the double plot in a Shakespearian tragedy. We hardly need even to recall that Malraux's pseudonym, as a tank commander in the French Resist-ance forces, was Berger, to realize that both father and son in the novel are portions of their creator; what is equally to be stressed is that, in examining himself, Malraux is also summing up the compos-ite career of a generation. Formally as well as substantively, *Les Noyers* is typical second generation fiction. More deliberately even than *Bread and Wine* or *The Power and the Glory*, it is a novel of successive encounters—with the constant aim of finding and present-ing the human image. The source of the son's knowledge about his father is the latter's notations on the theme he had entitled: "En-counters with Man."

The story Vincent Berger's son has to tell begins, familiarly enough, with a return and a suicide—Vincent's return in 1914, from Constantinople, where the first of his three main adventures had taken place; and the suicide of Vincent's father, old Dietrich Berger, squire of a large Alsatian estate and the eccentric leading citizen of the local community. This suicide, of course, is the event that causes Dietrich's brother Walter to change the topic of his annual colloquy from art to man. The colloquy is duly described in the novel's second section; but before arriving at it, the narrative pauses and circles back to sketch Vincent's Middle Eastern experiences. "Sketch" is the word: the prose throughout most of the first section of *Les Noyers* is sparse and jumpy; it presents notes rather than narrative, or perhaps recollections of recollections, recorded at a remote distance in space and time, hasty memories of a series of meaningful encounters, strung together in the manner of picaresque tales. Vincent has been teaching philosophy—a Nietzschean philosophy of action—at the University of Constantinople. Owing to his knowledge of Turkish history and affairs, the German Embassy—as an Alsatian, Vincent is a citizen of the (then) German Empire—appoints him to liaison work with the Young Turks of Enver Pasha. Vincent's sympathies and his lust for action, however, involve him with the Turkish elements further than his German superiors can countenance; he becomes a chief advisor to Enver Pasha and, in the way of the Malraux hero, acquires considerable authority within the revolutionary movement. In Europe as in the Middle East, Vincent begins to appear as a mysterious, even legendary figure of eminence (like T. E. Lawrence, on whom he is plainly, if only part' modeled). After guiding Enver to his first successes, Vincent sets forth on a journey through the Islamic world in search of the old Turkish Blood Alliance—the *Touran*—and in hope of revitalizing it. Nowhere does he find evidence that the alliance exists. And his final Asian encounter, a humiliating incident in far-off Ghazni where he is attacked by a madman, convinces him not only of the absence of any Blood Alliance but, by extension, of the failure of communication between men on which any alliance must be founded. He leaves Turkey and returns to Europe and to the Alsace, liberated from this particular dream but still dedicated to his larger quest for some mode of human alliance: and peculiarly ready to take part in the discussion his uncle has suddenly chosen: "Whether there exists any grounds upon which the notion of man might be based?"

The question (it has been noted), replacing as it does the original question about the eternal principles of art, reflects the crucial shift from the artistic concerns of the first to those of the second generation. To use the mythological allusions of the writers themselves, it is a shift from the image of the artist as Daedalus or as Orpheus to the image of the artist as Prometheus. Speaking of Joyce and of his artist-hero Stephen Dedalus, Francis Fergusson has observed the significance of the name: "When [Joyce] toys with the notion of a mythic parallel to his destiny he chooses not Prometheus but Dedalus. The artist in his flight is as impatient as Prometheus of divine restraints, but he is not, like Prometheus, attached to the service of humanity. . . . His being and his art are both self-con-

tained, and both 'free' alike of God and of man." [4] Those words are
generally applicable to most first generation writers. But they may
be virtually reversed in describing the generation that followed.
When Camus, for example, "toys with the notion of a mythic
parallel to his destiny," we have to say that "he chooses not Dedalus
but Prometheus," because, as an artist, he is exactly "attached to the
service of humanity." The whole group of writings that include
The Plague, The Rebel and two plays, is referred to by Camus as
"The Myth of Prometheus"; and Promethean tendencies, at least,
are detectable in Silone and the later Faulkner. In Malraux, they
become unmistakable.

It is Vincent Berger himself, in *Les Noyers*, who puts forward
the conception of art not as total aesthetic liberation but as a humanization of the world. Berger's remarks provide a philosophical
basis for contemporary fiction, with its rebellious and conversionary
aims; for Berger's point is precisely that great art remakes the universe for the sake of mankind. This is the idea we have already encountered in Camus's argument that art is "a fabricator of universes,"
and that in its habit of revolt art aims to construct a "substitute
universe" (words written almost a decade after *Les Noyers*). And
it is the idea behind Malraux's search for the human image in both
his *Psychology of Art* and *The Voices of Silence*. It is an idea that
perhaps goes astray when applied (for example) to the art and literature of the classical world; but it bespeaks with a kind of metaphysical passion the radical imperatives of the contemporary world.

> We know [says Vincent] we did not choose to be born and that
> we shall not choose to die. . . . When I say that each man feels
> forcibly the presence of destiny, I mean that he feels—and almost
> always tragically, at least at certain moments—the independence of
> the world in his regard. . . . To say stylized is to say humanized;
> what man would have done if he had been God. Man knows that
> the universe is not built to the human scale; and he wishes it were.
> And when he reconstructs it, it is according to the human scale that
> he does so. . . . Our art seems to me a rectification of the universe,
> a way of escaping from the human condition. The worst confusion
> seems to me to have come from the belief . . . that to represent a
> fatality is to submit to it. On the contrary—it is almost to overcome
> it! . . . In its essentials, our art is a humanization of the universe.

If to stylize is to humanize, then to humanize is to accomplish an act of conversion: from the antihuman to the human, from death to life. This conversion is the fundamentally creative act in which Malraux's contemporaries have so devotedly joined him.

Vincent's speech, at the same time, represents another and parallel development. Taken as the consequence of his Turkish adventure, it reflects a personal conversion similar to the one we followed at length in the career and the fiction of Ignazio Silone: a movement through and beyond politics. Malraux, like Silone, had engaged vigorously in the actual political battles of his time; and became, while doing so, a legendary figure in his own right, a vital symbol of the artist in action. Whether or not he was physically present during the upheavals in China during the nineteen twenties (Professor Frohock adduces reasons to doubt it), he was obviously a close student of them. And he was certainly active in the Loyalist Air Force during the Spanish Civil War, and during most of the thirties as an impassioned political spokesman in the struggle for social justice. He had manifested extraordinary personal courage in the advocacy of his anti-Fascist convictions; and, again like Silone, he had known physical pain and imprisonment.[5] Because of his strenuous immersion in immediate political history, all the novels Malraux included in the Pléiade edition of 1947—*The Conquerors, Man's Fate* and *Man's Hope*—were regarded upon their first appearance and for too long thereafter as stirring fictional documents in the great political and social revolutions of the post-war era. *Les Noyers* enforces what should have been evident earlier: a profound enlargement of that view.

It is now possible to see, as Joseph Frank has shrewdly remarked, that "Malraux's heroes . . . are not so much engaged in a battle against a particular social and economic form of life as against the limitations of life itself. To fight a war or revolution they may submit to social discipline; but they never confuse this limited battle with the eternal struggle that can only end in their defeat."[6] There were, perhaps, some slight traces of such a confusion in one or two of the earlier novels; there is none, in any case, in *Les Noyers de l'Altenburg*. By this time, Malraux and his hero had emerged from the temporal political battle, with the scars of physical attack and of humiliation, equipped to confront the eternal question. It is exactly the question raised, out of the wreckage of their political program, by Silone and his hero: "What is man? What is this human life?"

Or rather, it is a question about those questions. Not even, as yet, What is man? but rather, Does the question itself make sense? Malraux, in the French manner exemplified later by Camus, has gone at the great issues of the day armed primarily with a compassionate intellect, with *la raison* in its concern for man. His questions come from the head and have to do with logic and the scientific study of history; those of Silone seem to come from the heart and to return there. The vigor of Malraux's fiction is always a cold vigor, even when it is most anxious to expose the specifically human; but for all that, his extreme Gallic intellectualizing does Malraux no disservice. It enables him, on the contrary, to do something Silone could never do (he tried it, with unhappy results, in *The Seed Beneath the Snow*) and which, indeed, only a handful of Frenchmen and Germans have ever shown any real talent for doing. It enables him to fictionalize thought.[7] The second section of *Les Noyers*, the debate over the question about man's nature, is as lively and engrossing as any passage in contemporary fiction. And in it, Malraux's dramatic intellect doubles on itself and rises by its own energy to a suprarational intuition, an intuitive affirmation beyond the reasoned negative, of the continuance of human nature.

For by a kind of double paradox, the intellectual and scientific approach to the question both carries the day and is rejected as the truly fruitful approach; it demonstrates unanswerably that there is *no* continuity to human nature across the ages, that there are *no* grounds on which to base an idea of man as man—and these severely rational and well-documented findings are immediately dispelled from Vincent Berger's mind, as it turns to the mute testimony, outside the halls of the colloquy, of the immemorial Altenburg walnut trees. During the colloquy, one speaker voices the intellectual hope: "Something eternal remains in man, in thinking man . . . something I would call his divine element: it is his capacity to question the universe." But Möllberg, the Continent's leading ethnologist, produces a tremendous amount of evidence, from precultural times onward, to demonstrate the opposite—that between the cultures so learnedly cited there is no communication, no sharing of the fundamental presuppositions of human conduct and relationships; no common image of man whatsoever. Möllberg's long and majestic discourse, with its somber quasi-Spenglerian implications, closes the debate by destroying it; how is even debate possible, if communication is denied? Rationally persuaded and profoundly troubled, his mind sufficiently exhausted to be receptive to something like a mystical vision, Vincent Berger walks on the Altenburg hillside: and in the long spectacle of the walnut trees leading away to the Strassbourg cathedral, he sees imposed "the ideas of a will and of a metamorphosis without end." This is Vincent's "leap"—the leap of his faith; corresponding to that leap of faith across reason to God that agnostics from Nietzsche to Camus have regularly derided; but, illuminating in a single flash the secret motion of an age, it is a leap of faith not in God but in the continuing reality of an exclusively human nature.

In the third section of Vincent's career, as recollected by his son, this lightning glimpse of truth is translated into concrete terms and takes upon itself a forcible human shape. Here Malraux advances beyond knowledge to pity, and beyond compassion into the realm of companionship. The scene is the Eastern Front, in June of 1915. Lieutenant Berger is a staff officer at the German headquarters; he has been assigned as aide to a professor of chemistry who has come to the forward area to supervise an attack upon the Russian troops by the new gas he has recently invented. The attack is launched; the gas drifts across the valley into the Russian trenches; after an interval the German soldiers move forward to mop up. Then something extraordinary happens: the Germans are seen, no longer advancing, but returning, coming back toward their own lines, each one carrying the body of a gassed Russian infantryman. It takes Vincent many moments to grasp what has occurred; the dazed and appalled Germans can only babble, "It's not possible . . . it's not possible . . . you can't . . . you can't." And it takes him still longer to understand the stunning significance of the turn-around. When he does, Vincent abandons his charge and plunges into the inferno, seeking a Russian whom he himself may carry back on his shoulders —to partake with his German and Russian comrades of the tortured, ravaged fraternity they have suddenly embodied; to assert along with them a common humanity in the face of the unspeakable inhuman. Knowing that "the barrage of pity would not often be effective," he loses himself in the full experience of an epiphany he may never experience again.

No image in contemporary fiction—not the hugely allegorized image in Faulkner's *A Fable* nor the electrifying moment in the deaf-mute's hut in Silone's *Bread and Wine*—is more compelling than is this one of Malraux's as a dramatization of man's greatest potential quality: his charity, his capacity to humanize power by transmuting it into charity. Nowhere is the movement from death to life—and the latter as the common sharing of pain and of nourishment—more poetically conveyed. The misty horror of the gassed countryside takes its place beside the impenetrably dark, stench-filled prison of *The Power and the Glory* as one of the generation's supremely pictured settings for the heroic discovery of man's relation to man. And the metaphors of death, which were a major element in *The Royal Way*, are here intensified to a Dantesque eloquence:

> Apple trees scarred by men, killed just as the men were: deader even than the other trees, because more fertile. . . . Beneath them, the grass was black, with a blackness never before seen. Black were the trees which closed off the horizon, they too sticky with gas; black the woods before which there passed, running, the silhouettes of German soldiers. . . . Dead the foliage, dead the leaves, dead the earth across which the runaway horse disappeared in the wind at a gallop.

Man, in this novel, is defined as the only animal who knows it must die; and it is upon this scene, now invaded and possessed by death itself as the monstrous synthesis of every inhuman force, that Vincent is granted an answer to man's knowledge, the answer that forgives it: "the assault of pity," as the impulse that truly humanizes the human individual; and the assault of something more radical, more active, more creative. "Pity? he thought. . . . It was a profound impulse of a very different sort, an impulse in which anguish and fraternity mingled inextricably, an impulse which came from very far back in time." And Vincent, hurrying and stumbling through the apocalypse toward his own humanity, has a flashing reminiscence of the walnut trees of the Altenburg. The promise of that former moment has been fulfilled in the actual life of men; exultantly, even as he loses consciousness, Vincent feels he has touched at last upon "the sense of life." It is to experience the happiness of fraternal pain.

This theme, as readers of Malraux well know, had—after its first fitful appearance in *The Royal Way*—been an object of central dramatic focus in *Man's Fate* and the subsequent novels. Katow, in the climax of *Man's Fate*, giving up the cyanide that would have spared him a hideously cruel execution—giving it up to a fellow prisoner and explaining "with deep joy" to an astonished guard that there was not enough cyanide left for himself; the life-giving communication, in *Days of Wrath*, between Kassner and the unseen prisoner in the adjoining Nazi cell; the descent from the mountain in *Man's Hope*, the peasants carrying the wounded aviators down the precarious slope to safety—these moments, and other moments and allusions that clustered around them, had already comprised a swelling image of fellowship between men as the noblest answer to man's mutilated and imprisoned condition. And if the climactic scene in *Les Noyers de l'Altenburg* is perhaps even more memorable than those previous scenes, it is partly because the composition of the earlier scenes had made the episode in *Les Noyers* possible by steadily heightening Malraux's sense of the matter. It is partly, too, because the episode in *Les Noyers* enlarges on its predecessors, not only to engage, in effect, an entire people on a comprehensive stage, but to extend the principle of fellowship to mean fellowship with the enemy; and for Malraux, a French prisoner of the German Army in 1941, the act of writing about the heroic fraternity of German soldiers was itself a singular act of fraternizing with the enemy. But beyond all this, the experience recorded in *Les Noyers* has an especially forceful significance because it is presented in its impact upon the sensibility of a very remarkable man.

Vincent Berger begins as an adventurer in the tradition of Malraux's Garine and Perken; but he travels a long way. As another Garine, Berger would have ended his career with the failure of his search and the abandonment of his power in the Middle East. But that is only the prologue to his real career, as *The Conquerors* and *The Royal Way* were but the prologue to Malraux's—as, indeed, the sense of death and of defeat, the failure of communication and the shattering of the human image marked only the beginning, not the end, of the artistic career of the second generation. Berger continues to grow, until, through his later experiences and his response to them, he takes upon himself the complex structure of the hero of his time. He becomes Malraux's version of his generation's representative hero; and in both his affinities with the other versions we have inspected and his deviation from them, Berger serves to complete our understanding of the figure.

The picaresque saint appears in *Les Noyers* as a shaman. Vincent's son recalls a conversation he once had:

> "Do you know what a shaman is?" one of my Russian comrades asked me one day.
> "A Siberian medicine man, isn't he?"
> "Something more, too. Lenin was a great man, but not a shaman; Trotsky is less great, but he *is* a shaman. Pushkin, Robespierre, Goethe? None of them shamans. But Dostoevski, Mirabeau, Hölderlin, Poe: great shamans! There are little shamans, too, like Heine. Napoleon was not a real shaman: he believed too much in things. You find something of the shaman in geniuses, and also, of course, in idiots. Among us Russians, there is more of the quality than elsewhere. Well, the strength and weakness of Vincent Berger is that he was a bit of a shaman."

The passage is tantalizingly enigmatic; but from it, with the help of a pattern of allusions throughout the novel, we may hazard several inferences that bear upon the whole of our discussion. The names cited in the passage, one observes, are those of men of action or of artists; and the shaman is a person who (like Trotsky) combines the practical involvement in history with the poetic imagination that sees beyond history to realities of perhaps greater significance. The combination is precarious. The shaman, in fact, is a character of profound contradictions, and one liable to both strength and weakness; a character in whom great natural powers combine with a radical instability that exposes him equally to deep mystical insight and to extravagantly nonsensical behavior. He is a figure who is at once above and below the normally human: a figure, in short, whose variety of paradoxes we have seen embodied already in the heroes of Silone and Greene and Camus; a figure whom the heroes of Moravia and Faulkner (for opposite reasons) approximate but do not fully realize.

The other novelists we have considered customarily establish their paradoxes in moral, religious or even in legal terms: hence the recurring image of the dedicated character who is also a rogue, an outlaw. Malraux, however, has typically defined his protagonists in intellectual terms, in terms of their mental capacity, but in so doing, he describes a plainly analogous tension. In *The Royal Way*, the important design was provided by a contrast and a fusion between sight and blindness. In *Les Noyers*, it is provided by a contrast and a fusion between genius and idiocy ("You find something of the shaman in geniuses, and also, of course, in idiots"). Genius is represented at the Altenburg colloquy, for example; and the idiot who attacks Vincent Berger in the bazaar at Ghazni is recalled by later references to *idiotes* and *fous* and by a reminiscence of Berger's idol, Nietzsche, after he had gone insane. Berger, the shaman, has some of both extreme qualities. He is by no means the least radiant among the highly cultivated intellects at Altenburg, and he is also prone to hallucinations and has a noticeable strain of hysteria. But perhaps the key reference in the novel occurs during the colloquy, in the naming and celebration of the three novels and characters who have represented better than any others in the history of literature—so it is argued—the eternal condition of man and man's eternal aspirations. For primary among those three is *The Idiot* of Dostoevski.

Second and nearly equal is Cervantes' *Don Quixote*. The third choice is perhaps surprising: *Robinson Crusoe*. But borrowing and humanizing the three theological virtues, we may suggest that Crusoe stands for hope; as surely, Quixote and Myshkin divide between them the faith that leads to charity. In Quixote and Myshkin, we recognize the supreme instances in Western literature of the saintly *pícaro*—the holy wanderer, with his special combination of extraordinary spiritual gifts and extraordinary spiritual frailties; we recognize the type of the disturbing and even troublesome individual who is charity in action. In the novels Cervantes and Dostoevski wrote about their sublimely eccentric heroes, moreover, we recognize the literary ancestry of much of second generation fiction. For contemporary fiction, even while it is attempting to remodel the distracted world it deals with, is returning to the sources of the narrative tradition to find the means to do so. The episodic novel, the tale of successive encounters, the paradoxical hero and his ambiguous relation to the world he travels through: all these ele-ments which characterize the second generation are at least as old as the work which is usually taken as the chief ancestor of modern prose fiction in general—*Don Quixote*.

Only at the end of his recorded career does Vincent Berger enter the honorable company headed by figures like Quixote and Myshkin. But he belongs there, for like those figures Berger has chosen to resist the new disruptive forces of his day out of an impulse which is very ancient, very simple, and very human—"an impulse in which anguish and fraternity mingled inextricably, an impulse which came from very far back." He belongs there because he reveals the same kind of contradictions of character which justify the admission of his fictional contemporaries. In his strength and his weakness, Berger is an eccentric and an outsider in more ways than one; but he has submitted himself to the experience of humanity. He has fallen headlong into the sufferings of mankind, and from that fall he has acquired a sense of life that he is willing to share. It is in the inten-sity of his approach to "the intimate reality of others," that Berger has an intuition of the sacred. And that, in the literature of the day as in the literary tradition it has renewed, is what it has meant to be a saint.

NOTES

Chapter 1: *The Sense of Life*

1. "My intention was to write a chapter of the moral history of my country and I chose Dublin for the scene because that city seemed to me the centre of paralysis."—Joyce to Frank Budgen.

2. "It was with an almost triumphant harshness that [M. de Charlus] repeated in a level tone, stammering slightly and booming sepulchrally: 'Hannibal de Breauté, dead! Antoine de Mouchy, dead! Charles Swann, dead! Adalbert de Montmorency, dead! Baron de Talleyrand, dead! Sosthène de Doudeauville, dead!' And each time the word 'dead' seemed to fling upon the deceased a great spadeful of earth, hurled by a grave digger who was anxious to rivet them more firmly in the grave."—Proust, *The Past Recaptured.*

3. On the side of brilliantly perceptive praise, I commend the lectures delivered at the Library of Congress in 1956 by R. P. Blackmur; published by the United States Printing Office as *Anni Mirabiles: 1921-1925.*

4. Erich Auerbach, *Mimesis: The Representation of Reality in Western Literature* (Princeton, 1953), p. 551.

5. *Hudson Review,* Autumn, 1956.

6. The metaphysical basis of first generation fiction remains fully to be examined and defined. Meanwhile, I commend chapter two ("The Symbolistic Imagination") of Charles Feidelson's *Symbolism and American Literature* (Chicago, 1953).

7. Preface to *The Wings of the Dove.*

8. *The Man with the Blue Guitar,* section XXII.

9. Those premonitions were first notably articulated on a large scale in the startlingly prophetic manner of Henry James's later work: when, for instance, Merton Densher in *The Wings of the Dove* perceives dimly in rain-swept Venice, and in the context of the murderous intrigue he has embarked upon, an image of "the drawing-room of Europe, profaned and bewildered by some reverse of fortune."

10. Quoted by Philip Rahv in the introduction to *Great Russian Short Novels* (New York, 1951).

11. See the present writer's *The American Adam* (Chicago, 1955).

12. Cf. Daniel Aaron's *Men of Good Hope* (New York, 1951), p. 259—the summary of an essay by Brooks Adams.

Chapter 2: *Alberto Moravia: Eros and Existence*

1. *La Terza Generazione*, initiated in Rome in 1953, and dedicated to "solutions," other than political, of the cultural crisis of our time. The magazine was discontinued in 1957.

2. I should acknowledge here a sensible review of Moravia's career by Aldo Paladini, in the Milanese periodical *Settimo Giorno*, December 2, 1954.

3. The very form and the peculiarly haunting music of Elio Vittorini's brilliant *Conversazione in Sicilia* (1937) were a necessary and happy response to the Fascist challenge.

4. A collection of sixty-odd "short short stories" or anecdotes, published originally in newspapers and dealing with the comic or seedy side of the city of Rome. They have not all been translated into English. The one referred to here is "*Il Mediatore*."

5. Interview in the *New Yorker*, May 7, 1955.

6. In a review of Moravia's collection of articles, *Un Mese in URSS; L'Espresso* (Roman weekly), April 13, 1958. Milano continues: "For the massive facts of history . . . Moravia has the same dark respect that the phenomena of nature excite in others. This is one of the forms of Moravia's pessimism, on which his vigor as a novelist depends, as well as his analytic acumen and his anti-rhetoric." The book under review, incidentally, is the only collection of Moravia's journalistic writings yet published.

7. For this and for several other references, I am indebted to *Introduzione a Moravia* by Euralio de Michelis (Florence, 1954).

8. *Hudson Review*, Summer, 1951.

9. Paladini, *loc. cit.*

10. *Sentirsi vivo. Vivo* is only partly rendered by "alive"; it contains the note also of making one's presence felt, of being recognized and acknowledged.

11. After reading this chapter, which was published as a separate essay in *Modern Writing No. 3* (1956), Moravia addressed a letter to me, in English. I have permission to quote the following (dated April 13, 1957): "It is quite true that sex has been for me the key to open many doors. The fact is that I started to write in 1925 . . . and in that time there were very few or no values at all which, after the terrible crisis of the so-called twenties, resisted a close examination. Everything in this faraway time seemed tottering, inconsistent, contradictory and false. There were only a few things which seemed to me solid and true and these things were connected with nature and with the less objectionable and analysable and ineffable sides of the human soul. Among these things no doubt was sex, which is something primordial and absolute. I have said the word: absolute. Looking for the absolute, it was impossible to

find it then in the upper spiritual world but only in the depths of the un-conscious and of the lowest and most obscure instincts of man."

12. In the letter addressed to me by Moravia, and already quoted in part, he adds the following: "Ten years before Sartre's *Nausée*, I wrote *The Time of Indifference* which was an existentialist novel avant-la-lettre. From existence to being it is very difficult to pass; there is a big gap between the two. I tried hard to fill the gap, to cross the line between existence and being. Maybe I didn't succeed."

The present chapter is clear, I hope, in its conviction that the failure to cross the line in Moravia's novels is a failure of the characters and not of the author; that Moravia is dramatizing a failure, but not himself failing. In this respect, he may be compared with Chekov. The failure of will and nerve in Chekov's plays is a quality of his dramatis personae, and not of himself; hence Chekov may aptly and ironically call *The Cherry Orchard* "a comedy," as I would call most of the stories by Moravia.

Chapter 3: *Albert Camus: The Compassionate Mind*

1. "Descend still lower to climb still higher." Marguerite de Navarre, the sister of Henri IV, and the author of the *Heptameron*, was one of the so-called "Christian humanists" of the sixteenth century. Alongside Marguerite's remark (which is from a poem), we can place the contention of Camus that he has plumbed "the depths of our nihilism . . . search[ing] only for reasons to transcend it."

2. Cf. "*Non je ne suis pas existentialiste*," in *Les Nouvelles Litteraires*, November 13, 1945.

3. *Hudson Review*, Winter, 1953.

4. *Troilus and Cressida*, I, iii, 109 *et seq.*

In an interview published in the *New York Times Book Review* on February 24, 1957, Camus astonishingly declared that "Shakespeare had the innocence, the profound innocence of the sixteenth century, which took no account of good or evil and overflowed with vitality." This is another of the remarks by Camus that, as I have suggested earlier, make at least as much sense if reversed. Probably no century before or since has taken so severe an account of good and evil as did the sixteenth century, and "innocence" is hardly applicable to the tormented conscience that created King Lear.

5. Literary analogies and contrasts proliferate irresistibly around this representative man. The reference here, of course, is to the much-quoted remarks attributed to Margaret Fuller and Carlyle: "I accept the universe"; "Gad, she'd better!"

6. Camus's father, however—who died when Camus was an infant—was Alsatian, and his mother Spanish. Other nationalities and cultures appear in his background.

7. In the phrase of Pierre Henri Simon, *Noces* combines sensual pantheism with Stoic atheism. *Témoins de l'Homme* (Paris, 1951).

8.   . . . The young
In one another's arms, birds in the trees,
—Those dying generations—at their song,
The salmon-falls, the mackerel-crowded seas,
Fish, flesh, or fowl, commend all summer long,
Whatever is begotten, born and dies.

Yeats goes on in the poem, unlike Camus in *Noces*, to affirm the superior value of unaging intellect. The central idea of *Noces*—that "the spirit finds its reason in the body"—is exactly formulated by Yeats in "Among School Children," the poem that was his dialectical counterpart to "Sailing to Byzantium":

O body swayed to music, O brightening glance,
How can we know the dancer from the dance?

9. *Esprit*, January, 1950.

10. *"Explication de* L'Etranger," *Situations* I (Paris, 1947; first published in 1943). Most of my references to Sartre in this connection are drawn from this cogent analysis. Unhappily, as is well known, Sartre and Camus later engaged in a public controversy—rancorous on Sartre's side—after the appearance of *The Rebel* in 1951; and their ten-year friendship was formally dissolved. See Nicola Chiaramonte, *Partisan Review*, November, 1952; and Joseph Frank, *Hudson Review*, Winter, 1953.

11. The American reader would be excused, at this point, for hearing echoes of the old ballad "Sam Hall," a song Camus would surely honor as authentically absurd, especially in its last verse: "Oh the preacher he did come, he did come/ Oh the preacher he did come, and he talked of kingdom come/ Yes, he talked of kingdom come, damn your eyes."

12. I do not mean to say, at least without discussion, that this is a bad thing for a novel to do. We must also reckon with Camus's own curious but logical theory of the literary art: that a book is a kind of thrust of the spirit under very particular circumstances; so that circumstances warranting one type of expression at one moment may require something rather different at another.

13. The only passage in the novel where causal relations are asserted is the speech for the prosecution at Meursault's trial. The presence of such relations is one reason why Meursault feels that the speech is about someone else, not about himself.

14. In *The Idea of a Theater* (Princeton, 1949). Mr. Fergusson acknowledges a partial debt to Kenneth Burke for these terms; and both Mr. Fergusson and Mr. Burke are indebted to the *Poetics* of Aristotle.

15. This suggestion and the one following I owe to Mr. Robert Rechnitz, a member of my "pro-seminar" at Columbia University, 1956-57.

16. He is thus cousin to the American Laura in Katherine Anne Porter's splendid story, "Flowering Judas": Laura, who "is not at home in the world," who feels betrayed "by the disunion between her way of living and her feeling of what life should be," who looks on every man as a stranger, and "no matter what this stranger says to her, nor what her message to him, the very cells of her flesh reject knowledge and kinship in one monotonous word. No. No. No. In "Flowering Judas," as in *The Stranger*, the present tense absorbs all distinctions.

17. Cf. "Trends in Affectlessness," an analysis of *The Stranger* by Dr. Nathan Leites in the periodical *American Imago* VI (1947). "Affectless" is a tinny but

not altogether inappropriate word to describe Meursault; but like Camus's own phrase, "supernatural consolation," it betrays an unexamined assumption. Dr. Leites assumes there must be some unnatural psychic dislocation in Meursault to account for his behavior; he finds it in buried guilt feelings of Meursault as regards his father, and sees in the young man's death a suicide that is a mode of expiation and appeasement. But Meursault is a condemned man, not a suicide; the point of the novel is the ironic reasonableness of his absurd outlook; *he*, not the spectators at the court (who share Dr. Leites' notion of the normal), is the natural man.

18. Some of Camus's more graceless French opponents have traced the mental and stylistic sins they claim to find in him to his physical illness—to "the supposed condition of my respiratory system," as he has remarked. Sartre, on the contrary, seemed to relate the illness to an artistic achievement when he observed (in the remark already quoted) that the style of *The Stranger* "brings up each phrase out of nothing, by a sort of respiratory spasm."

19. Cited by Henri Peyre in *The Contemporary French Novel* (New York, 1955), p. 221.

20. In America, it was not surprisingly Herman Melville who confronted suicide with the greatest force of imagination. Hawthorne's Zenobia drowns herself in *The Blithedale Romance;* but the orgy of self-slaughter that concludes *Pierre* is far more wild and suggestive.

21. The feeling of absurdity may be illuminated by contrasting the following passages. Camus describes the sense of divorce between man and nature, the anguish of the separated self, in these words: "If I were a tree among trees, a cat among animals, this life would make sense, or rather this problem would not make sense—for I would be part of the world. I *would be* this world to which I now oppose myself with all my conscience." Against that, consider the organic union with nature celebrated by Henry David Thoreau—the sense that is still a luminous portion of the American temperament and tradition: "I go and come with a strange liberty in Nature, *a part of herself* [italics added]. . . . Sympathy with the fluttering alder and poplar leaves almost takes my breath away. . . . The fox, and skunk, and rabbit now roam the fields without fear." (From "Sounds," in *Walden.*) A tree among trees, a fox among foxes, Thoreau proclaims the union of which Camus fiercely combats the loss.

22. Translated by Walter Kauffman, in *The Portable Nietzsche* (New York, 1954), which he edited. Professor Kauffman writes that "the passage . . . may seem to be aimed at Kierkegaard—of whom Nietzsche, however, heard only in 1888, too late to acquaint himself with the ideas of the Dane." The passage was probably written in Italy not later than 1885.

23. I borrow the phrase from the title of Lawrance Thompson's study of Melville, *Melville's Quarrel with God* (Princeton, 1952). Working largely with materials outside of the European tradition exemplified by Camus, Professor Thompson none the less has elaborated out of Melville a pattern of attitudes and a recurring tension quite similar to those of Camus. In *The Myth,* Camus refers to *Moby-Dick* as a "truly absurd work," *i.e.,* a great work; its impact upon him is everywhere observable. There is, I should add, a most interesting chapter to be written on the parallels and contrasts between "the sour tradition" in America and European existentialism.

24. Some typically reckless exclamations of Luther, quoted here in full awareness of other elements in Luther and especially in the developing Lutheranism that helped balance them: "The nature of God demands that He should at first

destroy and annihilate everything that is in us"; "God cannot be possessed . . . except by the negation of everything that is in us"; "Whoever is not destroyed and brought back by the cross and suffering to the state of nothingness . . . abuses and dishonors the gifts of God. But whoever is annihilated by suffering ceases to do anything and knows that God is working in him and doing all." Luther bespoke an entire tormented culture and a century and a half of death-fever, but the Lutheran emphasis on death, annihilation, and nothing as vital doctrine ran counter to the greater and more ancient tradition represented by St. Thomas Aquinas and by his insistent formula that *grace does not destroy nature but perfects it.* That tradition is today testified to most persuasively by Jacques Maritain; but in fairness to Camus and his colleagues, it should be confessed that the contemporary Christian vision, both Catholic and Protestant and both in theology and in literature, has more a Lutheran than a Thomist air about it. The theological dialogue of our generation takes place outside the great tradition of theocentric humanism.

25. The French title, *Le Malentendu*, emphasizes the rational element in the play, and permits Camus the pun on the word *entendre*, which means both to understand and to hear. A connection is implied between deafness (that, for example, of the perhaps God-symbolizing old servant) and the inability or the refusal to understand: a connection also carried by the word *absurde* in its relation to *sourde* (deaf). Cf. *The Rebel:* "A deaf God is the only religious image for men in revolt."

26. In his study of nineteenth century literary themes, *The Romantic Agony*, (New York, 1933).

27. So Camus remarked during rehearsals, which I was privileged to witness, for a new production of *Caligula* in the winter of 1958. What emerged more clearly for me in the actual staging of the play was the extraordinarily rich theatrical element in the play's *content*, along with the pervasive element of the genuinely comic.

28. The comparison has been noted by Rachel Bespaloff, in the article cited earlier. Miss Bespaloff is less persuasive in seeing Tarrou as an extension of Scipio, in *Caligula*, and Rieux's indistinct old mother as the successor of Caesonia.

29. *Lettres à un Ami allemand*, published by the French underground press and reprinted by Gallimard, 1945.

30. This defining aspect of *The Rebel* has been somewhat obliterated in the English edition, which deletes part of the section on "metaphysical revolt" in what it refers to as "the interests of economy."

31. In a conversation with the author.

32. See especially "Dialogue," written in 1929 and included in *Between Man and Man* (Boston, 1955).

33. A remark made to this writer.

34. *The Reporter*, November 28, 1957.

35. *The Fall*, translated by Justin O'Brien (New York, 1957).

36. This notion played a large part in nineteenth century American writing, as I have indicated in *The American Adam*.

Chapter 4: *Ignazio Silone: The Politics of Charity*

1. The distinction in Silone's Italian is between *fede*—faith, including religious faith, a sentiment Silone will not appeal to—and *fiducia*, which he does assert: faith, in the sense of trust: "I have faith in that man."

2. Or, interchangeably, the Abruzzi (plural), from its division into three provinces—Teramo to the north, Aquila in the mountains, and Chieti near the Adriatic coast.

3. The diminutive form is Secondino, and so he is often called by Italian political historians—especially by Communist writers, who intend thereby a rather heavy joke. A minor meaning of *secondino* is subjailer, the person second in charge of a prison. With this pun, Communist commentators visit a small revenge on the apostate.

4. Violence and religious emotion are intimately related in the Abruzzo. Within living memory in neighboring Celano (the home of St. Thomas of Celano, author of *Dies Irae* and of a life of Saint Francis), a poor wretch who tried to steal the chalice of the town church was literally torn to pieces at the church door.

5. Among the peasantry of the Abruzzo, *sposo* or *sposa* (spouse) may signify husband, fiancé, suitor, lover, or simply a friendly acquaintance. Similarly, every encounter between a boy and a girl is called love-making *(fare l'amore)*. If a girl returns from the town pump where she has exchanged greetings with a boy she knows only slightly, she will say, when asked what she was doing, "*Ho fatto l'amore con Mario.*" (I was making love with Mario.) The poverty of Abruzzese speech has been a factor, both limiting and helpful, in Silone's narrative style.

6. There had perhaps been one dim precedent for concerted action in the Abruzzo—a Farmers' League that had died out by 1913, but had left its memory of possibilities.

7. In the Second World War, every cave hid an escaped prisoner of war. The present writer was engaged for some months in digging the refugees out and having them led to safety.

8. It has never been clear whether abdication was or is possible under Canon Law, though Celestino published an edict in advance claiming its propriety. The act was encouraged by the talented and self-interested Cardinal Caetani, who then promptly succeeded as Boniface VIII. But when, at the Jubilee of 1300, Boniface was heard to thunder, "I am Caesar, I am Emperor!" there were those who doubted openly that he was even the Pope. Boniface, whose feet Dante watched toasting in a lower circle of Hell, fell victim himself to intrigue and violence, on "the terrible day of Anagni," in 1303, when he was manhandled and his palace sacked by agents of French King Philip.

9. *E conobbi l'ombra di colui / che fece per viltate il gran rifiuto.* Other identities have been proposed for "*colui*," by scholars who have scrutinized every syllable of those lines. The consensus, however, favors the name of Celestino V, especially since Dante's words did reflect the general opinion of Celestino in the early fourteenth century.

10. B. Ciccardini, in the manifesto of the new periodical *La Terza Gener-*

azione, Rome, 1953. The rejection, or better, the effort at transcendence of politics by young Italian intellectuals dates from the defeat of the De Gasperi government in June, 1953.

11. Between 1917, when he came to Rome, and 1921, when he became a Communist, Silone had functioned as a journalist mostly with the Socialist paper *Avan-Guardia* in Rome, subsisting on the meager returns that newspaper writing could bring him. Under the name of Pasquini, he had also become known as a vigorous exponent of the extreme left of the Socialist youth movement.

12. This was its name until May 24, 1943, when, with the dissolution of the Comintern, it took the name it now holds: Italian Communist Party.

13. Gramsci won and Bordiga was kicked out of the Party—to be denounced later by Togliatti according to strict Communist ritual as "a Trotskyite swine, protected by the police and the Fascists." Bordiga was not a Trotskyite, he was only a bit old-fashioned: still something of a Social Democrat. And Gramsci, who opposed him, was not a Stalinist, only a futurist and something of a poet; nor was he radically hostile to Trotsky. Silone counts among the most impressive persons he has known both Gramsci and Trotsky.

14. At no time did the Italian Communist underground or the Italian Communists in exile try to cooperate with other radical Italian movements. Instead, the interradical warfare continued in Switzerland and France and even in New York, where refugee Communists and refugee Socialists reviled each other in the Italian language press.

15. "*La maniera di Béla veramente non é una bella maniera.*"

16. "Every revolution, every single one, without any exception whatever," says Uliva to Spina in *Bread and Wine,* "started as a movement for liberation and finished as a tyranny. For a long time I was tortured by that fact." Uliva kills himself. Perhaps the whole point of this present chapter is to explain why Silone, after arriving at Uliva's insight, did not kill himself but came back to life. In terms suggested within other contexts by certain modern critics, we might argue that in the suicide of Uliva, Silone purifies himself of the suicidal instinct in him—concentrating all his bias toward life in Pietro Spina.

17. The Communists who stayed in Italy left the Party or managed to be kicked out of it sooner than those operating in Switzerland and elsewhere; for they stayed closer to the truth of the experience and to the source of their initial involvement. They felt the betrayal more swiftly and sharply.

18. In which Mann's novelist, Gustav von Aschenbach, discovers that creativity requires a "descent into the abyss," the annihilation of all serenity and aestheticism.

19. See p. 24.

20. See pp. 73-74.

21. It is interesting that the Communist paper for which Silone once wrote is called *Unita,* and the liberal periodical to which he now contributes is called *Comunitá* (published by Adrian Olivetti).

22. Rather than *Abruzzo,* Cavalcanti (died 1300) wrote *Toscano.*

23. An edition in the original Italian was put out by a little press run in Paris by a group of Italian emigrants in 1934. For the first publication by a proper Italian firm (Mondadori of Milan), Silone revised *Fontamara* considerably. The novel was translated into seventeen languages other than German and English, including Russian (Moscow, 1935), Hebrew, Esperanto, Croa-

tian, and Finnish. The most complete bibliography of Siloniana is one compiled by Mlle. Jeanne Peret, of the University of Grenoble, in an appendix to a thesis on Silone. It was printed in part in the periodical *Fiera Letteraria* (Rome), August 14, 1955.

24. The question of "race"—*razza*—is a topic for prolonged meditation in *Bread and Wine*. The Italian word connotes class (the "race" of farmers, the "race" of landowners) and also type or kind (*"Che razza di viliaco sei tu?"* "What kind of a coward are you?"). Pietro Spina moves himself toward conscience when he realizes that "race" more properly signifies a way of being.

25. Writers who refused to submit their art to the Fascist censor and who did not have the advantage of peasant isolation turned their attention inwards and created a body of hermetic writing—obscure designs in poetry and passionate allegories in prose. We have already noted Moravia's development in this direction.

26. A well-disposed English critic once said that Silone is the kind of writer who reads better in translation. That is not strictly true, but it suggests something true—that Silone can be read most appreciatively in Italian by one for whom Italian is not his primary language, and who has not, therefore, been nourished since birth on its traditional idioms and rhythm. In almost precisely the same manner, the Italians and the French are less distracted than are the English by the wild native locutions of William Faulkner.

27. *Bread and Wine* begins with the sister of Don Benedetto, the priest, seated at her loom: "The shuttle bobbed backwards and forwards through the warp of red and black wool, from left to right and from right to left, to accompaniment of the rhythm of the treadle." This is Silone's artful manner of announcing the start of his narrative—of its action, and of the method that will control the action.

28. Silone's critical difficulties are with the neo-neo-Croceans rather than with the master himself or the ablest of his disciples. Silone and Croce are in some respects opposite sides of the same coin. The most distinguished Crocean in literary criticism, Francesco Flora, has made one of the few apt and appreciative (though for my taste somewhat excessively Marxist) evaluations of the art of Silone.

29. In 1955, Mondadori in Milan published a novel called *Vino e Pane (Wine and Bread)*, a version of the original so extensively revised by Silone that he thought it proper to revise the title as well.

30. In America, the novel was selected by the Book-of-the-Month Club.

31. The phrase is Martin Buber's, in *Between Man and Man*.

32. Silone sees an identical development in the excellent brief novel *The Seizure of Power*, by the exiled Polish poet and former anti-Nazi underground agent, Czeslaw Milosz (New York, 1955, in English). "The great theme of this sober and courageous novel," Silone writes, "is not the apparent struggle for power; actually it is the struggle for love." But Milosz' characters are rendered from the outset in primarily human terms; their humanity is drawn into the political struggle and survives it.

33. A good description of Silone's own manner of conversing. He sometimes makes visitors and interviewers uneasy, just because he prefers to "talk softly and with many pauses."

34. Cf. Martin Buber's description, in *Between Man and Man*, of what Buber regards as the kind of true "meeting" that is creative of life. The section is

called "Silence which is communication." "Just as the most eager speaking at one another does not make conversation . . . so for a conversation no sound is necessary, not even a gesture. . . .

What I am thinking of I will make clear by an example.

Imagine two men sitting beside one another in any kind of solitude of the world. They do not speak with one another, they do not look at one another, not once have they turned to one another. They are not in one another's confidence, the one knows nothing of the other's career, early that morning they got to know one another in the course of their travels. . . . The one is sitting on the common seat obviously after his usual manner, calm, hospitably disposed to everything that may come. . . . The other, whose attitude does not betray him, is a man who holds himself in reserve, withholds himself. . . . Imperceptibly the spell is lifted. But even now the man does not speak a word, does not stir a finger. Yet he does something. The lifting of the spell has happened to him—no matter from where—without his doing. But this is what he does now: he releases in himself a reserve over which only he himself has the power. Unreservedly communication streams from him, and the silence bears it to his neighbor. Indeed it was intended for him, and he receives it unreservedly as he receives all genuine destiny that meets him. He will be able to tell no one, not even himself, what he has experienced. What does he now 'know' of the other? No more knowing is needed. For where unreserve has ruled, even wordlessly, between men, the word of dialogue has happened sacramentally."

The passage from *Bread and Wine* is virtually a moment-by-moment dramatization of Buber's remarks, with a little more narrative detail and a little less mystical flow.

In response to a question, Silone recently wrote me as follows: "Yes, I knew Martin Buber in Zurich in 1934, after the appearance of *Fontamara*, and I saw him several times later in Ascona (Ticino). I have read several of his books, and *perhaps* they have exercised a good influence on me. I say *perhaps* sincerely, because I am not sure about it. When I talked with Buber, we found ourselves in easy agreement." Silone adds that he may reflect on this question in a future essay.

35. "These things Jesus spake and departed, and he did hide himself from them"; John, XII, 36. The latter phrase is the title of the mystery play Silone composed in 1944, based on *Bread and Wine*.

36. New York, 1954.

37. *The Invisible Writing*, p. 279. Koestler's report is slightly tinged with resentment, but tinged more strongly with perplexity and wistfulness. "We did indeed become quite good friends," he adds, "but it has always remained a somewhat frustrating kind of friendship."

38. Published simultaneously in German (Zurich), Italian (Lugano, Switzerland), French, and English (Harper & Bros., New York). It was brought out by Mondadori in Italy in 1950. It has also been translated into Swedish, Danish, Spanish, and Portugese.

39. The distinction made here and throughout the novel is pretty much the same as the one Martin Buber makes between what he calls the "I-It" relation, in which utility is paramount, and the "I-Thou" relation, in which communion takes place.

40. The construction of English does not permit the precise effect gained

by the infinitive form in Italian; the word *go*, for instance, is an indicative as well as an infinitive form in English.

41. Silone writes in a letter: "If I was able to overcome the great material and moral difficulties of isolation in Zurich, especially after breaking with the Communist Party, it was in large part due to several friends, among them Marcel Fleischmann, with whom I lived for ten years as though in my own home. . . . And I should mention, in addition to religious Socialists like Martin Buber and Leonhard Ragaz, and on the different intellectual plane of a critique of Marxist ideology, the ideas of Georges Gurvich, which brought me back to liberal and federalistic socialism."

42. From another letter to this writer.

43. *Encounter*, September, 1955.

44. "Today," Silone is quoted as continuing, "it is officially admitted that there had been murders, massacres, etc. I don't want to preach heroism. I simply want to state that there has been a break with tradition. None of the great suffering of the Russian people in this period has found any expression whatever."

45. The title remains somewhat enigmatic for me. In the story, it refers to a handful of blackberries that the peasant Martino picks and offers to Rocco, near the end of the first part. Symbolically, it may stand for the same thing the figures of bread and wine stand for: a communion of spirit through a sharing of physical food; with an emphasis upon the simplicity of the food available to the poor folk the story deals with.

Chapter 5: *William Faulkner: The Hero in the New World*

1. In an interview with Jean-Bloch Michel; London *Observer*, November 17, 1957.

2. This chapter does not attempt a full-scale consideration of the whole of Faulkner's work, and in this respect it differs from the other chapters in the book. I am concerned here with a single aspect—a crucial aspect, as it seems to me, and the one that best reveals Faulkner's participation in the artistic enterprise of his generation. But to isolate a single aspect is to invite a misunderstanding both of Faulkner and of my purpose: which this caveat may help to prevent. Most of Faulkner's writings, in any case, have been pretty thoroughly investigated already, and the kind of full-scale discussion that would now be desirable must either be written by Professor Carvel Collins or must await Professor Collins's release of his multitudinous findings on Faulkner's life and times and career.

3. In a lecture delivered in November, 1957, in a series sponsored by the United States Embassy in London, and reprinted in *The Young Rebel in American Literature* (London, 1959).

4. Once the enormous differences between the hot-hearted Southerner and the cool-spirited New Englander have been granted, there appear likenesses

that extend from the verbal and superficial to the radical. Faulkner's first book (a book of poems) borrowed the title of Hawthorne's last completed novel, *The Marble Faun.* And in the midst of that comedy of horrors, *As I Lay Dying,* there emerges a situation surprisingly reminiscent of the one in *The Scarlet Letter:* a love affair between a minister (Dimmesdale, Whitefield) and a married woman, resulting in an illegitimate child (Pearl, Jewel) and a lifetime of pride, remorse, and selfless service. The common element, however, is the concern with the drama of moral passion.

5. Sartre's most elaborate nonfictional and nondramatic description of the picaresque saint is in his massive essay on Jean Genet, the gifted writer who has also explored several brands of criminality. Sartre calls Genet and the book he wrote about him *Saint Genet, Comédien et Martyr* (1952); and in the book, Sartre stresses the crucial connection between sainthood and roguery—with all the attendant paradoxes—beyond anything elsewhere proposed in his generation.

6. *Atlantic Monthly,* June, 1947; reprinted in Peyre's *The Contemporary French Novel.*

7. The title of a book. Published in Paris in 1948.

8. The volume, which introduced Faulkner to Italy, also contained an intelligent essay on Hemingway and a splendid analysis of *Moby-Dick.*

9. *Mannen Utan Vag,* poems composed in 1939 and 1940.

10. Richard Chase, in his interesting book, *The American Novel and Its Tradition* (New York, 1957), argues that American fiction is peculiarly and perennially a fiction of tensions and contraries rather than of resolutions. His argument (which at one point is directed against me) is well supported by several major instances—*Moby-Dick,* for example, and *The Sound and the Fury;* and the support is the more impressive just because they are so major. But I cannot agree, as a matter of fact, that unresolved dualism has been the high and steady concern of American fiction; nor do I think, as a matter of theory, that the fiction would be of greater stature if such were the case.

11. Faulkner belongs also with Conrad and James, with Hawthorne and Charles Brockden Brown, with Webster and Marlowe and with Virgil, and so on. My historical point should not be taken too strenuously.

12. We learn more about him from other stories in *Go Down, Moses.*

13. I omit detailed consideration of "The Bear" as a timeless psychic drama. It is a treasure chest for psychologists in criticism. Though I do not count myself among such critics, I should note that "The Bear" does have several distinct "levels" or dimensions of meaning; and that somewhere between the moral dimension and the mythic (the dimension concerned with power), there is a psychological one. Object after object that scholars say are recurring symbols in the dream legends of the unconscious are scattered through the story: the forest, the tree, the rifle, the bear, and a score of others. As to the rebirth of Ike, Carl Jung may be quoted: "The birth of the hero is not that of an ordinary mortal, but a rebirth from a mother-spouse . . . because only through her does he share in immortality." This second mother, Jung says, is often an animal and even an animal normally thought of as male, like Hiawatha's mother, who first appears as the Great Bear of the Mountains. As to the next phase: traditionally, according to Joseph Campbell, it is a psychic journey through "a dream landscape of curiously fluid, ambiguous forms, where he must survive a succession of trials." This is nearly an exact description of the fourth section of *The Bear.* The paradigm of literary analysis of this kind, adapting the psychological meaning to other and more important ones, is

Newton Arvin's analysis of *Moby-Dick*, in his book *Herman Melville* (New York, 1950).

14. *Kenyon Review*, Autumn, 1951.

15. There are, of course, factual differences. Mary, for instance, is the corporal's half-sister, not his mother. But the effort to see any *distance* between the original and the copy is defeated by scenes like the one in which the corporal is implicitly identified with two other persons, both of whom have died. Beyond that, the lack of distance is felt increasingly in the texture of the prose.

16. "Pure and Impure Poetry," in *Selected Essays* (New York, 1958).

17. "The Stillness of *Light in August*," *Partisan Review*, Fall, 1957.

Chapter 6: *Graham Greene: The Religious Affair*

1. These phrases were first brought to my attention by Mr. Carl Haffenreffer, then a student at Princeton. I believe they occur in one of Eliot's discussions of Matthew Arnold.

2. Oxford, 1925. The thirty short poems had already appeared in half a dozen periodicals, most of them published in or near Oxford. The title comes from Edna St. Vincent Millay: "It is not enough that yearly, down this hill, / April / Comes like an idiot, babbling and strewing flowers."

3. From the title essay in *The Lost Childhood and Other Essays* (London: 1951).

4. James is alleged to have said: "So here it is at last, the distinguished things."

5. Prologue to *The Lawless Roads*.

6. *The Man Within* (1929), *The Name of Action* (1930), *Rumor at Nightfall* (1931), *Stamboul Train* (1932), *It's a Battlefield* (1934), and *England Made Me* (1935). Greene has excluded the second and third items from the uniform edition published in England by William Heinemann.

7. *The Lost Childhood*, p. 69.

8. *Ibid.*, p. 99.

9. This notion will be developed in rather different terms by Robert Kelly of the University of Indiana, in a forthcoming study. I am indebted to Mr. Kelly for several stimulating conversations about Greene.

10. In *The End of the Affair*, the writer Maurice Bendrix, who on occasion speaks for Graham Greene, is asked about this: "You used the stream of consciousness in one of your books. Why did you abandon the method?" "Oh, I don't know," Bendrix replies in his supercilious way. "Why does one change a flat?" Because, one supposes, one does not belong there.

11. The film version of *Brighton Rock*, so I am told, introduced a suggestive change in the matter of the phonograph record. The words recorded by Pinkie in the film go something like this: "You may think I love you, but to me you are just an ugly brat, and I hate you." When Rose plays the record (a moment left to our appalled imagination in the book), the needle sticks in the

groove, and the voice is heard saying, "You may think I love you I love you I love you . . ." It is a device that hints at the mixture of loathing and attraction that the bewildered Pinkie feels.

12. See above, pp. 77-79.

13. Miss Frances Ebstein, a former student of mine, has quoted Heidegger suggestively to say of Pinkie that he was not so much born and bred as "ejaculated into existence."

14. The image of enemy troops fraternizing is widespread in contemporary fiction. It recurs in *The Heart of the Matter*, is an actual event and a key experience in Malraux's *Les Noyers de l'Altenberg*, and is elaborated into book-length allegory in Faulkner's *A Fable*.

15. I am indebted to Mr. Herbert Haber, a former student of mine, for this phrase and for working out in detail a theory we shared about the structure of *Brighton Rock*.

16. Greene achieves a telling effect, for those who remember this particular interchange, when, at the end, the description of the execution is juxtaposed with a picture of the chief of police moaning cravenly over his aching tooth in the dentist's office.

17. Greene felt about Trollope, it will be recalled, that his characters *existed* with added force, since they existed not only for each other "but also in a God's eye." This is the sense he tries to impart to the members of this novel's society. "Here you could love human beings nearly as God loved them, knowing the worst."

18. This notion is interestingly proposed by Marie-Béatrice Mesnet in *Graham Greene and the heart of the matter* (London, 1954).

19. Quoted by Marie-Béatrice Mesnet, *ibid.*, p. 102.

20. Since *The Heart of the Matter*, Greene has published two novels—*The End of the Affair* (1951) and *The Quiet American* (1956); two plays—*The Living Room* (1953) and *The Potting Shed* (American edition, 1957); and two entertainments, *Loser Take All* (1955) and *Our Man in Havana* (1958). He has also composed an original film script for *The Third Man*, which has since appeared as fiction (1950); and a script from his short story of 1936, "The Basement Room" (*The Fallen Idol*, 1950).

21. *Partisan Review*, Summer, 1957.

22. Even the titles of the two plays reverse each other's paradox. The irony of *The Living Room*'s title lies in the festering death hovering just outside the room. The title of the second play has an opposite intention. Combined with the name of Potter, the former servant who has a crucial clue to the play's secret, *The Potting Shed* echoes the name of the burial site for suicides—Potter's Field. But the shed itself, though it had been the scene of the suicide, is more importantly the site of James Callifer's resurrection; echoing in its title a name associated with death, the play in fact discloses the secret of a life.

Epilogue: *The Shared Reality: The Shadow of André Malraux*

1. *The Walnut Trees of Altenburg.* I use the French title, since the novel—first published in Switzerland in 1943—has not been translated; quotations in this section have been translated by the writer.

2. The quotation is from W. M. Frohock's *André Malraux and the Tragic Imagination* (Stanford, 1952), to which I also owe my knowledge of the essay cited. For many other items of information and for a number of stimulating insights. I am uncommonly grateful to Professor Frohock.

3. Greene's Oliver Chant journies only as far as the revolutionary turmoils of nearby Trier, and his mission collapses. It would be five years before Greene would in actual fact take the larger step of braving his own jungle, in the Liberian journey.

4. *The Human Image in Dramatic Literature* (New York, 1957), pp. 78-79.

5. Another chapter might be written on the image of the legal process and prison in second generation fiction, a follow-up to Thoreau's chapter on "My Prisons." The sense expressed by Garine, in *The Conquerors*, of the remote absurdity of the court that convicted him and of its preposterous obeisance to some Sphynx-like force corresponds both to the reaction of Meursault to his trial in *The Stranger* and to the reminiscence of Silone, described earlier.

6. "Malraux and the Image of Man," an article on *Les Noyers* by Joseph Frank in *The New Republic*, August 30, 1954.

7. A phrase suggested by Newton Arvin, in a conversation with the author.

INDEX